sbt in Action

sbt in Action

THE SIMPLE SCALA BUILD TOOL

JOSHUA SUERETH
MATTHEW FARWELL

MANNING
SHELTER ISLAND

For online information and ordering of this and other Manning books, please visit
www.manning.com. The publisher offers discounts on this book when ordered in quantity.
For more information, please contact

> Special Sales Department
> Manning Publications Co.
> 20 Baldwin Road
> PO Box 761
> Shelter Island, NY 11964
> Email: orders@manning.com

Manning Publications Co.
20 Baldwin Road
PO Box 761
Shelter Island, NY 11964

Development editor: Jennifer Stout
Technical development editors: Patrick Touhey, Matt Momont
Copyeditors: Tiffany Taylor,
Linda Recktenwald
Proofreader: Melody Dolab
Technical proofreader: Thomas Lockney
Typesetter: Dottie Marsico
Cover designer: Marija Tudor

ISBN 9781617291272
Printed in the United States of America
1 2 3 4 5 6 7 8 9 10 – EBM – 20 19 18 17 16 15

contents

preface

It's 2012-ish and I'm in the middle of bootstrapping Typesafe, the company behind Scala. I get a call from Manning about more book ideas for Scala. At the time, I was working on one of the least understood and most important tools in the Scala ecosystem: sbt. sbt was a build tool that had some rough edges, but was amazingly powerful and elegant in its core idioms. After a quick chat with Michael Stephens at Manning, we decided to put a proposal together and see if we could find a second author. While I really wanted to see an sbt book, as the community desperately needed one, at the time my commitments at home and work were too much for a new book. This lead to us eventually finding Matthew as a second author, and I'm very glad we did. Matthew has been great to work with and brings his own unique humor that I very much appreciated throughout the book writing process.

For some reason, I tend to wind up as "the build guy" for my day job. This inevitably happens due to two "flaws" in my personality:

- A desire to understand everything I use
- A desire to improve my daily workflow

At Typesafe, this meant I was thrown into using sbt. At the time I was a "Maven guy," having fallen in love with the notional simplicity of lifecycles, plugins, and declarative builds. In fact, I had forks of most major Maven plugins at my company to tweak/work around issues we discovered. When I first picked up sbt, I didn't like it.

The documentation at the time was sparse, and the idioms for the build were by far a lot different from what I was used to. However, as I started diving in, asking lots of questions of Mark Harrah, my coworker and the inventor of sbt, I found something beautiful underneath the rough exterior. sbt had (whether on purpose or by accident) turned into an automation delivery vehicle for your development experience.

By this, I mean that sbt allowed me to control and tune my build for my most common tasks, with an emphasis on interaction. In other words, sbt was not a "one shot" build; it was something you ran like an IDE, and it made coding Scala so much better than any other IDE at the time.

I'm so glad we were able to write this book to show you the vision of what I saw in this little tool. It still has some rough edges here and there, but I hope you'll see the beauty and what I consider the future of build tools.

JOSH SUERETH

When Manning approached me about helping out with a book about sbt, I jumped at the chance. I'd contacted Manning to help with another book, and they suggested that I help with this one. I knew Josh through the Scala community, and I knew his reputation, so working with him would be great.

I've always been interested in code quality and software that helps me develop more easily. I like Larry Wall's idea of being "productively lazy." I've contributed to a number of open source projects to help with quality, such as Scala-IDE, JUnit, and most notably Scalastyle, the style checker for Scala that I wrote because I hate having to remember to put a copyright header on each source file.

The first real build tool I used was Make. Before that it was simple shell scripts. Make is great as long as you don't have to build on multiple platforms. For me, the problems with Make are summed up in one project: Perl. There isn't one makefile for Perl; it is generated by a 25,000-line shell script according to your system's capabilities. Now, admittedly, Perl is built for a huge number of systems, but 25,000 lines to create a makefile? Really?

When I saw Apache Ant for the first time, it was a revelation. By abstracting out the differences between operating systems to the JVM, you didn't need to worry if your system was being built on Microsoft Windows or Linux. And then came Maven. Maven took the abstraction even further—you said "This is a Java project; build it" rather than "I want to compile my Java." But Maven was still a bit clunky for all of the custom tasks we had as part of our build.

Then I started using Scala. Some of the Scala developers used sbt, and I wanted to know more. I immediately saw the usefulness of some of the things that sbt was doing. First, the ~ operator has more rapid feedback. I loved saving a file and having my sbt tell me my unit tests had failed. What could be better than something automatically telling you that you had screwed up? Second, I loved the fact that the code was written in a statically typed language—I didn't have to wait two hours for my build to fail with what would have been a compilation error.

We started writing the book in January 2013, and the result of that work is before you now. I hope you enjoy it.

I feel that the importance of build tools in a project is often underestimated. A good build tool will help you with your project. A bad build tool will get in your way.

MATTHEW FARWELL

acknowledgments

When we signed up to write this book, we didn't know how much effort it would require, or how long it would take. We started in 2013, and not only did we have to write the book, but sbt was changing underneath us as we wrote! It was Josh's second book, so he had some idea, but Matthew had no idea. Without the assistance of many people, this book would definitely not be in your hands or on your screen right now. It's much more likely that we would still be working on it.

From day one of the project, help has poured in, and all of it has been not only appreciated but essential. If we've forgotten anyone, please accept our sincere apologies. In no particular order, we'd like to thank the following people for their work and support.

Manning Publications

Many thanks to publisher Marjan Bace for accepting the initial proposal of two new and inexperienced authors. He helped the book take its first, and most important, step.

Thanks to Christina Rudolph and Michael Stephens, who were the first two people we talked with about the book.

Our development editor Jennifer Stout deserves a medal for the marathon work she did. Her patience and encouragement were invaluable. Special thanks to Candace Gillhoolley and Ana Romac for their marketing efforts.

Thanks also to many other members of the Manning team who helped us during production: Mary Piergies, Tiffany Taylor, Sharon Wilkey, Janet Vail, Melody Dolab, and Linda Recktenwald. And thanks to our technical editors Patrick Touhey and Matt

Momont, as well as to our technical proofreader Thomas Lockney. Their work was invaluable in making our work better.

The sbt team

Without sbt itself, this book wouldn't have been possible (or necessary). We'd like to thank the legion of volunteer developers responsible for the development of sbt. First, Mark Harrah, who started the sbt project and has carried it for most of its life. There are too many other contributors to mention, but we should at least mention Grzegorz Kossakowski, Eugene Yokota, Indrajit Raychaudhuri, Dale Wijnand, Nepomuk Seiler, Alexey Kardapoltsev, and of course Josh.

The reviewers

Thanks to our MEAP readers for their comments and corrections to the book and to the following reviewers who read the manuscript at various stages during its development and gave helpful feedback to our editors and to us: Alexander Myltsev, Bret Ikehara, Chad Michael Davis, Chris Nauroth, Dusan Kysel, Eric Weinberg, Iain Campbell, Joost den Boer, Logan Hauenstein, Michael Schleichardt, Mike Dalrymple, Nicolas Jorand, Ricky Yim, Tobias Kaatz, and William Wheeler; also to Mark Harrah, Sergii Vozniuk, Sergii Kuku, Philippe Genevès, Nicolas Jorand, and everyone who participated in the book's Author Online forum.

about this book

sbt takes the concept of a reliable build tool and extends it in two ways—using a DSL written in the Scala language and as an interactive development environment. *sbt in Action* is a step-by-step introduction to sbt. The text includes numerous real-world examples designed to demonstrate the power and flexibility of sbt, along with best practices for using it.

This book is intended for professional developers who want practical, battle-tested advice on how to get their own projects built using sbt. Developers building applications with sbt will typically use several related technologies as part of their projects. A book that provided complete information on each of these would fill many volumes. To avoid killing more trees than necessary, we assume that the reader is familiar with the JVM, and to a certain extent the Scala language syntax. However, we don't feel that the reader needs too much knowledge about either of these. A wealth of information is available on these elsewhere.

Our focus is sbt and the problems it solves—the building and development of Scala and Java projects.

Roadmap

Chapter 1 talks about the need for a standard reliable build tool. We talk about some of the other options available for building Scala and Java projects, comparing and contrasting them with sbt. We end the chapter with our beliefs: why we use sbt

Chapter 2 introduces sbt—how to get started with it and basic usage. We introduce the basic commands and the basic concepts of tasks and settings. We show how to run your unit tests. This chapter will get you up and running with sbt.

Chapter 3 is a deeper dive into the core concepts of sbt: settings, tasks, and projects. We'll see how to reuse values, introducing the notion of build dependencies. We'll also use an Excel analogy to illustrate setting reuse. We'll write our first custom task to create a Java properties file as part of your build. We'll also introduce the notion of configurations, which are namespaces for settings and tasks.

Chapter 4 covers the default build—all of the default settings and tasks that mean that sbt gives you a standard build out of the box. We walk through compile, run, test, package, and publish to see how they work.

Chapter 5 covers how to test your code and how to use sbt to speed up your development. It also covers how to use different test frameworks within sbt. We cover Specs2, ScalaCheck, JUnit, and ScalaTest. We'll perform some integration testing using the ScalaTest Selenium DSL. We'll also cover how to get nicely formatted reports from your tests.

Chapter 6 goes for a deeper dive into the library made available by sbt for IO: sbt.IO. If you do any complex custom tasks in sbt, this library will do most of the heavy lifting for you.

Chapter 7 has more information about how to help developers develop using sbt. We create an sbt command which performs database migration through the sbt console as an example of how you can use sbt to help with non-build tasks which aid developers.

Chapter 8 covers plugins and external libraries—how to reuse components created by others in your build, and how to not reinvent the wheel.

Chapter 9 covers debugging your build—what to do when things go wrong.

Chapter 10 covers automating workflows. We create a simple release command which performs a number of checks on your project, then builds, creates, and pushes a version control tag. This is an example of how a workflow can be created to increase safety on your build.

Chapter 11 covers how to define plugins and when and how to reuse your build code. We cover how to create the plugin and how to test it, along with how to use configurations in your plugin and how to create incremental tasks. We cover the Auto-Plugin interface, which allows dependencies between plugins.

Chapter 12 shows how to distribute your projects. We publish a library to a company repository and create a native package (a deb file, but this could also be an rpm or msi file).

Code conventions and downloads

When we present source code in the book, we use `Courier typeface like this` to separate it from normal text. Sometimes, when the context is not clear, the code is prefixed with the file name. These will appear in **bold typeface**.

Much of the source code shown in the earlier part of the book consists of fragments designed to illustrate the text. When a complete segment of code is given, it's shown as a numbered listing; code annotations accompany some of the listings.

The source code for the example applications in this book is available to download via Manning's website, www.manning.com/books/sbt-in-action. It is also available from the GitHub website at https://github.com/jsuereth/sbt-in-action-examples.

Author Online

Purchase of *sbt in Action* includes free access to a private web forum run by Manning Publications where you can make comments about the book, ask technical questions, and receive help from the authors and from other users. To access the forum and subscribe to it, point your web browser to www.manning.com/books/sbt-in-action. This page provides information on how to get on the forum once you are registered, what kind of help is available, and the rules of conduct on the forum.

Manning's commitment to our readers is to provide a venue where a meaningful dialog between individual readers and between readers and the authors can take place. It is not a commitment to any specific amount of participation on the part of the author, whose contribution to the AO remains voluntary (and unpaid). We suggest you try asking the authors some challenging questions lest their interest stray!

The Author Online forum and the archives of previous discussions will be accessible from the publisher's website as long as the book is in print.

About the authors

JOSH SUERETH is a senior software engineer at Typesafe and the author of Manning's *Scala in Depth*. He is the author of several open source Scala projects, including the Scala automated resource management library, the PGP sbt plugin.

MATTHEW FARWELL is a senior software developer at Nexthink. He is the author of Scalastyle, the style checker for Scala, and is a contributor to JUnit and the Eclipse Scala IDE. Matthew lives in Lausanne, Switzerland, with his gorgeous wife and gorgeous daughter.

about the cover illustration

The figure on the cover of *sbt in Action* is captioned "Habit of a Pilgrim of Mecca called Saquaz, who carries aromatic water to sell." The illustration is taken from Thomas Jefferys' *A Collection of the Dresses of Different Nations, Ancient and Modern* (4 volumes), London, published between 1757 and 1772. The title page states that these are hand-colored copperplate engravings, heightened with gum arabic. Thomas Jefferys (1719–1771) was called "Geographer to King George III." He was an English cartographer who was the leading map supplier of his day. He engraved and printed maps for government and other official bodies and produced a wide range of commercial maps and atlases, especially of North America. His work as a map maker sparked an interest in local dress customs of the lands he surveyed and mapped, which are brilliantly displayed in this four-volume collection.

Fascination with faraway lands and travel for pleasure were relatively new phenomena in the late 18th century and collections such as this one were popular, introducing both the tourist as well as the armchair traveler to the inhabitants of other countries. The diversity of the drawings in Jefferys' volumes speaks vividly of the uniqueness and individuality of the world's nations some 200 years ago. Dress codes have changed since then and the diversity by region and country, so rich at the time, has faded away. It is now often hard to tell the inhabitant of one continent from another. Perhaps, trying to view it optimistically, we have traded a cultural and visual diversity for a more varied personal life, or a more varied and interesting intellectual and technical life.

Manning celebrates the inventiveness and initiative of the computer business with book covers based on the rich diversity of regional life of two centuries ago, brought back to life by illustrations from old books and collections like this one.

Part 1

Why SBT?

In Part 1, we'll go over a bit of history, including why you would want a tool like sbt rather than other available build tools. We'll cover some of the advantages and disadvantages of each approach. Then we'll get you up and running with sbt.

Why sbt?

This chapter covers

- Why use a build tool?
- Apache Ant
- Apache Maven
- Gradle
- Why sbt?
- Interactivity/reactivity of sbt

In this chapter we're going to explore why someone would use sbt (Simple Build Tool) to give a bit of a background to this book. If you're convinced that you need to use sbt, you can probably skip this chapter. We'll cover why you'd want an automated build and what other options you have for Scala and Java development. Finally, we'll compare these other options to sbt and show why we think sbt is a good option for a large range of builds but especially for Scala builds.

For the impatient: sbt is a build tool that creates a stable build platform and increases developer productivity by taking the good ideas from other build tools such as

- Minimal configuration—default project layouts
- A number of built-in tasks (test, compile, publish)

3

and adding new features:

- A reactive development environment. (You change your source code, and sbt reruns your tests.)
- Allowing developers to use the Scala REPL on their projects.
- Faster compilation through incremental compilation and caching.
- Automatic recompilation with different versions of Scala.

Let's start at the beginning.

1.1   Why a build tool?

If you spend any time working in a team of software developers, you'll notice one thing: people make mistakes. Have you ever heard the old joke about asking 10 economists a question and getting 11 different answers? It's like that when you have a list of things to do: if you have 10 things to do, you'll make 11 mistakes doing them.

Another thing you'll notice is that people are different. Bob isn't the same person as Ted. When we look at Bob's workstation, everything is organized and tidy. Everything is where it should be. No icons on his desktop. Ted, however, can't see his screen background for the icons. Don't know why he bothers having one in the first place.

One thing is absolutely certain. If you ask Bob to do a build of the product, you'll get a different product than if you ask Ted. But you can't tell which will have fewer bugs.

A few years ago, one of our project teams had an "automated" build. It was 10 or 12 Windows batch files, which built and deployed a web application; it compiled the Java, built the web application, and deployed it to the server. This took a developer about 1.5 to 2 hours to do correctly; it was a lesson in how not to automate. Each developer had to do this for each change. Then two developers came in over the weekend and rewrote these scripts, using a build tool called Apache Ant. The time for a full build dropped from 1.5 hours to (wait for it) 8 minutes. After the experience with batch scripts, the increase in speed and reliability due to the use of Ant was very welcome. One of the fundamental principles of agile development is getting rapid feedback, and this applies to building your code as well. If you have to wait an hour for a deployment, it becomes less and less interesting to experiment and try new approaches. Subsequently, with gradual refactoring the build time was reduced to 3 minutes for a full build, including running more than 1000 unit tests.

This shorter time encouraged experimentation. You could easily try something out. You may say that there isn't much difference between 8 minutes and 3 minutes, but for fun we'll do the calculation: let's say a developer builds five times a day. There are six people in the team, so each day we save 5 * 5 * 6 minutes = 2.5 person hours. Over a year (200 days), this is 500 person hours, or about 60 person days.

But speed wasn't the only reason we wanted a better build system; we also wanted reproducibility. If a build is reproducible, then it doesn't matter if Bob builds the project and deploys it to the integration server or if Ted does it. It produces the same result. When the build was rewritten as described previously, *it didn't matter who did the final build.* It didn't matter what software was installed on the developer's machine, which versions of the libraries they had, which version of Java they happened to have installed, and so on. If there was a problem with that version of the software, then we could reproduce exactly the build that had a problem, so we at least had a chance to fix the bug.

Later, at a different company, there was another automated build system. His name was Fred.[1] His job was to build the product, in all of its various combinations. Every day, he would come in, check out all of the sources, and enter the numerous commands to build the product. And then he'd do it again, with a slightly different combination for a slightly different version of the build. If any of the builds failed, it was his job to tell the developers that something went wrong. This was his job. Fred was an intelligent person and, frankly, he deserved better—and indeed he could have spent his time much better elsewhere. In fact, he ended up writing his own build system to automate the builds. And he could have saved the time taken to write and maintain that as well if he'd used a standard build tool.

Hopefully you'll agree that you need build automation. You can automate your build perfectly well with a shell script (or batch script). But why have a specific tool for this purpose? Well, it comes back to a number of factors:

- *Reproducibility*—Automating your build gives you time to do real work.
- *Less to do*—A good build tool should give you a framework to work in. For instance, you should have sensible defaults. Maven is a good example of this; the default is to use src/main/java for Java source code and src/test/java for Java test code. You shouldn't need to specify every last option to every last javac command.
- *Experience*—This is an underrated factor. You can stand on the shoulders of giants—or at least on the shoulders of people who've done similar things over and over again. A good build tool is a distillation of developer wisdom. You can use the collected experience in a build tool such as Apache Ant, Apache Maven, or indeed sbt to enforce good practices in your project. For instance, Maven and sbt automatically run your tests before you package. If any of the tests fail, the build doesn't succeed. This helps you increase quality in the project, which is generally seen as a good thing.
- *Portability*—A good build tool should protect you from differences between systems. If you develop on a Windows machine, but the nightly build happens on a Linux box, you shouldn't have to care about that. And (again), it should produce the same result whatever the machine. If you're using a shell script for the build, then it definitely won't work on both Windows and Linux.
- *A good ecosystem*—A good build tool should allow you to extend your build easily. Do you use an automated style checker? Is it easy to plug into your build with minimal effort? The less work you have to do to, the better.

---

[1] The names have been changed to protect the guilty.

Let's look at some of the popular build tools available for Scala and Java projects, and then you'll see how they compare against sbt. Please note that both authors of this book have extensive experience with all of the build tools mentioned here, and Josh in particular is co-author of the Scala Maven plugin. Neither of us have anything against these build tools; we just want to use the right tool for the job.

1.2   *Apache Ant*

Apache Ant originally came from the Apache Tomcat project in early 2000. It was a replacement for the Unix make build tool and was created because of a number of problems with the Unix make command. The main problem was that make consisted of only shell commands. This caused a lot of problems for the Tomcat project, because this was built in multiple places by multiple people—the maintainers couldn't predict what sort of operating system Tomcat would be built on. So James Duncan Davison wrote Ant (Another Neat Tool) to help with these portability problems. Ant uses a configuration file called a build file, usually build.xml. It looks something like this:

```xml
<?xml version="1.0"?>
<project name="Hello" default="compile">
  <target name="clean" description="remove generated files">
    <delete dir="classes"/>
  </target>
  <target name="compile" description="compile the Java source code">
    <mkdir dir="classes"/>
    <javac srcdir="src" destdir="classes"/>
  </target>
  <target name="jar" depends="compile" description="create a jar file">
    <jar destfile="hello.jar">
      <fileset dir="classes" includes="**/*.class"/>
      <manifest>
        <attribute name="Main-Class" value="com.xx.Hello"/>
      </manifest>
    </jar>
  </target>
</project>
```

This build file defines a build with three targets (effectively tasks), which are clean, compile, and jar. If you execute the jar target

```
$ ant jar
```

then Ant will first execute the compile target (because jar depends on compile) and jar target. In this case, Ant will do the following:

- Create the classes directory if it doesn't exist already
- Compile all Java sources in src to the classes directory
- Collect all of the class files generated and place them in a jar file, along with a manifest file

The main innovation of Ant was the "pure Java" approach. All of the tasks are defined in Java, not in the form of a Unix shell or Windows command line, so the same project could be built on multiple platforms with the same results, and you didn't have to maintain different build scripts. As you can see in the previous example, the tasks are referred to in the build file through an XML element; for instance:

```
<delete dir="classes" />
```

This deletes the directory classes and all of its contents. In a make file on a Windows system, this would be something like

```
> rmdir /Q /S classes
```

or on a Unix system

```
$ rm -rf classes
```

At the time Ant was a real step forward, and almost overnight it became the de facto build tool for Java.

As we said earlier, the advantage of Ant is its portability. But it has a number of limitations:

- Ant doesn't have any defaults for project layout: where to put Java files, JUnit tests, and the like. This means that every build is different, and you need to read the build.xml to find out what's going on.
- Ant doesn't have a workflow defined by default. In the previous example, the jar target depended on the compile target, but we had to explicitly say this. This increases the verbosity of build files with Ant because you always have to say everything. This doesn't encourage good practice: it's easy to accidentally comment out the tests.
- The build files don't allow reassignment to variables. This means you can't have loops or simply have a default value that's reassigned somewhere else. Again, this makes Ant awkward to work with when you have a complex build.
- Although Ant has tight integration with the Ivy dependency manager, its use still has to be explicitly specified.
- It's not easy to define a new task. You need to define a Java class or set of classes, compile them, produce a jar, and then include that jar on the Ant classpath on every build machine. If there are multiple machines, this can be a problem—for instance, an open source project where you have no idea who will download and compile your project.

Quite a few of these limitations are addressed in Apache Maven, which we'll look at now.

1.3   Apache Maven

Apache Maven is a command-line build system used extensively by Java and JVM users. The word *maven* means "accumulator of knowledge" in Yiddish.

> **Maven's objectives**
>
> Maven's primary goal is to allow a developer to comprehend the complete state of a development effort in the shortest period of time. In order to attain this goal, there are several areas of concern that Maven attempts to deal with:
>
> - Making the build process easy
> - Providing a uniform build system
> - Providing quality project information
> - Providing guidelines for best practices development
> - Allowing transparent migration to new features
>
> This is from "What is Maven?" (http://maven.apache.org/what-is-maven.html).

Maven is an "opinionated" build system; it guides you into its way of doing things. It was originally designed to address some of the Ant limitations as set out previously. For example, it defines a set of defaults for the placement of Java source files; by default you put your Java production code in src/main/java and the test code in src/test/java. You can change these defaults, but most people don't. If you don't change these defaults, no configuration is required for the source code directories. This makes for an easy build experience if your build follows the Maven standard configuration story.

1.3.1   Build definition

The build definition in Maven uses XML. This is an example build definition, called a POM (Project Object Model):

```
<project>
 <modelVersion>4.0.0</modelVersion>
 <groupId>com.mycompany.app</groupId>
 <artifactId>my-app</artifactId>
 <version>1.0</version>
 <name>Maven text project</name>
 <packaging>jar</packaging>

 <dependencies>
  <dependency>
   <groupId>junit</groupId>
   <artifactId>junit</artifactId>
   <version>4.11</version>
   <scope>test</scope>
  </dependency>
 </dependencies>
</project>
```

This defines a project called my-app, version 1.0, and we've declared a dependency on the JUnit unit-testing library, version 4.11. Maven does declarative dependency management: you declare your dependencies in the Maven configuration file (called pom.xml). When you build your project, it will download the relevant jars from the central repository and include those in the build. It will also download and include their dependent jars (called transitive dependencies), and their dependent jars, and so on. No more saving your dependent jars to your source code version control system. The main advantage of having declarative dependency management is not that it saves a few bytes of disk space, but that when you change the dependencies (by upgrading a version, for instance), all of the transitive dependencies also get upgraded automatically. The versions on the central repository are the definitive versions of those dependencies, which means that once you've downloaded JUnit version 4.11, it will never change. If there are bug fixes, the version number will change.

1.3.2 *Maven workflow—default lifecycle*

Maven has a good default workflow. Each task is executed after the tasks that should precede it. If you're packaging your project, then it will by default compile your production code, compile your test code, execute your tests,[2] and, if they succeed, package the project. This is a much better story than with Ant, because none of it needs to be configured; you get it for free. This is called the default lifecycle.

A Maven lifecycle is a series of sequential phases. Each phase can contain zero or more tasks (in Maven terms, a *goal*). When you execute a phase in Maven, it will execute all of the preceding phases before executing that phase. Simple, eh?

The main lifecycle in Maven is called the default lifecycle, and it's used for project construction and deployment. These are some of the phases in the default lifecycle:

- *Validate*—Validate that the project is correct and all necessary information is available.
- *Compile*—Compile the source code of the project.
- *Test*—Test the compiled source code by using a suitable unit-testing framework. These tests shouldn't require the code to be packaged or deployed.
- *Package*—Take the compiled code and package it in its distributable format, such as a jar.
- *Integration test*—Process and deploy the package, if necessary, into an environment where integration tests can be run.
- *Verify*—Run any checks to verify that the package is valid and meets quality criteria.
- *Install*—Install the package into the local repository for use as a dependency in other projects locally.
- *Deploy*—This is done in an integration or release environment; it copies the final package to the remote repository for sharing with other developers and projects.

---

[2] Unless, of course, you haven't defined any tests, but that's another problem.

When you execute

```
$ mvn package
```

it will execute all of the goals for the validate phase, then all of the goals for the compile phase, then the test phase, and then the package phase. There are 23 phases in the default lifecycle, but most of them don't have any goals assigned to them. They exist so that you can assign goals to them, to execute things in the right place.

A goal is actually a goal within a plugin. Maven has a plugin architecture so that you can add a new plugin and then have it be executed in the correct place in your build. This is how Maven gets its flexibility. You can either use an existing plugin (such as the Java compiler plugin) or create a new one to perform some specific task for your build. For the default lifecycle, these goals are executed for a particular phase when you're building a jar project, as shown in table 1.1.

Table 1.1 Maven phases mapping to sbt tasks

Phase	Plugin:goal
process-resources	resources:resources
compile	compiler:compile
process-test-resources	resources:testResources
test-compile	compiler:testCompile
test	surefire:test
package	jar:jar
install	install:install
deploy	deploy:deploy

This means that during the test phase you're executing the testCompile goal of the compiler plugin. This is a different but similar goal to the one executed during the compile phase. The testCompile goal compiles everything in src/test/java and includes on its classpath the sources compiled during the compile phase.

By default, Maven has three lifecycles:

- *Default*—Project construction and deployment
- *Clean*—Project cleaning
- *Site*—Project site (documentation) construction

This information was taken from "Introduction to the Build Lifecycle": http://maven.apache.org/guides/introduction/introduction-to-the-lifecycle.html.

1.3.3 *Adding another task to a Maven build*

Your default build is great, but how do you add to it? To execute something else during the build, you attach a plugin goal to the phase that you want. For instance, it's common to want to run integration tests after the packaging is done. You can add a plugin goal to the verify phase, which is similar to the test phase but executed after the package phase. You can add an execution of the `failsafe` plugin (similar to the `surefire` plugin, which executes automated unit tests) to execute your integration tests:

```
<plugin>
    <artifactId>maven-failsafe-plugin</artifactId>
    <version>2.12.4</version>
    <executions>
     <execution>
       <phase>verify</phase>
       <goals>
        <goal>verify</goal>
       </goals>
     </execution>
    </executions>
</plugin>
```

Now when you execute `mvn install`, it will run your integration tests, using the goal failsafe:verify in the verify phase. This will use the default configuration for `failsafe`. You can also add configuration parameters for a plugin. This configuration can be any of the following:

- Per user (useful for specifying default repositories or credentials)
- For a number of projects (through the use of a parent POM), which allows you to define configurations for multiple projects
- For a single project
- For a single goal, to define the configuration for that goal, so that different goals for the same plugin can have different configurations
- For multiple executions of the same goal in different phases, so that each execution of the goal in that plugin can have a different configuration

1.3.4 *Advantages of Maven*

For a simple, standard project, Maven is great. It requires only a few lines of XML, and you're up and running. You get a wealth of great plugins that do a myriad of things. The default build does what you'd expect. The default configurations are pretty good, and most of the plugins are fairly configurable.

Maven gives you a stable base with which to work. It's well known and pretty well understood. Lots of good, reliable software has been built with Maven.

1.3.5 *Limitations of Maven*

The configuration is XML based, which is great, except when you want to do something that requires options that aren't available. For a project that requires nonstandard operations or tasks, things sometimes get awkward. If there's a standard plugin that does what you want it to do, great. If the required option exists for the plugin you're using, then that's also great. If it doesn't, then the fun starts.

As an illustration, let's look at the Maven Jetty plugin, which runs a Jetty HTTP server. This is often used to run integration tests for web servers. You can run your tests against a real server.

This plugin has options to run Jetty either in-process (as a separate thread) or as a separate process. If you run it as in-process, you can't specify command-line arguments to the Java command line, so you can't (for instance) specify the amount of memory that's required for the Jetty; you have to be content with the amount allocated to Maven.

If you run it as a different process, then the server isn't run in the background and the Maven process waits for the Jetty to stop before continuing. Your tests don't get run until the server has stopped.

This isn't a criticism of the Jetty plugin; by the time you read this, this problem may have been fixed, but it illustrates the point: you're stuck with the plugin as it's written. If you need to change the plugin, you can write your own, run a modified version of the plugin, or live with the limitations. And it's not simple to create your own plugin with Maven.

Also, Maven is a command-line tool. Apart from some specific cases, there's very little interaction between you and Maven. It's designed this way: it's a build tool and nothing else. This contrasts with sbt, which is designed to both give you a stable build and be an interactive development environment.

1.4   Gradle

Gradle is the new kid on the block for JVM-based builds, at least compared to Apache Ant and Maven, and is an upgrade compared to them.

1.4.1   What is Gradle?

Gradle takes a similar approach to sbt—the build is constructed using a DSL. In the case of Gradle, it's using the Groovy language. The conventions used in Gradle are the same as in Maven; if you use src/main/java, then you don't need to specify the source location. The DSL and the sensible defaults mean that the Gradle build files are more concise than those of either Ant or Maven. Let's look at an example:

hello-gradle/build.gradle

```
apply plugin: 'java'

repositories {
    mavenCentral()
}

dependencies {
    compile group: 'commons-collections', name: 'commons-collections',
     version: '3.2'
    testCompile group: 'junit', name: 'junit', version: '4.11'
}
```

As you can see, the Gradle build files are a lot clearer and easier to read than the equivalent Maven pom.xml.[3] First you specify that you'll be using the Java plugin; this installs a number of tasks such as `compileJava` and `compileTestJava` and `jar`. The name of this project is taken from the final part of the path. If your file is called /foo/bar/hello-gradle/build.gradle, the name of the project will be `hello-gradle`. In the previous build, you're using external dependencies, so you need to explicitly set the repositories that you'd like to search—Maven central. And you're using the commons-collections for your main compilation and JUnit for your test classes. For your dependencies, Gradle acts pretty much like Maven: it downloads the dependencies from the repository, caches them locally, and you're ready to go.

1.4.2 Gradle workflow

Gradle also has a pretty good default workflow, similar to Maven. If you execute `gradle build`, the following tasks are executed:

```
$ gradle build
:compileJava
:processResources UP-TO-DATE
:classes UP-TO-DATE
:jar
:assemble
:compileTestJava UP-TO-DATE
:processTestResources UP-TO-DATE
:testClasses UP-TO-DATE
:test UP-TO-DATE
:check UP-TO-DATE
:build
BUILD SUCCESSFUL
Total time: 3.68 secs
```

Gradle uses the term *task*, similarly to Ant, but by default there are dependencies between the tasks. Executing `build` will execute all of the previous tasks. This is what you want in the vast majority of cases. Therefore, you don't need to explicitly wire the dependencies between tasks, as you do with Ant.

1.4.3 Adding another task to a Gradle build

Adding to your default build is simpler in Gradle. The Gradle DSL is written in Groovy, so you have the power and flexibility that come with that. To define a task, you can add

hello-gradle/build.gradle

```
task hello << {
    println("hello")
}
```

and then execute it:

---

[3] At least we think so.

```
$ gradle hello
:hello
hello
BUILD SUCCESSFUL
Total time: 3.199 secs
```

You can also make a task depend on another one:

hello-gradle/build.gradle

```
task goodbye(dependsOn: hello) << {
    println("goodbye")
}
```

```
$ gradle goodbye
:hello
hello
:goodbye
goodbye
BUILD SUCCESSFUL
Total time: 3.199 secs
```

1.4.4   *Advantages of Gradle*

Gradle is a great build system. It fixes most of the problems associated with Maven and provides the flexibility to add new tasks easily and quickly. It isn't as mature as Maven, but there are still plenty of plugins that give you the option of doing what you need. Lots of good, reliable software has been built with Gradle.

1.4.5   *Limitations of Gradle*

Although Gradle is a great improvement over both Ant and Maven, we, the authors, believe there are three areas that make sbt a better development experience:

- Interactive console features
- Better extensibility
- Type safety

We believe that sbt has a number of features that enhance the developer experience. Gradle lacks some of the advancements in developer experience that sbt has pushed, such as "run a given task on source code changing" or "try to recompile only the tests affected by my latest change." These features are a core focus for both the sbt core developers and plugin authors, leading to an ecosystem that offers a great out-of-the-box experience. Although Gradle excels at defining repeatable automation, we feel it still needs improvement when it comes to the full user experience of *developing*, where building is but one step in a workflow and releasing is but another.

Second, Gradle's task dependency mechanism isn't explicit. There's a distinction between regular Gradle tasks and incremental tasks, which require the user to annotate what dependencies a task needs to run. This limits user visibility into how tasks are wired together and creates two APIs for defining tasks: the simple and the advanced.

Additionally, we feel sbt offers better extensibility of its existing tasks and settings due to the visibility and extension options offered within sbt.

Finally, Gradle's groovy DSL lacks type safety. The authors of this book, and the authors of sbt, believe that type safety is a necessity for any large project, including any large build, to avoid the "sole owner syndrome," where one person understands the layout of a build and is required to do code review/training of anyone coming onto a project.

1.5 Why sbt?

After all of that, why have a new build tool? Why not simply add a new Ant task, a new Maven plugin, or a new Gradle task? There are a number of reasons.

As we've said already, a build is not a fixed, standard beast. In our experience with hundreds of different projects of different sizes and shapes, there are almost always some parts of a build that don't fit into a standard framework. The bigger the project, the more likely it is that you'll need custom tasks. The same is true of when the tasks should be executed. Even the most standard of the build tools, Maven, finds it necessary to have most of the default phases in its primary lifecycle be empty so that you can insert a task into the correct place in the build, whatever your definition of *correct* is for this task in this project. So two things that we like to have in our builds are flexibility and the ability to insert custom tasks easily.

Also, communication between tasks is hard in Ant/Maven and to a certain extent in Gradle. If you have one task that uses the output of another, you're looking at creating an intermediate file. With sbt, each task has an output (be it a value or a file) and explicit dependencies, which means that sbt can execute tasks *in parallel by default*. It uses the dependency tree to ensure that tasks are executed in the right order.

1.5.1 How sbt works

Let's take a quick look at how sbt works. sbt consists of two things: tasks and settings. And that's it, except for the details.[4]

sbt tasks

sbt is built around tasks. Unlike Maven, there are no phases, goals, or executions, just tasks. You want to do something, you execute a task. You want to ensure that a task runs after another task, you add an explicit dependency between the tasks. If you want to use the results of a task in another task, you push the output from one task into another. The results of one task are automatically available in dependent tasks. The output of an sbt task is a value (which can be of any type), so this can be passed around with ease. Multiple tasks can depend on the output of the same task. By default, sbt runs all of the tasks in parallel, but by using the dependency tree, it can work out what should be sequential and what can be parallel. Those people used to

---

[4] Hence this book.

sequential builds are sometimes surprised by the parallel-by-default nature of sbt, but it can speed up your build.

The task-oriented nature of sbt is actually more similar to Ant or Gradle than Maven. But unlike Ant, sbt puts in place a default structure and layout. Out of the box you get your `compile` task, `test` task, and `publish` task, and these work as expected: if you run the `test` task, sbt will run the `compile` task beforehand. The `compile` task compiles Scala and Java by default. The layout is similar to that of a standard Maven project.

A task in sbt is Scala code. There isn't any intermediate XML; you write the code directly in your build configuration. This gives you all of the power of Scala in your build and avoids lots of portability problems.

sbt settings

A setting in sbt is just a value. This could be the name of the project or the version of Scala to use.

Let's look in more detail how sbt compares to Maven, Ant, and Gradle.

1.5.2   *Plugin architecture vs. tasks*

Let's look at some of the differences between the plugin style architecture and sbt tasks.

How to define an sbt task

In sbt, it's easy to add a custom task to a build, and if you use it in more than one place, it's relatively easy to add a plugin that can be used from more than one place. Configuration and tasks are defined using a combination of declaration and standard Scala code. As an example, you'll define a task in sbt that takes the output of a shell command and retrieves the first line:

```
val gitHeadCommitSha = taskKey[String]("Determines the current git commit
    SHA")

gitHeadCommitSha := Process("git rev-parse HEAD").lines.head
```

We're not going to explain the details here (you'll have to wait for chapter 3 for that), but that's all it takes to define a new task.

Note that this code appears directly in the build definition file, so as soon as it's checked into the version control system, it's available to the other users of the project, including your continuous integration system.

Once your task is generic enough or useful enough, you can turn the task into a plugin, which means that you can share the task definition via a repository. This is similar to the Maven model.

Defining a Maven plugin

How do you define a custom task in Maven? Well, all of the Maven configuration is done in XML, and you can only execute defined plugins. This means that if you can't find a plugin that does what you want, you'll have to resort to one of the plugins that allows custom code execution (such as the Ant[5] or Groovy plugins). If you're doing standard stuff, this isn't necessarily a problem, but as we said previously, there are almost always tasks in a build that require something that doesn't fit within the existing Maven plugin structure. One example would be the example from chapter 5, where we take our packaged jar and deploy it to an integration server. If your Maven plugin doesn't support the parameter you want, or the plugin simply doesn't exist, life gets harder. To define a custom task in Maven, you must create a new plugin.

To create a plugin, you need to do the following:

1 Read up on how to define a Maven plugin (see Guide to Developing Java Plugins at http://maven.apache.org/guides/plugin/guide-java-plugin-development.html).

2 Define a mojo. This takes the form of a bit of Java code, such as this:

```
package sample.plugin;

import org.apache.maven.plugin.AbstractMojo;
import org.apache.maven.plugin.MojoExecutionException;
import org.apache.maven.plugins.annotations.Mojo;

/**
 * Says "Hi" to the user.
 */
@Mojo( name = "sayhi")
public class GreetingMojo extends AbstractMojo {
    public void execute() throws MojoExecutionException {
        getLog().info( "Hello, world." );
    }
}
```

- You then create a Maven project definition:

```
<project>
  <modelVersion>4.0.0</modelVersion>

  <groupId>sample.plugin</groupId>
  <artifactId>hello-maven-plugin</artifactId>
  <version>1.0-SNAPSHOT</version>
  <packaging>maven-plugin</packaging>

  <name>Sample Parameter-less Maven Plugin</name>

  <dependencies>
    <dependency>
      <groupId>org.apache.maven</groupId>
      <artifactId>maven-plugin-api</artifactId>
      <version>2.0</version>
    </dependency>
  </dependencies>
</project>
```

---

[5] The irony of having a Maven plugin that executes Ant tasks is not lost on us, because Maven was designed to replace Ant.

3 You then compile and package this plugin and deploy it to your local Maven repository so that you can use it. If you want to be able to use it from other development machines or your Jenkins server, you need to deploy it to a repository that they can get to as well.

Now you can use your plugin.

Does Ant do any better?

Does Ant do any better? Not really. To define an Ant task, you go through a similar process to Maven: first you extend a class `org.apache.tools.ant.Task` and then implement the `execute()` method, which does the work. After this, you have distribution problems similar to Maven's, though; you need to make this class available to all instances of Ant that you're going to use (all development machines, Jenkins, and so on). But this is harder than with Maven because there's no standard method for distributing plugins via a repository as there is with Maven.

And what about Gradle?

As you saw earlier, defining a task in Gradle is relatively simple. But the difference between incremental and regular tasks sometimes makes it awkward to use.

1.5.3   *Phases vs. task dependencies*

One area that always causes confusion with Maven is the order of execution of tasks or goals. It seems simple enough: a goal is executed in a phase, and the phases are executed sequentially. But at a more fine-grained level it gets complicated. If you have two tasks executed within a phase, which gets executed first? If the two are in the same pom.xml, there's an implicit order of execution: the first gets executed first and the second, second. But if there's a default goal assigned to that phase, then this will get executed before anything you specify in your POM. If you want to execute something before a default goal in a phase, you need to completely duplicate the configuration for that plugin in your pom.xml, effectively replacing the default configuration.

This implicit order of execution can cause problems when it comes to parallelizing your build. If there are dependencies between Maven goals (say one goal produces a file that's consumed by another), then you can't parallelize your build with Maven.

With sbt, you have to specify an explicit dependency between tasks. This enables sbt to run tasks *in parallel by default*. If task A depends on task B, and task C also depends on task B, then sbt runs task B and then runs tasks A and C in parallel. One other option that a Maven user has is to define a custom lifecycle. This isn't simple, and, in essence, you'll be doing exactly what sbt does out of the box.

1.5.4   *Passing information around your build*

Passing information between different tasks is hard in Maven and Ant. If you do have dependent tasks, then you'll probably want to pass information between them. This is relatively easy in sbt but harder in Maven, because you usually have to pass information through an intermediate file. In sbt, you can simply return the information from the first task as the return value of the task. For the example of the Git process discussed previously, we retrieved the HEAD for Git for our project and returned it as the return value for the task. If we make this a dependent task for another task, this information automatically becomes available. This makes chaining tasks a lot easier.

This is another area where sbt comes into its own. You know that the task has executed because you have the value. It's not certain when a task or goal will execute in Maven.

1.5.5 Working with Scala

Until now, we've spoken only about issues that can apply equally to Scala and Java builds. Ant, Maven, and Gradle all have excellent Scala plugins, and Scala can be compiled equally well with all of the build tools mentioned here. A Scala build tool requires the same things as a Java build tool, but there are a couple of additional problems that come with Scala builds.

Cross-compilation for multiple Scala versions

The most prominent example is cross-compilation. First, a bit of background: Scala (the library) is binary-compatible between minor version releases, so 2.10.0 is compatible with 2.10.1, but 2.10.0 isn't compatible with 2.9.1. Why do you care? Well, you can't use version 2.10.1 of the Scala library with a project that has been compiled against 2.9.1. Say your project is a utility jar that's used in two other projects, one of which is compiled against 2.9.1 and one against 2.10.1; you'll have to produce two versions of your jar, compiled against 2.9 and 2.10.

With Ant, Maven, and Gradle, this starts to get difficult. Gradle and Maven do better than Ant, but sbt has built-in options for this sort of thing. You can tell sbt to cross-compile directly in the build definition:

```
scalaVersion := "2.10.1"

crossScalaVersions := Seq("2.8.2", "2.9.2")
```

Now when you compile, by default it will compile using the 2.10.1 compiler against the 2.10.1 release of the Scala library, but you also have the option of compiling against 2.8.2 and/or 2.9.2. This will automatically pick up the dependencies with the correct library version. This option isn't restricted to the Scala versions, either; if you have one version of a dependency for your 2.10.1 version and a different version for 2.9.1, this is easy to include in sbt:

```
                                            Decide which dependencies to
                                            include based on Scala version

libraryDependencies += (scalaBinaryVersion.value match {
  case "2.10" => "org.specs2" %% "specs2" % "2.0"      ◁——— Use 2.0 of specs2 with 2.10.
  case "2.9.1" => "org.specs2" %% "specs2" % "1.12.4"  ◁—┐
})                                                        │ Use 1.12.4 with 2.9.1.
```

In this example, when you compile against 2.10.x, you're going to use version 2.0 of the specs2 testing library. When you compile against 2.9.1, version 2.0 isn't available, so you'll have to use an older version, 1.12.4.

Lots more classes in Scala

The Scala compiler tends to generate more classes (.class files) than would be generated by the equivalent program written in Java. This is due to how Scala generates code for closures and other constructs that aren't supported directly in the JVM, which it must simulate. The concrete effect is that the JVM takes longer to get up and running with Scala code—and not only on compilation but on test startup as well. Gradle, Ant, and Maven are command-line tools, so every time you run them, they need to start from scratch (read slow). But sbt is designed to run as an interactive environment, so it doesn't need to restart each time.

Slow Scala compilation

One of the frustrations of Scala is the compilation speed, which is seen by some (most?) developers as slow, at least compared to Java. sbt has good incremental compilation; it recompiles only those files that have changed. And if you use it in console mode (see section 1.6, "Interactivity"), then it gets even quicker. Maven, Ant, Gradle, and sbt in command-line mode all suffer from the slowness of the JVM startup.

These are examples of how sbt is, in general, more suited to building Scala projects than the other available build tools.

1.5.6   *Multiproject builds*

sbt is also designed specifically for multiproject (sometimes called multimodule) builds. These are builds that include more than one artifact. One example could be a project that contains a client and a server, which communicate via a set of web services. In this case, it makes sense to have three projects: the client, the server, and a common library that includes all of the common classes, such as the payloads for the services.

Maven and Gradle also do a pretty good job of this. For example, if project A depends on projects B and C, then Maven can compile and run the tests for projects B and C in parallel, if you tell it to do so. It then builds project A. sbt does better: it will *compile* B and C in parallel and then compile A in parallel with running the tests for B and C. If the tests for B or C are long running, then the build for A can finish before those for B and C.

Multimodule Maven builds have one more limitation: the submodules need to know about the parent module. If A depends on B and C, then the POM for A will contain references to B and C. But you also need to declare in your POMs for B and C that A is their parent. The modules also need to be in a strict hierarchy in the filesystem; B and C need to be subdirectories of A.

sbt doesn't have this restriction. You can declare B a submodule of A without B knowing about A. The directory containing B doesn't need to be a subdirectory of A;

it can be elsewhere on the filesystem—on another machine, perhaps. You can even specify a dependency on a remote Git source code repository; sbt will download and compile the project for you.

We'll look at this in chapter 3, "Core Concepts."

1.5.7　*Dependency resolution*

Maven and sbt have slightly different dependency resolutions. sbt uses Ivy for its dependency resolution, whereas Maven uses Aether. Gradle uses its own dependency resolution mechanism. For 95% of the tasks, you won't notice it, but it does have some caveats, so read appendix A for those.

1.6　*Interactivity/reactivity of sbt*

There's one major area that we haven't mentioned much until now: the interactive nature of sbt. We didn't mention it in our comparison because Maven, Gradle, and Ant aren't really interactive environments.

1.6.1　*Quicker compilation and testing cycle*

As well as creating a good, stable build, sbt can be used in console mode, so you can run it in a command window somewhere and leave it. This improves compilation speed (no JVM startup slowness and better incremental compilation) and generally improves reactivity. sbt can be executed with a task on the command line:

```
$ sbt compile
```

This will execute the compile task and then exit. If you don't specify a task, sbt enters console mode and you can execute tasks by typing them into the prompt:

```
$ sbt                                                          <──  Runs sbt
[info] Loading project definition from /home/mfarwell/code/sbt/
➥sbt-in-action-examples/chapter2/project
[info] Set current project to preowned-kittens (in build
➥file:/home/mfarwell/code/sbt/sbt-in-action-examples/chapter2/)
> compile                                                      <──  Compiles
[info] Compiling 3 Scala sources to /home/mfarwell/code/sbt/
➥sbt-in-action-examples/chapter2/target/scala-2.10/classes...
[success] Total time: 3 s, completed 15-May-2015 09:32:55
> update                                                       <──  More commands
[info] Updating {file:/home/mfarwell/code/sbt/sbt-in-action-
➥examples/chapter2/}chapter2...
[info] Resolving org.fusesource.jansi#jansi;1.4 ...
[info] Done updating.
[success] Total time: 0 s, completed 15-May-2015 09:33:01
```

1.6.2　*Quicker compilation and testing cycle*

When you're in sbt in console mode, you can use the ~ method to continually execute a task. If you prefix any command with ~, sbt will execute the command and then wait for source file changes. When a source file changes, it will re-execute the task and so on. And obviously, if a task depends on another task, it will do that task first:

```
$ sbt                                                    ⟵── Runs sbt
[info] Loading project definition from /home/mfarwell/code/sbt/
➥sbt-in-action-examples/chapter2/project
[info] Set current project to preowned-kittens (in build
➥file:/home/mfarwell/code/sbt/sbt-in-action-examples/chapter2/)
> ~test                                                  ⟵── Runs tests
[info] Compiling 1 Scala source to /home/mfarwell/code/sbt/
➥sbt-in-action-examples/chapter2/target/scala-2.10/test-classes...  ⟵┐
[info] LogicSpec                                                      │
[info]                                               sbt compiles sources
[info] The 'matchLikelihood' method should              and test sources.
[info] + be 100% when all attributes match        ⟵
[info] + be 0% when no attributes match
[info]                                               sbt executes
[info]                                               the tests.
[info] Total for specification LogicSpec
[info] Finished in 22 ms
[info] 2 examples, 0 failure, 0 error
[info]                                                        sbt waits for
[info] Passed: Total 2, Failed 0, Errors 0, Passed 2          source code
[success] Total time: 8 s, completed 15-May-2015 09:37:22     changes.
1. Waiting for source changes... (press enter to interrupt)  ⟵┘
```

Here we've executed ~test, which will compile our sources, compile our test sources, execute the tests, and then wait for more changes. When you change the source file, the whole cycle gets run again. Obviously, sbt recompiles only the necessary files each time, and if you use the ~testQuick command rather than ~test, it will execute only those tests that have been affected by the changed sources. This cuts down on the change/compile/test cycle. sbt gives you immediate feedback on how you're doing. You'll see more about this in chapter 4, "Testing."

1.6.3   *sbt and the Scala REPL—the console command*

One of the things that Scala developers love is the Scala REPL. REPL stands for Read-Evaluate-Print Loop. It allows you to type Scala expressions that are evaluated immediately, and to try things out and explore. If you type Scala at the command line, this starts the Scala REPL, and you can enter Scala code and see what the results are:

```
Welcome to Scala version 2.11.1 (Java 1.7.0_76).
Type in expressions to have them evaluated.
Type :help for more information.

scala> val l = List(1,2,3)                  ⟵────────── Defines a value
l: List[Int] = List(1, 2, 3)

scala> l.map(i => i + 1)         ⟵──  Calls a method using it and shows the results
res0: List[Int] = List(2, 3, 4)
```

You can also have tab completion of methods (similar to Ctrl-spacebar in Eclipse or IntelliJ). This is useful, but sbt makes it even more useful in the context of a project. sbt has a console command, which starts the REPL from sbt, but sbt will put all of your dependencies on the classpath so you can use it to evaluate and explore the available APIs in your project.

1.7 *Summary*

In this chapter you've seen that a build tool should provide the following:

- *Reproducible builds*—It doesn't matter who does the build.
- *Minimal configuration*—Get up and running fast.
- *Encouragement of good practices*—For example, it should run tests before packaging.
- *Portability*—It should run on almost any machine.
- *A good ecosystem*—There's less work for the developers.

sbt ticks these boxes, and in addition it provides an interactive environment that increases developer productivity by offering these features:

- *Faster compilation times*—Lower startup times and incremental compilation.
- *Easy addition of custom tasks*—They're right there in the build definition.
- *Faster compile/test cycles through the use of the ~ command*—Quicker feedback.
- *The ability to explore your project using the Scala REPL*—Again, quicker feedback.

You've seen that although Apache Ant, Apache Maven, and Gradle are excellent tools, they don't quite give you the flexibility or functionality you need to build a Scala project. Let's go learn about sbt.

Getting started 2

This chapter covers

- Testing code in a live interpreted session
- Automatically running tasks when sources change
- Filtering what tests to execute using `testOnly`
- Providing discoverable usage using tab completion
  and an `inspect` command

The simple build tool (sbt) is used for building Java and Scala projects; its purpose is to allow users to skillfully perform the basics of building and to customize endlessly. sbt, at its core, provides a parallel execution engine and configuration system that allow you to design an efficient and robust script to build your software. sbt aims, above all, to be consistent in the basic concepts so that once you learn the concepts, you don't have to unlearn them as you dive further into the build system.

sbt is a highly interactive tool, meant to be used during all stages of the development process. It provides interactive help and autocomplete for most services and promotes a type of autodiscovery for builds. Although you can use sbt as a command-line tool, it doesn't really shine until you use its shell.

Throughout this book, you'll be designing an sbt build for a sophisticated website called preowned-kittens.com that handles the resale of pet kittens. The website attempts to find ideal owners by matching buyer survey questions to known statistics of happy pet owners and behavior characteristics of the kittens. As you add features to the website, you'll add new testing and debugging features to the build to ensure the entire preowned-kittens.com team is able to work effectively.

To start working on your website, you need to first install sbt.

2.1 Setting up sbt

sbt provides installation packages for most operating system variants at http://www.scala-sbt.org/download.html. The examples in this book were written using sbt version 0.13.5, downloadable at https://repo.scala-sbt.org/scalasbt/native-packages/sbt/0.13.5/sbt-0.13.5.zip. Although you're free to try the latest version, we recommend sticking to the one used in the book.

> **Windows users**
>
> If you're using Windows, there's a fast path to setup. You can download the MSI from http://scalasbt.artifactoryonline.com/scalasbt/sbt-native-packages/org/scala-sbt/sbt/0.13.5/sbt.msi and run the installation script. After setup, be sure to reboot your machine so that the PATH environment variable is correct. You can skip to the "Running sbt" section.

After downloading the zip file, extract it into a safe application location, such as C:\Users\Me\apps or /home/me/apps. You should see something like this in the extracted directory:

```
sbt/
  bin/
    sbt                                    Launcher script
                                           for Linux/Mac
    sbt-launch.jar              ◁───────   Launcher
    sbt.bat                     Launcher scripts for
    sbt-win                     Windows/Cygwin
    ...
  license.txt
```

Everything needed to run sbt is in the sbt/bin directory. This directory consists of the actual sbt launcher and convenience scripts that provide easier configuration of the Java runtime. The sbt/bin directory must be placed in the PATH to use sbt via the command line.

2.1.1 Setting the PATH in bash (for Linux/Mac)

In order for the operating system to find the newly downloaded sbt installation, you have to point it at the script files. First you need to locate the local shell setup file for your user:

- If you're using bash, open ~/.bashrc.
- If you're using KSH or SH, open ~/.profile.

Add the following lines to your setup file (near the bottom):

```
SBT_HOME=/path/to/your/zip/extraction
PATH=$PATH:$SBT_HOME/bin
export PATH
```

Close your current terminal window and open a new one.

2.1.2 *Running sbt*

Now that the path is set up, you can run the sbt script. First create a new directory for an sbt project. Make one called kittens in the home directory.

When running sbt for the first time, you should see the following output:

```
$ sbt
Getting org.scala-sbt sbt 0.13.5 ...
downloading http://repo.typesafe.com/typesafe/ivy-releases/org.scala-sbt/sbt/
    0.13.5/jars/sbt.jar ...
  [SUCCESSFUL ] org.scala-sbt#sbt;0.13.5!sbt.jar (254ms)
downloading http://repo.typesafe.com/typesafe/ivy-releases/org.scala-sbt/
    main/0.13.5/jars/main.jar ...
  [SUCCESSFUL ] org.scala-sbt#main;0.13.5!main.jar (1876ms)
downloading http://repo.typesafe.com/typesafe/ivy-releases/org.scala-sbt/
    compiler-interface/0.13.5/jars/compiler-interface-bin.jar ...
MANY MORE DOWNLOADS
5 artifacts copied, 0 already retrieved (24386kB/59ms)
[info] Loading project definition from /home/jsuereth/kittens/project
[info] Updating {file:/home/jsuereth/kittens/project/}default-b242f1...
[info] Resolving org.fusesource.jansi#jansi;1.4 ...
[info] Done updating.
[info] Set current project to preowned-kittens (in build file:/home/jsuereth/
    kittens/)
>
```

This is sbt downloading the actual pieces needed to run the build. By default, sbt includes only the bare minimum it needs to launch builds. The first time you run a project, sbt needs to download the remaining portions required, as well as compile the local project's build definition. This process happens only the first time a dependency is needed or when your build changes.

Exit out of sbt by using the exit command. Now when running sbt in this directory, you should see the following output:

```
jsuereth@jsuereth-work-i7:~/kittens$ sbt
[info] Set current project to kittens (in build file:/home/jsuereth/kittens/)
>
```

Notice how sbt was much quicker in loading and didn't download any additional pieces. This is because you compiled them in your previous session. Now let's talk about what the > means. This is the sbt command prompt. Here is where you'll interact with your build and, optionally, define portions of it. Let's work on defining your first build.

> **Interactive development**
>
> sbt is designed to be a highly interactive build tool. To take full advantage of its merits, it's best to use the sbt shell often during development. Even when using an IDE for writing code, having the sbt shell live can drastically improve the development environment. Throughout the book there will be lots of sbt shell session examples to encourage this type of interactive development and learning.
>
> Although this book makes no assumptions about which IDE or text editor to use, it may be easiest to start with a lightweight text editor, like the Sublime text editor (http://sublimetext.com).

2.2 Setting up a build

Every project using sbt should have two files:

- project/build.properties
- build.sbt

The build.properties file is used to inform sbt which version it should use for your build, and the build.sbt file defines the actual settings for your build. Create and fill in these two files with the following contents:

project/build.properties: `sbt.version=0.13.7`

build.sbt:
```
name := "preowned-kittens"

version := "1.0"
```
Empty line between settings was mandatory prior to sbt 0.13.7

These files configure the version of sbt used for the build and set the name and version of the project itself. We'll cover the syntax of these settings in more detail later. For now, type this code into your editor and get a feel for sbt in action.

> **Build files optional**
>
> Because sbt includes settings for a default project, it requires no build files to run for the simplest of builds. But it's a good practice to always manually create the project/build.properties and build.sbt files.

Now that you have the skeleton of the build in place, take a look at it inside sbt. Rerun the `sbt` command in the kittens directory. You should see the following output:

```
$ sbt
[info] Loading project definition from /home/jsuereth/kittens
[info] Set current project to preowned-kittens (in build file:/home/jsuereth/
    kittens)
>
```

When starting up, sbt now informs you that it's using the project preowned-kittens rather than default-174241. This is thanks to the name setting you added in the build.sbt file.

Now that you have sbt running with a project build file, let's see what it's able to do. sbt comes with a comprehensive help menu, so take a look at it in figure 2.1.

```
> help

  help                        Displays this help message or prints detailed help on requested
commands (run 'help <command>').
  about                       Displays basic information about sbt and the build.
  tasks                       Lists the tasks defined for the current project.
  settings                    Lists the settings defined for the current project.
  reload                      (Re)loads the project in the current directory
  projects                    Lists the names of available projects or temporarily
adds/removes extra builds to the session.
  project                     Displays the current project or changes to the provided
`project`.
  set                         Evaluates a Setting and applies it to the current project.
  session                     Manipulates session settings.  For details, run 'help session'.
  inspect                     Prints the value for 'key', the defining scope, delegates,
related definitions, and dependencies.
  ; <command> (; <command>)*  Runs the provided semicolon-separated commands.
  ~ <command>                 Executes the specified command whenever source files change.
  last                        Displays output from a previous command or the output from a
specific task.
  last-grep                   Shows lines from the last output for 'key' that match 'pattern'.
  exit                        Terminates the build.
  show <key>                  Displays the result of evaluating the setting or task associated
with 'key'.

More command help available using 'help <command>' for:
  !, -, <, alias, append, apply, eval, iflast, reboot, shell
```

Figure 2.1   sbt's comprehensive help menu

There are a lot of options here! We'll return to some of these and investigate as needed. But for now the three most important command-line options are these:

- tasks—Lists the tasks you can run on the build
- settings—Lists the settings you can modify for the project
- inspect—Displays information about a given setting or task

Let's look at each.

2.2.1   *Tasks*

Tasks are things that sbt build can do for you, like compiling a project, creating documentation, or running tests. We'll look at these in more detail later. For now, let's look at what sbt provides out of the box:

```
> tasks

This is a list of tasks defined for the current project.
It does not list the scopes the tasks are defined in; use the 'inspect'
    command for that.
```

```
Tasks produce values. Use the 'show' command to run the task and print the
    resulting value.

    clean           Deletes files produced by the build ...
    compile         Compiles sources.
    console         Starts the Scala interpreter with the ...
    consoleProject  Starts the Scala interpreter with the sbt ...
    consoleQuick    Starts the Scala interpreter with the ...
    copyResources   Copies resources to the output directory.
    doc             Generates API documentation.
    package         Produces the main artifact, such as a ...
    packageBin      Produces a main artifact, such as a ...
    packageDoc      Produces a documentation artifact, such ...
    packageSrc      Produces a source artifact, such as a ...
    publish         Publishes artifacts to a repository.
    publishLocal    Publishes artifacts to the local repository.
    run             Runs a main class, passing along args ...
    runMain         Runs the main class selected by arg ...
    test            Executes all tests.
    testOnly        Executes the tests provided as arguments ...
    testQuick       Executes the tests that either failed ...
    update          Resolves and optionally retrieves ...

More tasks may be viewed by increasing verbosity. See 'help tasks'.
```

As you can see, there's a lot available right off the bat. Again, we'll take note of all the possible tasks you can run and focus on the ones you'll be using immediately. Try out the following compile task:

```
> compile
[info] Updating {file:/home/jsuereth/kittens/}default-19b869... ◄─── Log output
[info] Resolving org.fusesource.jansi#jansi;1.4 ...
[info] Done updating.
[success] Total time: 0 s, completed Dec 26, 2012 8:17:30 PM
```

Result of the task

sbt keeps track of how long all tasks take to run. It's a good goal to keep build times as low as possible.

Because the project is still empty, the compile command returns immediately. You'll create a hello world program and watch the compile task do something useful. First you need to know where to put the source code. For that, you can check the settings help.

2.2.2 Settings

Run the settings help on the sbt command line and see if that points you to where source code for the project should go:

```
> settings

This is a list of settings defined for the current project.
It does not list the scopes the settings are defined in; use the 'inspect'
    command for that.
```

```
autoCompilerPlugins              If true, enables automatically  ...
autoScalaLibrary                 Adds a dependency on scala-library ...
baseDirectory                    The base directory. Depending on ...
classDirectory                   Directory for compiled classes ...
crossPaths                       If true, enables cross paths, ...
fork                             If true, forks a new JVM when ...
initialCommands                  Initial commands to execute ...
javaHome                         Selects the Java installation used ...
javaSource                       Default Java source directory.
libraryDependencies              Declares managed dependencies.
managedResourceDirectories       List of managed resource directories.
maxErrors                        The maximum number of errors, such ...
name                             Project name.
offline                          Configures sbt to work without ...
organization                     Organization/group ID.
publishArtifact                  Enables or disables publishing ...
publishTo                        The resolver to publish to.
resourceDirectory                Default unmanaged resource ...
scalaHome                        If Some, defines the local Scala ...
scalaSource                      Default Scala source directory.
scalaVersion                     The version of Scala used for building.
sourceDirectories                List of all source directories ...
sourceDirectory                  Default directory containing sources.
target                           Main directory for files generated ...
unmanagedBase                    The default directory for manually ...
unmanagedResourceDirectories     Unmanaged resource directories ...
unmanagedSourceDirectories       Unmanaged source directories, which ...
version                          The version/revision of the current ...
```

More settings may be viewed by increasing verbosity. See 'help settings'.

Again, there are a lot of default settings. We'll make another note to return here when needed and focus on the goal of adding some source code. Because we're into the Scala language, let's look more at the following scalaSource setting (for those interested in Java, the javaSource setting provides the same function as scalaSource):

```
> scalaSource                                    ⊲—— Type the setting name into the sbt prompt.

[info] /home/jsuereth/kittens/src/main/scala     ⊲—— The current value of the setting
```

The output tells you that Scala source files should go under the src/main/scala directory under your build directory. Here is where you'll put the first bit of source code for the preowned-kittens website.

Next you'll add a hello world application to the preowned-kittens project. To do so, create a file in src/main/scala like the one shown here:

```
src/main/scala/PreownedKittenMain.scala
object PreownedKittenMain extends App {
  println("Hello, sbt world!")
}
```

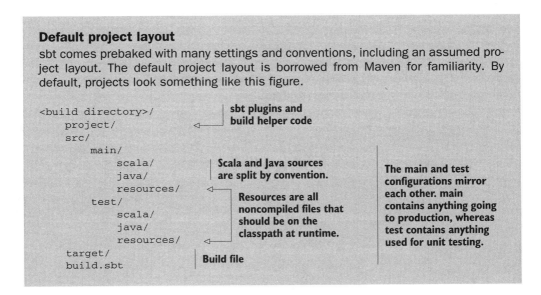

Default project layout

sbt comes prebaked with many settings and conventions, including an assumed project layout. The default project layout is borrowed from Maven for familiarity. By default, projects look something like this figure.

```
<build directory>/
    project/              ┌── sbt plugins and
    src/                  └── build helper code
        main/
            scala/        │ Scala and Java sources
            java/         │ are split by convention.
            resources/
        test/             │ Resources are all
            scala/        │ noncompiled files that
            java/         │ should be on the
            resources/    │ classpath at runtime.
    target/
    build.sbt             │ Build file
```

The main and test configurations mirror each other. main contains anything going to production, whereas test contains anything used for unit testing.

This Scala object extends the scala.App class, allowing it to be used as a main entry point to an application. It does one thing when run: prints the sentence "Hello, sbt world!" Run sbt's compile command and make sure the build sees this file:

```
> compile
[info] Compiling 1 Scala source to /home/jsuereth/kittens/target/scala-2.10/
    classes...
[success] Total time: 1 s, completed Dec 26, 2012 11:03:15 PM
```

This time, running compile isn't quite instantaneous. It takes ~1s to compile this Scala file.

Now that you have your first Scala code compiled, you can use sbt to run the code. To run this application in sbt, use the run task in the sbt console:

```
> run
[info] Running PreownedKittenMain
Hello, sbt world!
[success] Total time: 0 s, completed Dec 26, 2012 11:05:00 PM
>
```

Here you can see that the run task found the PreownedKittenMain application you just built and runs it locally. The output from the application is printed directly to the console, and then the sbt prompt returns when the application is done.

2.3 Running code

There's nothing like kicking the tires on some new code you wrote to make sure it does what's expected. A lot of software development is compiling and running code, to make sure it does what was expected.

In sbt, running code can take on a few different flavors. Here's a nonexhaustive list of options:

- Run any applications (as you saw with `PreownedKittenMain`).
- Open a Scala interpreted session against your current codebase.
- Run any tests defined on the project.

Interacting with code in the interpreter

One of the greatest advantages offered in sbt is the ability to explore a project through the Scala REPL (a.k.a. Scala console or Scala interpreter). This provides a command-line interface where you can directly construct classes, call methods, and see what happens.

Next you'll work on defining the entities for your preowned-kittens website and explore the API using the interpreter.

The preowned-kittens website is all about kittens. These kittens need to be matched up with buyers. The premise is that the buyers will list a set of preferences for the kittens they wish to buy, such as "kid friendly," "female," and so on. You need to be able to determine which kitten matches a buyer's preferences and how strong that match is. You'll use sbt to do a bit of exploratory coding in this regard.

First create a models.scala file in the src/main/scala directory of the project with the following content:

src/main/scala/models.scala

```
case class Kitten(id: Long,
                  attributes: Seq[String])
case class BuyerPreferences(attributes: Seq[String])
```

These classes are pretty simplistic right now. Each has a set of attributes, and each kitten has some sort of unique ID that's used to identify where it came from. This is far from being a complete data model for kittens, but it's a good way for you to start using code within sbt.

Now that you have a basic data model, see if you can make a function that detects how likely a kitten is to be a good match with a buyer. To do this, first start the Scala interpreter against your current project. Run the `console` task in sbt and you should see the following output:

```
> console
[info] Compiling 2 Scala sources to /home/jsuereth/kittens/target/scala-2.10/
    classes...
[info] Starting scala interpreter...
[info]
Welcome to Scala version 2.10.0 (OpenJDK 64-Bit Server VM, Java 1.6.0_24).
Type in expressions to have them evaluated.
Type :help for more information.

scala>
```

Now you're running an interpreter directly against your project. Instantiate a kitten and see what happens:

```
scala> val tabby = Kitten(id = 124,
     |        attributes = Seq("female", "tabby", "kid-friendly"))
tabby: Kitten = Kitten(124,List(female, tabby, kid-friendly))
```

What you typed into the interpreter

Result variable | **Result type** | **Result toString**

In this case, you've created a variable called `tabby` that is of the type `Kitten`, and the `toString` method returns `Kitten(124,List(female, tabby, kid-friendly))`.

Now you can make a buyer preferences object:

```
scala> val prefs = BuyerPreferences(List("male", "tabby", "kid-friendly"))
prefs: BuyerPreferences = BuyerPreferences(List(male, tabby, kid-friendly)
```

Now that you have kitten and buyer preferences, you can experiment with creating a function to determine how likely a match the kitten is to the buyer. Because you're in the interpreter, you don't need to create a method directly; you can start experimenting with function calls and see what they return directly. Pressing the Tab key will even display possible functions that can be called. Here's a sample session attempting to discover a good `matchLikelihood` method:

```
scala> prefs.attributes.map(attribute =>
     tabby.attributes.contains(attribute))
res1: Seq[Boolean] = List(false, true, true)
```

First you take all the buyer's preferred attributes and check the kitten to see whether it matches each attribute individually. The result is a list of Boolean values, denoting whether the kitten has a given attribute. This list is helpful, but you need to convert it to some kind of likely match score that you can use to compare different kittens for a given buyer and find the best result. Try to determine the percentage of attributes that match:

```
scala> res1 map (matched => if(matched) 1.0 else 0)
res2: Seq[Double] = List(0.0, 1.0, 1.0)

scala> res2.sum / res2.length
res3: Double = 0.6666666666666666
```

The first thing you must do to grab the percentage of similar preferences is convert the Booleans to 0.0 or 1.0 values. Now, you can take the average of the value in the list, and this should tell you the percentage of attributes that matched a given kitten. For the example, you had two matches ("tabby" and "kid-friendly") and one non-match ("male").

This algorithm looks like a good first step toward our goal of enlightened kitten shopping. You'll translate this into a method on the project. Create a new src/main/ scala/logic.scala file with the following contents:

```
src/main/scala/logic.scala
object Logic {
  def matchLikelihood(kitten: Kitten,
                      buyer: BuyerPreferences): Double = {
    val matches = buyer.attributes map { attribute =>
      kitten.attributes contains attribute
    }
    val nums = matches map { b => if(b) 1.0 else 0.0 }
    nums.sum / nums.length
  }
}
```

Now exit the running Scala interpreter and start a new one to try out the new method:

```
scala> :q
[success] Total time: 1214 s, completed Jan 21, 2013 12:55:51 PM
> console
[info] Compiling 1 Scala source to /home/jsuereth/kittens/target/scala-2.10/
    classes...
[info] Starting scala interpreter...
[info]
Welcome to Scala version 2.10.1 (OpenJDK 64-Bit Server VM, Java 1.6.0_24).
Type in expressions to have them evaluated.
Type :help for more information.

scala>
```

> **Always remember to exit the Scala interpreter**
> When sbt is running the Scala interpreter, the prompt will show scala> versus the usual >. If you're editing project code and need to see the changes in the interpreter, remember to always exit (using the :q command) and return to the console.

Now the new file is compiled and you're back in the interpreter. You can use the up-arrow key to rerun your previous code to create the kitten and buyer preferences.

```
scala> val tabby = Kitten(id = 124, attributes = Seq("female", "tabby",
    "kid-friendly"))
tabby: Kitten = Kitten(124,List(female, tabby, kid-friendly))
scala> val prefs = BuyerPreferences(List("male", "tabby", "kid-friendly"))
prefs: BuyerPreferences = BuyerPreferences(List(male, tabby, kid-friendly))
```

Try out the new logic method:

```
scala> Logic.matchLikelihood(tabby, prefs)
res1: Double = 0.6666666666666666
```

As you can see, the result is the same as when you tested in the console.

Now that you have your first function for the used-kittens website, you can write some tests to make sure it behaves as you desire.

Experiment-driven development

A lot of modern frameworks advocate test-driven development. Although this approach is certainly viable within sbt, it also allows a more interactive approach I like to call experiment-driven development. As demonstrated in this section, a lot of development within sbt involves a level of experimentation in the Scala console before committing to a particular implementation or API design. With sbt, a more common development model is as follows:

- Experiment with an implementation/API inside the console.
- Copy the best implementation into the project code.
- Write exhaustive unit tests to ensure behavior matches requirements.
- Improve the implementation based on unit test discoveries.

2.4 Testing code

Although there are many options available for testing Scala code, for the purpose of this chapter you'll use the specs2 library (http://specs2.org). You'll see more testing libraries later. For now, declare a dependency on this specs2 in your build and get some testing going. Add the following line to build.sbt:

```
libraryDependencies +=
  "org.specs2" % "specs2_2.10" % "1.14" % "test"
```

For now, the syntax with % and strings may look a bit arcane, so take it as a given. The syntax and rules for dependencies, including testing versus compile-time dependencies, are covered in appendix A, "Ivy."

Now that you've altered the build, you need to tell the sbt console to load the new changes. If the console is still open from the previous section, use the `reload` command to update the build:

```
> reload
[info] Loading project definition from /home/jsuereth/kittens/project
[info] Set current project to preowned-kittens (in build file:/home/jsuereth/
    kittens/)
>
```

This will ensure that any changes to build.sbt are compiled and incorporated in the console.

Make sure to reload

Any change to the build.sbt file or files in the project/ directory won't be immediately available within the sbt console. The `reload` command tells sbt to re-examine the project definition and rewire the project. When you edit an sbt build, you'll need to reload.

Now that the build has been updated to include the specs2 library, you can create a unit test using it. Remember that in the previous section you defined the match-Likelihood method:

```
src/main/scala/logic.scala
object Logic {
  def matchLikelihood(kitten: Kitten,
                        buyer: BuyerPreferences): Double = {
    val matches = buyer.attributes map { attribute =>
      kitten.attributes contains attribute
    }
    val nums = matches map { b => if(b) 1.0 else 0.0 }
    nums.sum / nums.length
  }
}
```

You'll define a new specs2 test for the method. Create the following file in the src/test/scala directory (not the src/main/scala directory):

```
src/test/scala/LogicSpec.scala
import org.specs2.mutable.Specification

object LogicSpec extends Specification {
  "The 'matchLikelihood' method" should {
    "be 100% when all attributes match" in {
      val tabby = Kitten(1, List("male", "tabby"))
      val prefs = BuyerPreferences(List("male", "tabby"))
      val result = Logic.matchLikelihood(tabby, prefs)
      result must beGreaterThan(.999)
    }
  }
}
```

Now you can run the test using the test command in sbt:

```
> test
[info] Compiling 1 Scala source to /home/jsuereth/kittens/target/scala-2.9.2/
    test-classes...
[info] LogicSpec
[info]
[info] The 'matchLikelihood' method should
[info] + be 100% when all attributes match
[info]
[info]
[info] Total for specification LogicSpec
[info] Finished in 37 ms
[info] 1 example, 0 failure, 0 error
[info]
[info] Passed: : Total 1, Failed 0, Errors 0, Passed 1, Skipped 0
[success] Total time: 3 s, completed Jan 21, 2013 2:05:32 PM
>
```

You can see that sbt automatically compiles the test and runs it. The output from specs2 is quite detailed, outlining every test and specification that passes. One of the benefits of using a testing framework like specs2 is the robust output for errors. Note: testing is covered in more depth in chapter 5.

2.4.1 *Running tasks when sources change*

One of sbt's most powerful features is the ability to rerun a task when it detects that a source file has changed. Try this out with writing new tests.

First type ~test in the sbt console. You should see the following output:

```
> ~test
[info] LogicSpec
[info]
[info] The 'matchLikelihood' method should
[info] + be 100% when all attributes match
[info]
[info]
[info] Total for specification LogicSpec
[info] Finished in 50 ms
[info] 1 example, 0 failure, 0 error
[info]
[info] Passed: : Total 1, Failed 0, Errors 0, Passed 1, Skipped 0
[success] Total time: 1 s, completed Jan 30, 2013 10:17:15 PM
1. Waiting for source changes... (press enter to interrupt)
```

sbt is now in watch mode. It will continue to examine the filesystem until it detects a change. Add a new test and see what happens.

In LogicSpec.scala, add the following test:

```
"The 'matchLikelihood' method" should {
  "be 0% when no attributes match" in {
    val tabby = Kitten(1, List("male", "tabby"))
    val prefs = BuyerPreferences(List("female", "calico"))
    val result = Logic.matchLikelihood(tabby, prefs)
    result must beLessThan(.001)
  }
}
```

After saving the file, you should see the following output in sbt:

```
1. Waiting for source changes... (press enter to interrupt)
[info] Compiling 1 Scala source to /home/jsuereth/projects/sbt-in-action/
    chapter1/target/scala-2.9.2/test-classes...
[info] LogicSpec
[info]
[info] The 'matchLikelihood' method should
[info] + be 100% when all attributes match
[info] + be 0% when no attributes match
[info]
[info]
[info] Total for specification LogicSpec
[info] Finished in 85 ms
[info] 2 examples, 0 failure, 0 error
[info]
[info] Passed: : Total 2, Failed 0, Errors 0, Passed 2, Skipped 0
[success] Total time: 10 s, completed Jan 30, 2013 10:21:39 PM
2. Waiting for source changes... (press enter to interrupt)
```

When sbt detected that the file changed, it rebuilt all the files necessary and reran all tests. After completing the `test` task, it returned to waiting for new source changes. This powerful behavior can be used with any sbt task.

2.4.2   *Selecting tests with interactive tasks*

Another core feature of sbt is the ability to interact with the build via command-line autocomplete options on tasks. Let's discover what other tasks are available for testing.

In the sbt console, type `test` and then click `<tab>`. You should see the following:

```
> test
::              test:          testFrameworks   testListeners
    testLoader       testOnly          testOptions       testQuick
```

Several of these are related to setting up and running tests, but there are three that catch the eye: `test`, `testQuick`, and `testOnly`. You've already seen the `test` task. The `testQuick` task will be covered later, so let's look into `testOnly`.

Type `help testOnly` into the sbt console. The following shows up:

```
> help testOnly
Executes the tests provided as arguments or all tests if no arguments are
    provided.
```

Let's see this task in action. In the console type `testOnly <tab>`. You should see the following:

```
> testOnly
—              LogicSpec
```

The console lists all the possible tests that could be filtered as arguments to `testOnly`. Because there's only one, it's displayed along with a generic "test all" option. You'll use `testOnly` on the one test:

```
> testOnly LogicSpec
[info] LogicSpec
[info]
[info] The 'matchLikelihood' method should
[info] + be 100% when all attributes match
[info] + be 0% when no attributes match
[info]
[info]
[info] Total for specification LogicSpec
[info] Finished in 76 ms
[info] 2 examples, 0 failure, 0 error
[info]
[info] Passed: : Total 2, Failed 0, Errors 0, Passed 2, Skipped 0
[success] Total time: 1 s, completed Jan 30, 2013 10:46:34 PM
```

The output is exactly the same as before because there's only one test. But once you start adding tests, or if you're working on fixing a particular bug, this feature becomes a good friend. It gives you a powerful way to do test-driven development. You can continue coding until sbt's watch feature (~) combined with `testOnly` indicate that you've finally managed to pass your tests.

2.5 *Summary*

sbt provides a quick and powerful means to get started with a Scala project and rapidly start developing, testing, and debugging your code. You saw that sbt is an interactive build tool, improving your development process through convenient means of working with the build, specifically by

- Testing code in a live interpreted session
- Automatically running tasks when sources change
- Filtering what tests to execute using `testOnly`
- Providing discoverable usage using tab completion and an `inspect` command

Although some build tools stop at providing a repeatable build that can be used on a continuous integration server, sbt goes a step further and adds a new level of interaction and customization for the developer. Throughout this book, you'll learn how to better configure sbt's existing settings and to add your own interactive behavior. Let's move on to chapter 3, where you'll learn the fundamental concepts of sbt and how you can define your own behavior.

Part 2

Understanding sbt's core concepts

In Part 2, we'll help you understand the Core Concepts of sbt. We'll start with the fundamentals: settings and tasks. Then we'll move on to the default build.

Core concepts

3

This chapter covers

- Configuring settings, tasks, and projects
- Reusing values across settings
- Learning the core concepts of an sbt build
- Adding additional projects to the preowned-kittens build

In chapter 2, you set up an initial sbt project and used the command line to perform basic operations. This chapter focuses on taking this build beyond the out-of-the-box defaults and into something that you can call your own. As you go, you'll learn the core of sbt, the fundamental concepts that pervade any build. These are the components you can use to construct any build you want, and indeed they're the mechanism by which sbt provides a default build. After reading this chapter, given sufficient time, you could implement sbt's default build, although we don't recommend that you do so!

3.1   *Creating builds*

As you may recall from chapter 2, the preowned-kittens build defines two files:

- *project/build.properties*—This file defines the sbt version.
- *build.sbt*—This file defines the actual build.

Let's look at the build.properties file you defined:

```
sbt.version=0.13.5
```

Although this file can be used to specify several things, it's commonly used only to specify the sbt version. For the preowned-kittens build, we're using sbt 0.13, the latest release of sbt. More important is the build.sbt file.

The core of the preowned-kittens build is its build.sbt file. Here's what you ended up with at the end of the last chapter:

Project settings

```
name := "preowned-kittens"

organization := "com.preowned-kittens"          Prior to sbt 0.13.7, a blank line
                                                 was required between settings.
version := "1.0"

libraryDependencies += "org.specs2" % "specs2_2.10" % "1.14" % "test"
```

Every sbt build is created by defining a group of settings, projects, and definitions. The preowned-kittens build includes only the build settings for the root project. We'll talk more about defining builds with multiple projects later in the chapter; for now, let's look into how to configure the preowned-kittens project.

3.2   *Defining settings*

Settings are the bread and butter of sbt builds. They're the mechanism by which you configure sbt to perform the work you need for your build. sbt reads all the settings defined in your build at load time and runs their initializations, which produce the final setting values used for your build. In chapter 2, you configured the name of the used-kittens project with the setting shown in figure 3.1 .

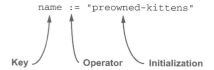

Figure 3.1   Configuring the name of the preowned-kittens build file. This sets the project name to the string literal "preowned-kittens".

A setting consists of three parts: a key, an initialization, and an operator that associates the key and initialization. A setting is used to change an aspect of the build or add functionality. In figure 3.1, you're altering the default name of the project to be preowned-kittens.

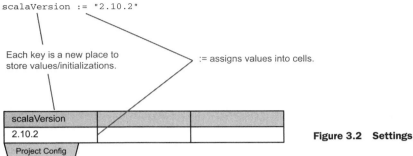

Figure 3.2 Settings with sbt defaults

The best way to think of settings is like a Microsoft Excel spreadsheet. Each key is analogous to a cell in the spreadsheet. You can place a value inside this cell. The value can either be a simple value, like a string, an integer, and so on, or it can be computed from other cells. The major caveat here is that in sbt settings have specific types, like `String`, `Int`, and `ModuleID`, and only values of those types can go into a cell. Let's look at a more complete analogy in figure 3.2.

The type (shape) of the `name` key is `String`, so `name` can only be assigned initializations that produce `String` values. Although the figure shows these settings as the first in the "spreadsheet," in reality sbt provides a default value for you, which you can override. The real spreadsheet looks something like figure 3.3.

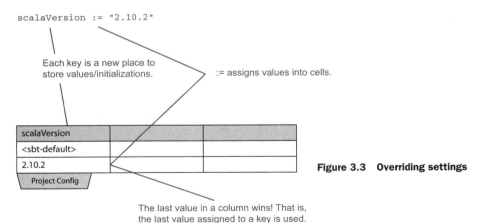

Figure 3.3 Overriding settings

Typesafe settings

In sbt, every key has one and only one type. Any value placed into a setting must match the exact type. This prevents mismatched data from being passed around the build.

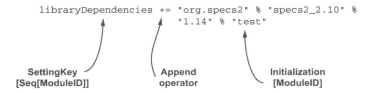

```
libraryDependencies += "org.specs2" % "specs2_2.10" %
                       "1.14" % "test"
```

SettingKey   Append   Initialization
[Seq[ModuleID]]   operator   [ModuleID]

Figure 3.4   To write a test for your new project, you added the specs2 testing library.

You're going to adapt the build from chapter 2 to include another testing library. In chapter 2 you needed to write a test for your new project. To do so, you added the specs2 testing library with the setting in figure 3.4 to get figure 3.5.

> **Defining dependencies**
> sbt provides a convenient syntax for defining dependencies on remote artifacts using the % method. This method is used to create `ModuleID` instances. To define a `ModuleID` in sbt, write `"groupId" % "artifactId" % "version"` and it will automatically become an instance of a `ModuleID`. For more information on remote artifacts and how sbt uses Ivy for general dependency management, see appendix A.

This setting adds the specs2 module to the sequence of library dependencies for the project. The `libraryDependencies` key holds a value of type `Seq[ModuleID]`. The `+=` operator is used to take the previous value assigned to the `libraryDependencies` setting and append the new `ModuleID` value to it. This is similar, in a spreadsheet, to taking the value of a previous cell to compute the next value. Try to visualize this, as shown in figure 3.5.

There are two operators to append values to existing settings that contain a sequence of items: `+=` and `++=`. The `++=` operator works similarly to the `+=` operator,

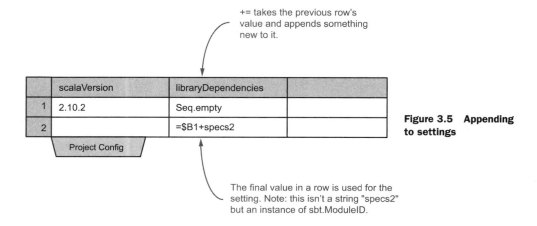

Figure 3.5   Appending to settings

but instead of adding a single value, it adds multiple values given as a sequence. In this example, more than one library can be added using the ++= operator:

```
libraryDependencies ++= Seq(
  "junit" % "junit" % "4.11" % "test",
  "org.specs2" % "specs2_2.10" % "1.10" % "test"
)
```

This setting appends not only the specs2 library but also the JUnit library, the standard Java unit-testing framework.

3.2.1 *Initializations*

Sometimes a setting value is duplicated in more than one location. For example, in the preowned-kittens build, you'd like to depend on a utility library. This library is part of your project but external to this build. This utility library is versioned with the same version number as your preowned-kittens website project because you'd like to evolve both the website and utility library together, for now. This includes building and publishing them at the same time, with the same version numbers.

Ideally, the version number should be specified in one location and reused everywhere. This is what initializations are for.

In sbt, an initialization is a Scala expression that can produce a value, and it may use other settings to do so. The += operator from before can accept an initialization of a ModuleID that uses the version setting.

Take a look at figure 3.6, which shows an example of adding the common library to your preowned-kittens build.

An *initialization* is an expression that produces a value and may use other settings to do so. You can access the value of another setting using the value method, as in figure 3.7.

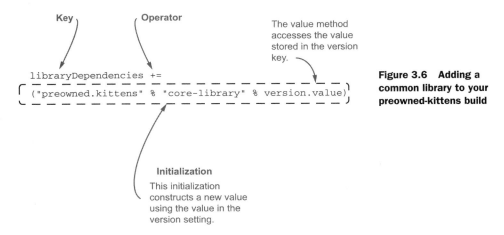

Figure 3.6 Adding a common library to your preowned-kittens build

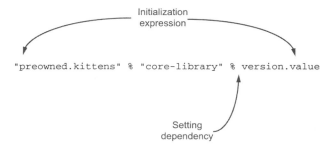

```
"preowned.kittens" % "core-library" % version.value
```

Figure 3.7   You can access the value of another setting using the `value` method. In this example, the initialization receives the value of the version setting. This expression generates a new `ModuleID` with that setting.

Initializations are code

Initializations are Scala code. You can read environment variables, properties, files, or anything else available in the JVM. sbt attempts to run all the initializations for a build when it starts. Any failures in an initialization will cause the build to fail to load, so make sure to catch exceptions as needed when defining initializations for settings!

Initializations can be created from more than one setting. Because the utility library is all part of the `preowned-kittens` project, it shares the same organization as the preowned-kittens website. You can modify the previous expression to make use of this shared organization when depending on the core library, as in figure 3.8.

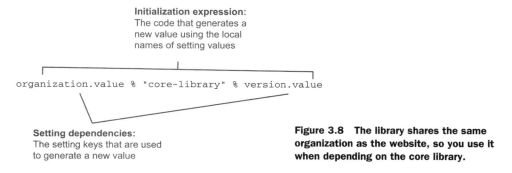

```
organization.value % "core-library" % version.value
```

Figure 3.8   The library shares the same organization as the website, so you use it when depending on the core library.

In this initialization, both the `organization` and `version` settings are declared as dependencies using their keys. During build initialization, as sbt resolves settings, it pulls the values for `organization` and `version` and uses these values to create this `ModuleID`. Using the spreadsheet analogy, this is a mechanism of declaring a dependency on the "last row" of a column in the settings spreadsheet. Take a look at figure 3.9.

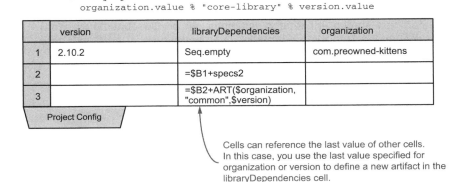

Figure 3.9 **Mapping setting dependencies to a spreadsheet**

Circular references

Because sbt can use values of one setting to instantiate another, it's possible to create circular references. If, for example, `name` depends on `version` and `version` depends on `name`, then the build will fail to load. This is similar to trying to define a spreadsheet cell that computes its own value based on itself.

To recap, in sbt there are three operators used to create settings:

`:=`	Assigns an initialization expression to a key. Overrides any previous value.
`+=`	Appends an initialization expression to the existing sequence in a key.
`++=`	Appends an initialization of a sequence of values to the existing sequence in a key.

These operators are used to construct all settings, but they need to be modified slightly when used with tasks.

One operator to rule them all

In sbt all settings can be implemented in terms of the `:=` operator. For example, `foo += bar.value` is just `foo := foo.value + bar.value`.

3.3 Creating and executing tasks

Builds are about accomplishing tasks, from running a compiler to generating zip files for distribution. Tasks are the means to repeatedly perform some operation, like compiling your project, generating documentation, or running tests. In sbt a task is like a

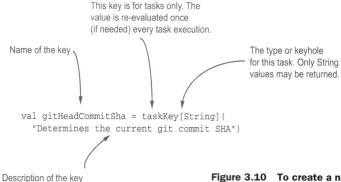

This key is for tasks only. The
value is re-evaluated once
(if needed) every task execution.

Name of the key

The type or keyhole
for this task. Only String
values may be returned.

```
val gitHeadCommitSha = taskKey[String](
    "Determines the current git commit SHA")
```

Description of the key
displayed in the sbt console

Figure 3.10   To create a new task in sbt, you first need to create a new key that can store the value of the Git commit.

setting that runs every time you request its value. That is, every time you make a request to sbt's task engine, each task required will be run once for that request.

For the preowned-kittens website, you'd like to display the version of the code on the website. This project is stored using the Git version control system. Git is a distributed version control system that can handle nonlinear history and is efficient at merging. The best version number you can get from Git is what is called a commit hash. This is an autogenerated hash string of elements composing a commit. This hash can uniquely represent the version of the code you're building.

You can look up the Git commit hash when you build and then generate a new version.properties file that the website can read at runtime. This way, you'll always be aware of what code you're using.

To create a new task in sbt, first you need to create a new key that can store the value of the Git commit, as in figure 3.10.

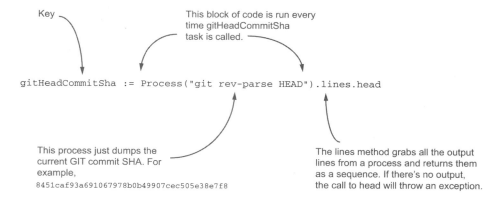

Key

This block of code is run every
time gitHeadCommitSha
task is called.

```
gitHeadCommitSha := Process("git rev-parse HEAD").lines.head
```

This process just dumps the
current GIT commit SHA. For
example,
8451caf93a691067978b0b49907cec505e38e7f8

The lines method grabs all the output
lines from a process and returns them
as a sequence. If there's no output,
the call to head will throw an exception.

Figure 3.11   After defining a new key to contain the Git SHA, you can define a new setting that will grab the value of the SHA and place it in the setting.

This is a *definition* in sbt. A definition defines a variable or method for reuse within sbt settings. In sbt, definitions are compiled first and can reference previous definitions. That's why definitions are defined using the = operator and not the := operator. A definition isn't assigning a value into a setting but is defining some Scala code to help define the build.

Because settings are executed after definitions, settings can refer to any definition in the build file. For style reasons, it's best to declare value definitions, like TaskKeys, before using them so maintainers of your build understand what you're doing.

After defining a new key to contain the Git SHA, you can define a new setting that will grab the value of the SHA and place it in the setting, as in figure 3.11.

The way to think of this process is that the definition (=) is constructing a new slot where computed build values can go. The setting (:=) is constructing a function that will compute the value for the slot when needed.

Parallel task execution

Unlike a lot of modern build tools, sbt separates defining the computation of a value from the slot that stores the value. This is to aid in parallel execution of builds. sbt uses a parallel execution strategy and needs to ensure that values inside key slots are available before they're used. These unconventional conventions allow sbt to parallelize and fragment your build in a safe manner. The beauty is that to increase parallelism in builds, all you need to do is create more intermediate tasks and sbt will attempt to run them in parallel if it can.

The gitHeadCommit task, when run, returns the current Git commit SHA. Look at the following example:

```
> show gitHeadCommitSha
[info] 99df7ebfe75327c2144605e94898e220d1fbcf72
```

The show command displays the result of the task.

toString of the task result, in this case the commit SHA

Handling errors in tasks

Tasks are expected to do things that may fail, like create files, run programs, and communicate over the network. When a setting fails, it prevents the build from loading. When a task fails, it stops the current task execution with an error. Other tasks in the build will continue to execute.

Now that you have the Git commit SHA in a task key, you can use that value in another task.

3.3.1   *Task dependencies*

Just as settings may depend on other settings, tasks may also depend on settings as well as the output from other tasks. When the user requests a task to be executed, sbt will run all of the dependent tasks (once) and pass their values to the requested task. Figure 3.12 shows what happens when you create a task that generates the properties file that contains the Git version.

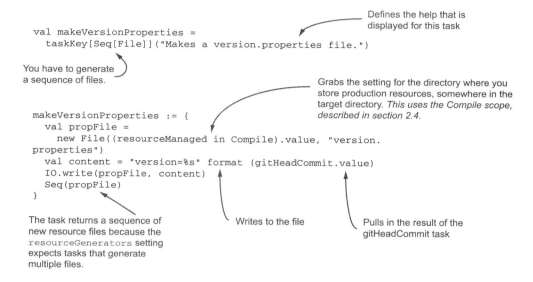

Figure 3.12   Creating a task that generates the properties file that contains the Git version

There's a lot going on in this figure! First you create a new `TaskKey` to store the initialization of the task. Next you define how the task executes. This task defines a new `java.io.File` object for where to write the properties file using a location provided by the sbt standard build (described later). It then calls `IO.write` to write a string into that file.

When tasks collide: parallel execution

sbt executes tasks in parallel if it can. Therefore, if you have `taskA`, which depends on `taskB` and `taskC`, sbt will try to execute `taskB` and `taskC` at the same time. This can be trivially proven using the following tasks:

```
val taskA = taskKey[String]("taskA")
val taskB = taskKey[String]("taskB")
val taskC = taskKey[String]("taskC")
taskA := { val b = taskB.value; val c = taskC.value; "taskA" }
taskB := { Thread.sleep(5000); "taskB" }
taskC := { Thread.sleep(5000); "taskC" }
> taskA
[success] Total time: 5 s, completed 22-Sep-2013 17:19:31
```

The total time taken if `taskB` and `taskC` were executed serially would be 10 seconds; clearly, the tasks are being executed in parallel. If B also depended on C, you'd need to explicitly declare this in the definition of `taskB`; otherwise your build could fail.

If you do declare that B also depends on C, then the tasks will be executed serially, not in parallel:

```
taskB := { val c = taskC.value; Thread.sleep(5000); "taskB" }
> taskA
[success] Total time: 10s, completed 22-Sep-2013 17:25:38
```

sbt also checks for cycles in the list of tasks to execute. If you have

```
val taskX = taskKey[String]("taskX")
taskX := { val y = taskY.value; "taskX" }
val taskY= taskKey[String]("taskY")
taskY := { val x = taskX.value; "taskY" }
```

then sbt will give you

```
[error] Cyclic reference involving
[error]     {file:/C:/code/sbt/sbt-in-action-examples/chapter3/}root/
        *:taskY
[error]     {file:/C:/code/sbt/sbt-in-action-examples/chapter3/}root/
        *:taskX
```

What's interesting is that you can make use of the values computed in other tasks using the `value` method, the same way you did for settings. Now when the make-version-properties task is called, sbt will first execute the `git-head-commit` task before running the `make-version-properties` task with its value.

Everything makes a value!

As you've seen, in sbt everything generates a value. Tasks and settings both produce values that can be used in other tasks and settings. It's rare in sbt that a task doesn't return something to be used in other tasks. This design allows great flexibility and power when defining complex builds. It also drastically simplifies parallel building.

Finally, you need to wire this properties file in the runtime classpath for your website. To do that, you can use the `resourceGenerators` key, as shown in figure 3.13.

The sbt default build (described in detail later) has hooks that allow tasks to generate sources or resources for a project. The `resourceGenerators` setting is defined as a setting that stores all the tasks used to generate resources. sbt uses this setting to generate resources before bundling production jar/war files or running tests.

This setting makes use of the `Compile` configuration for the resource generators. You've seen the `Key in Configuration` syntax twice now; let's look into what it means.

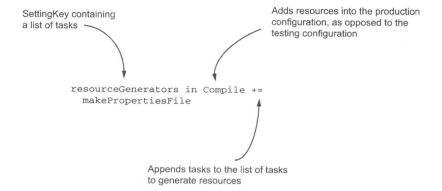

SettingKey containing
a list of tasks

Adds resources into the production
configuration, as opposed to the
testing configuration

```
resourceGenerators in Compile +=
      makePropertiesFile
```

Appends tasks to the list of tasks
to generate resources

Figure 3.13   You need to tell sbt to include this properties file in the runtime classpath for your website. To do that, you can use the `resourceGenerators` key.

3.4   *Using configurations*

Configurations are namespaces for keys. These are similar to adding new pages to a spreadsheet. They allow the same key, or column, to be reused to serve different purposes. sbt comes with several configurations in the default build; see table 3.1.

Table 3.1   sbt default configurations

Configuration	Purpose
Compile	These settings and values are used to compile the main project and generate production artifacts.
Test	These settings and values are used to compile and run unit-testing code.
Runtime	These settings and values are used to run your project within sbt.
IntegrationTest	These settings and values are used to run tests against your production artifacts.

These configurations are used to split settings and tasks across higher-level goals. For example, the task defined at `sources in Compile` collects the source files that will be compiled for your production artifacts, whereas `sources in Test` defines the source files that will be compiled to run your unit tests.

To return to the spreadsheet analogy, configurations create new worksheets, as in figure 3.14.

Configurations provide consistencies between tasks within sbt. A given flow of tasks can be repeated across two different configurations. Also, tasks in one configuration can depend on tasks in another configuration. Because sbt runs all tasks in parallel by default, configurations can be used to create mirror tasks that can run in parallel.

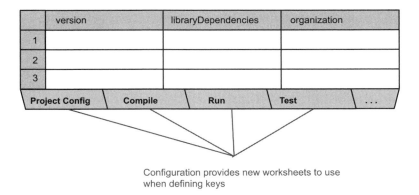

Configuration provides new worksheets to use
when defining keys

Figure 3.14 Configurations as worksheets

Configurations provide one means to namespace settings and tasks, but there's
another mechanism you can use: defining with subprojects.

> ## A wealth of configurations
> Although `Test` and `Compile` are the most commonly used configurations, sbt also
> defines `Default`, `Pom`, `Optional`, `System`, `Provided`, `Docs`, and `Sources`. These are
> discussed in greater depth in chapter 4.

3.5 Defining with subprojects

So far, your build has dealt with a single sbt project. But in coding you've noticed a bit
of clutter forming in the code base. In particular, you're shipping around a single
project that defines both your analytics application and your website.

You'd like to split the preowned-kittens website into two parts:

- The website
- The data analytics

In addition, these two applications both need to refer to some common code. To
make these changes, you'll have to tweak your current build and project layout quite a
bit. First you'll define a new subproject called `common`. This project is where you'll
move your existing code and tests.

To create a new project within sbt, add the line indicated in figure 3.15 to your
build.sbt file.

You've created a new subproject to contain the common code. All the code you've
written so far is common code, so you can move your existing code into the common
project. Because all of the code and resource files are found under the src/ directory,
you can move this directory to common/src/.

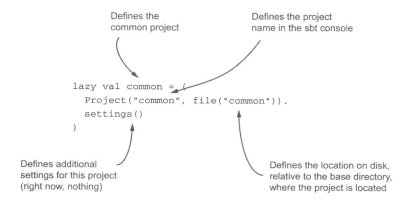

Figure 3.15   Splitting the common code out of the website project

After creating the new subproject, restart sbt and try to interact with it. First run the `reload` command in the sbt prompt so your new build.sbt definition is compiled and loaded:

```
> reload
[info] Loading project definition from /home/jsuereth/projects/sbt-in-action/
    chapter3/
[info] Set current project to preowned-kittens (in build file:/home/jsuereth/
    projects/sbt-in-action/chapter3/
)
```

Next run the `projects` command to see if your new subproject shows up:

```
> projects
[info] In file:/home/jsuereth/projects/sbt-in-action/chapter3/
[info]          common
[info]        * default-33d8c8
```

Now you can see that you have two projects defined: `default-33d8c8` and `common`. `common` is the project you just defined, but where did this `default` project come from?

Well, earlier you weren't constructing `Project` instances, yet sbt was creating a project for you. This is usually referred to as the root project, and it represents the same directory where the build.sbt file is found.

Projects need their own directories

In sbt, the default project settings assume that each project has its own base directory. Each project in your build should have its own base directory that's different from any other project. Within this base directory, you'll find the directories for source code, testing code, and so on.

Now that you have the new project defined, try to rerun the tests that are now located in the common project. To do so, in the sbt console you need to prefix the test task with the project name and a / character, like this:

```
> common/test
[info] Updating {file:/home/jsuereth/projects/sbt-in-action/chapter3/
    }common...
[info] Resolving org.fusesource.jansi#jansi;1.4 ...
[info] Done updating.
[info] Compiling 3 Scala sources to /home/jsuereth/projects/sbt-in-action/
    chapter3/common/target/scala-2.10/classes...
[info] Compiling 1 Scala source to /home/jsuereth/projects/sbt-in-action/
    chapter3/common/target/scala-2.10/test-classes...
[error] /home/jsuereth/projects/sbt-in-action/chapter3/common/src/test/scala/
    LogicSpec.scala:1: object specs2 is not a member of package org
[error] import org.specs2.mutable.Specification
[error]                   ^
[error] /home/jsuereth/projects/sbt-in-action/chapter3/common/src/test/scala/
    LogicSpec.scala:3: not found: type Specification
[error] object LogicSpec extends Specification {
[error]                          ^
[error] /home/jsuereth/projects/sbt-in-action/chapter3/common/src/test/scala/
    LogicSpec.scala:4: value should is not a member of String
[error]    "The 'matchLikelihood' method" should {
[error]                                   ^
[error] three errors found
[error] (common/test:compile) Compilation failed
[error] Total time: 6 s, completed May 6, 2013 8:29:42 PM
```

The syntax common/test refers not to the directory structure but to the task within sbt to run. In this case, you're telling sbt to run the default test task within the common project.

The test task is failing against the common project because it can't find the specs2 testing library. The reason is that you haven't defined the settings for this project to find specs2.

The root directory is the default target for settings found in the build.sbt file. This means that all the configuration you have so far for testing applies only to code in the root project. All that configuration needs to be added to the common project for it to compile. First add the library dependencies for specs2. Edit the common project setting to be the following:

```
lazy val common = (
 Project("common", file("common"))
 settings(
   libraryDependencies +=
       "org.specs2" % "specs2_2.10" % "1.14" % "test"
 )
)
```

New settings go inside the project settings block.

Now rerun the common/test task. Remember to first reload the build in the sbt prompt:

```
> reload
[info] Loading project definition from /home/jsuereth/kittens/project
[info] Set current project to preowned-kittens (in build file:/home/jsuereth/
    kittens/)
```

Then run the common/test task:

```
> common/test
[info] Updating {file:/home/jsuereth/projects/sbt-in-action/chapter3/
    }common...
[info] Resolving org.fusesource.jansi#jansi;1.4 ...
[info] Done updating.
[info] Compiling 1 Scala source to /home/jsuereth/projects/sbt-in-action/
    chapter3/common/target/scala-2.10/test-classes...
[info] LogicSpec
[info]
[info] The 'matchLikelihood' method should
[info] + be 100% when all attributes match
[info] + be 0% when no attributes match
[info]
[info]
[info] Total for specification LogicSpec
[info] Finished in 24 ms
[info] 2 examples, 0 failure, 0 error
[info]
[info] Passed: : Total 2, Failed 0, Errors 0, Passed 2, Skipped 0
[success] Total time: 5 s, completed May 6, 2013 8:48:10 PM
```

Now everything is succeeding again! You can start adding the new analytics and website projects to the build, as shown here:

```
lazy val analytics = (
 Project("analytics", file("analytics"))
 dependsOn(common)                          ◁──────────────┐
 settings()                                                │
)                                                          │
                                        **Defines a dependency
                                        from these projects to
                                        the common project**
lazy val website = (
 Project("website", file("website"))                       │
 dependsOn(common)                         ◁──────────────┘
 settings()
)
```

Project dependencies are defined using the dependsOn method of Project.

Now that you've defined the new projects with dependencies, you can watch sbt in action. First reload your build in the sbt prompt:

```
> reload
[info] Loading project definition from /home/jsuereth/kittens/project
[info] Set current project to preowned-kittens (in build file:/home/jsuereth/
    kittens/)
```

> **Project definition order matters!**
>
> Just like any other Scala object, any values defined can't be referenced before they're declared. Because of this, it drastically simplifies life to declare projects using `lazy vals`. It's such a common issue with circular references that we recommend always using `lazy vals` to define projects. A rule of thumb is that if you see an `Exception-InInitalization` when starting an sbt, you should do a quick grep of your build.sbt files for a `val` without the `lazy`.

Now clean the `common` project and then compile the `website` project:

```
> common/clean
[success] Total time: 0 s, completed May 6, 2013 8:56:45 PM
> website/compile
[info] Updating {file:/home/jsuereth/kittens/}common...
[info] Resolving org.fusesource.jansi#jansi;1.4 ...
[info] Done updating.
[info] Updating {file:/home/jsuereth/kittens/}website...
[info] Resolving org.fusesource.jansi#jansi;1.4 ...
[info] Done updating.
[info] Compiling 3 Scala sources to /home/jsuereth/kittens/common/target/
    scala-2.10/classes...
[success] Total time: 2 s, completed May 6, 2013 8:56:54 PM
```

Notice that sbt compiles the `kittens` project, even though you didn't explicitly ask it to. In sbt, across all projects, tasks are structured as a dependency graph. sbt will ensure that tasks from one project are executed before they're used by another project.

> **Pervasive parallelism**
>
> In sbt, the fundamental unit of concurrency is the task. If you want to improve the parallelism of your builds, you need to have more tasks that can run simultaneously. One of the easiest ways to do this is to ensure you use lots of loosely coupled sub-projects. This splits up the compilation tasks and can let sbt use more processors. This can be dramatic for Scala compilation, which doesn't usually make use of more than one or two cores.

Now that you've split the project into subprojects, you can start to share settings between them. Let's look at a few techniques to simplify defining your project's builds.

Directories and project layout!

You may have noticed that you did not create any of the directories for the subprojects. sbt will generate necessary directories on demand, but it's good to know where it expects to find files. Here's the directory layout for the `preowned-kittens` project so far:

```
<root>/
    <build.sbt files defining total project structure>
    project/
        <sbt plugin files + .scala helper libraries>
        target/
            <your sbt build, compiled>
    common/
        <build.sbt with configuration specific to the common project>
        src/
            main/
                scala/
                    <scala/java code for production>
                resources/
                    <files that should be on the classpath for the common
                project>
            test/
                scala/
                    <scala/java code for unit testing>
                resources/
                    <files that should be on the classpath when unit
                testing
        target/
            <generated files from the build for the 'common' project.
    analytics/
        <similar to common>
    web/
        <similar to common>
```

3.6   *Putting it all together*

sbt is built on top of Scala, an expressive language with a lot of nice features. You can start using these to reduce clutter in your build and ensure that it's easy to maintain. You'll start by reducing some of the clutter in creating your projects.

For the preowned-kittens site, all of the project names correspond exactly with directory names. This convention helps the developers find the correct project and know how to interact with the build. Rather than copying the name/directory string in several places, you can create a helper method that will construct your base project settings.

Open your build.sbt file and add the following definition at/near the top of the file (remember to leave blank lines around it):

```
def PreownedKittenProject(name: String): Project = (
  Project(name, file(name))
)
```

This constructs a method called `PreownedKittenProject` that takes in the name of the project and returns a new `sbt.Project` object where the location and name are the same. Now update your project definitions to use this new method:

```
lazy val common = (
  PreownedKittenProject("common").
  settings(
    libraryDependencies += "org.specs2" % "specs2_2.10" % "1.14" % "test"
  )
)

val analytics = (
  PreownedKittenProject("analytics").
  dependsOn(common).
  settings()
)

val website = (
  PreownedKittenProject("website").
  dependsOn(common).
  settings()
)
```

Notice that the `dependsOn` and `settings` calls are unchanged for each project. This is because the new `PreownedKittenProject` method returns a base-level project, which you can further refine with dependencies and settings. This means any settings or configuration you place in the `PreownedKittensProject` method will be applied to all projects you construct using that method.

You're going to update the `PreownedKittensProject` method so that the default organization, version, and testing libraries are included for all the projects. Your build file should now look like the following (after some moving/removals of extraneous settings):

```
def PreownedKittenProject(name: String): Project = (
  Project(name, file(name)).
  settings(
    version := "1.0",
    organization := "com.preownedkittens",
    libraryDependencies += "org.specs2" % "specs2_2.10" % "1.14" % "test"
  )
)

lazy val common = (
  PreownedKittenProject("common").
  settings()
)

val analytics = (
  PreownedKittenProject("analytics").
  dependsOn(common).
  settings()
)
```

```
val website = (
  PreownedKittenProject("website").
  dependsOn(common).
  settings()
)

val gitHeadCommitSha = taskKey[String]("Determines the current git commit
    SHA")

gitHeadCommitSha := Process("git rev-parse HEAD").lines.head

val makeVersionProperties = taskKey[Seq[File]]("Creates a version.properties
    file we can find at runtime.")

makeVersionProperties := {
  val propFile = (resourceManaged in Compile).value / "version.properties"
  val content = "version=%s" format (gitHeadCommitSha.value)
  IO.write(propFile, content)
  Seq(propFile)
}
```

Now that you have the version and testing libraries shared across projects, it's time to decide what to do about the version properties task. For the preowned-kittens build, you should have only one version.properties file in the common project that can be used in both the analysis and website projects. This will help you detect if you're talking to a compatible version at runtime.

The Git commit SHA (version), on the other hand, is something that's not specific to the common project but to the build itself. It could be that other tasks may want to make use of the gitHeadCommitSha task later. Go ahead and migrate the version .properties generation into the common project and the gitHeadCommitSha into the build itself, rather than attaching it to a particular project.

First move the gitHeadCommitSha task to be defined on the build itself. To do this, you add the in ThisBuild qualifier to the task key when you define the setting. Modify the existing setting in build.sbt to look as follows:

```
gitHeadCommitSha in ThisBuild := Process("git rev-parse HEAD").lines.head
```

Now that the task is attached to the build itself, you only have to define it once, but all projects can make use of its results. This is great for files/settings that are truly shared across all projects, because it means sbt will execute the task only once for all projects that request the value. Also it means that you don't have to redefine the setting in every project that needs it. By default, if sbt doesn't find a task/setting for a key in a given project, it will fall back to task/settings defined in the build itself.

The makeVersionProperties setting is still defined on the root project. Let's move that to the common project. Modify your build.sbt by copying and pasting the make-VersionProperties setting into the settings() block of the common project. The new common project definition should look like this:

```
lazy val common = (
  PreownedKittenProject("common").
  settings(
```

```
  makeVersionProperties := {
    val propFile = (resourceManaged in Compile).value /
   "version.properties"
    val content = "version=%s" format (gitHeadCommitSha.value)
    IO.write(propFile, content)
    Seq(propFile)
  }
 )
)
```

Now you've dramatically cleaned up the build. Take a look at the final build (note that I've rearranged some pieces and added comments to clarify sections of the build), shown in the following listing.

Listing 3.1 Full multiproject build

```
name := "preowned-kittens"

// Custom keys for this build.

val gitHeadCommitSha = taskKey[String]("Determines the current git commit
    SHA")

val makeVersionProperties = taskKey[Seq[File]]("Creates a version.properties
    file we can find at runtime.")

// Common settings/definitions for the build

def PreownedKittenProject(name: String): Project = (
  Project(name, file(name))
  settings(
    version := "1.0",
    organization := "com.preownedkittens",
    libraryDependencies += "org.specs2" % "specs2_2.10" % "1.14" % "test"
  )
)

gitHeadCommitSha in ThisBuild := Process("git rev-parse HEAD").lines.head

// Projects in this build

lazy val common = (
  PreownedKittenProject("common").
  settings(
    makeVersionProperties := {
      val propFile = (resourceManaged in Compile).value /
     "version.properties"
      val content = "version=%s" format (gitHeadCommitSha.value)
      IO.write(propFile, content)
      Seq(propFile)
    }
  )
)

val analytics = (
  PreownedKittenProject("analytics").
  dependsOn(common).
```

```
    settings()
)

val website = (
  PreownedKittenProject("website").
  dependsOn(common).
  settings()
)
```

Now that the build is complete, you can reload it into your sbt console and kick the tires a bit:

```
> reload
[info] Loading project definition from /home/jsuereth/projects/sbt-in-action/
      chapter3/project
[info] Set current project to preowned-kittens (in build file:/home/jsuereth/
      projects/sbt-in-action/chapter3/)
>
```

Now run the name setting:

```
> name
[info] website/*:name
[info]   website
[info] analytics/*:name
[info]   analytics
[info] common/*:name
[info]   common
[info] kittens/*:name
[info]   preowned-kittens
```

Tasks/settings with no prefix are run across all projects in a multiproject build.

\<project>/\<scope>:\<setting>

Value of the setting

* means the default setting.

The root project name defaults to the directory name for the project.

By default, sbt will run unprefixed settings/tasks against all projects defined in the build. This is known as *aggregation* in sbt. In addition to automatically aggregating subprojects, sbt automatically generates a root project. This is a default project defined against the root directory of the build, in this case the kittens directory. The root project is the one responsible for aggregating the other projects. It's recommended for multimodule projects to avoid building code in the root project. It should instead be used to simplify working with the subprojects, which are the stars of any sbt build.

You're now well on your way to creating a powerful and concise build.

3.7   *Summary*

In sbt, the whole build is a key/initialization pairing of projects. Each project consists of a list of these settings, which are executed when the build is first loaded. Some of these settings contain repeatable blocks of code, called tasks. Tasks are executed once, as needed, for every action passed into sbt. To enable reuse of key values, configurations provide a mechanism to shard, or namespace, your tasks and settings. Finally, projects provide a way to modularize portions of the build and isolate dependencies between code.

The core of sbt is settings, tasks, configurations, and projects. Using just these concepts, you can construct any build for any project, using whatever flow of tasks you desire. Chapter 4 looks at the settings, tasks, and configurations that sbt provides by default so you don't have to create your builds from the ground up.

The default build 4

This chapter covers

- Arranging source files
- Dealing with dependencies (libraries)
- Compiling Scala and Java code
- Running individual tests
- Packaging your code

In the previous chapter, you learned the nuts and bolts: tasks, settings, projects, and builds. This chapter covers the structure of the building: the default build. Unlike the previous chapters, you won't add much to the preowned-kittens project, but instead you'll investigate *how* the existing build works so you know *where* to add new features.

We'll deconstruct the build from the general tasks you need to accomplish, back to the pieces that make it up. Let's walk back through the tasks you ran in chapter 2 and see what sbt does to execute them. We'll walk through the tasks compile, run, test, package, and then publish.

4.1 Compiling your code

One of the primary purposes of a build tool is to compile code. But in order to compile code, sbt first needs to know a few things. You can ask sbt what it needs using the `inspect tree` command on the sbt prompt. First go back to the kittens folder you created earlier for your projects. Then start sbt in this directory. When the prompt appears, type `inspect tree compile:compile`:

```
> inspect tree compile:compile
[info] compile:compile = Task[sbt.inc.Analysis]
[info]   +-compile:compile::compileInputs = Task[sbt.Compiler$Inputs]
[info]   | +-*/*:javacOptions = Task[scala.collection.Seq[java.lang.String]]
[info]   | +-compile:classDirectory = target/scala-2.10/classes
[info]   | +-compile:dependencyClasspath =
      Task[scala.collection.Seq[sbt.Attributed[java.io.File]]]
[info]   | +-*/*:compileOrder = Mixed
[info]   | +-*:compilers = Task[sbt.Compiler$Compilers]
[info]   | +-compile:sources = Task[scala.collection.Seq[java.io.File]]
[info]   | +-*/*:sourcePositionMappers =
      Task[scala.collection.Seq[scala.Function1[xsbti.Position,
      scala.Option[xsbti.Position]]]]
[info]   | +-*/*:maxErrors = 100
[info]   | +-compile:compile::streams =
      Task[sbt.std.TaskStreams[sbt.Init$ScopedKey[_ <: Any]]]
[info]   | | +-*/*:streamsManager = Task[sbt.std.Streams[sbt.Init$ScopedKey[_
      <: Any]]]
[info]   | |
[info]   | +-compile:scalacOptions =
      Task[scala.collection.Seq[java.lang.String]]
[info]   | +-compile:incCompileSetup = Task[sbt.Compiler$IncSetup]
[info]   |
[info]   +-compile:compile::streams =
      Task[sbt.std.TaskStreams[sbt.Init$ScopedKey[_ <: Any]]]
[info]      +-*/*:streamsManager = Task[sbt.std.Streams[sbt.Init$ScopedKey[_
      <: Any]]]
[info]
```

The command's output is an ASCII tree detailing which tasks/settings the `compile` task depends on and what values those settings/tasks return. This command is available against any sbt task/setting, and it's an amazing resource when learning how a new project works.

Figure 4.1 shows the same output in a more book-readable form.

As shown in this more easily readable tree, compilation requires three things:

- A sequence (list) of source files
- A sequence (list) of libraries
- A sequence (list) of compiler configuration options

Let's look at each individually, starting with sources.

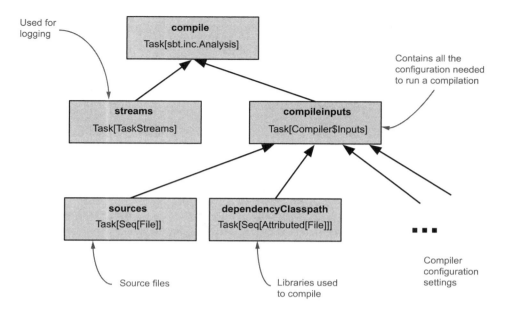

Figure 4.1   A more book-readable format of an ASCII tree detailing what tasks/settings the `compile` task depends on

4.2   *Finding your sources*

Almost every software project, at least those using Scala and/or Java, includes source code. Therefore, you first need to understand how to organize your sources in sbt. As it does for many other aspects of a build, sbt applies certain conventions when looking for your source code. But you can easily customize the way sources are organized, if necessary.

> **Convention over configuration**
>
> It has become a widely adopted paradigm in software engineering to make it as easy as possible for the users to get simple things done by minimizing the number of explicit decisions necessary through conventions. On the other hand, it should still be possible to get complex things done by defining nonstandard aspects through configuration.

4.2.1   *Standard organization of sources*

Let's take a look at the `sources` task and determine the source layout conventions from there. A simple run of `inspect tree sources` reveals the structure shown in figure 4.2.

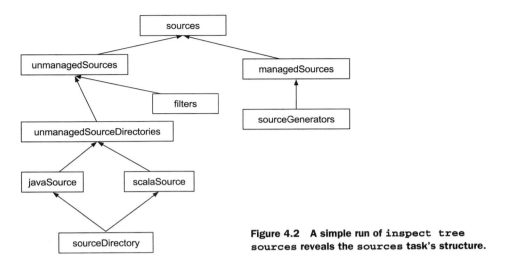

Figure 4.2 A simple run of `inspect tree sources` reveals the sources task's structure.

You can see that the list of sources is taken from two aggregates:

- *unmanagedSources*—A discovered list of source files using standard project conventions
- *managedSources*—A list of sources that are either generated from the build or manually added

For sbt, the unmanaged sources are discovered *by convention.* This is akin to memory management. Unmanaged means you (not sbt) have to do the work of adding, modifying, and tracking the source files, whereas managed source files are ones that sbt will create and track for you.

Unmanaged sources make use of a set of file filters and a default set of directories to produce the sequence of source files for the project. As shown in the dependency tree, the directories defined by the `javaSource` and `scalaSource` settings make up the set of directories where sbt looks for sources. Let's see what these settings are by default (the convention):

```
> show javaSource
[info] <project-dir>/src/main/java
> show scalaSource
[info] <project-dir>/src/main/scala
```

By default, the set of sources that sbt uses for a project comes from the src/main/java directory and the src/main/scala directory. These directories are scanned for files, and those files that pass the default filters are used in compilation.

Of course, there are the production source files, also referred to as the *compile sources.* Those are the .scala and .java files that will be compiled and whose binary artifacts will go into production. In addition, many projects also contain *compile resources,* which are files that are also needed at runtime but don't need to be compiled. Well-known examples include .properties and .xml files to configure your logging system.

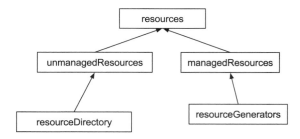

Figure 4.3   The dependency tree for the `resources` task

These resources aren't compiled but are copied or included alongside the binary artifacts. When the context allows for it, we won't always make a precise distinction between sources and resources and sometimes refer to both as sources.

Similar to how sbt has a `sources` task to collect sources, there's a corresponding `resources` task, which collects all the files that should be available at runtime. Figure 4.3 gives you a look at the dependency tree for the `resources` task. We don't include the full output of `inspect tree resources` for space reasons.

Similar to the `sources` task, the `resources` task comprises two sets of files:

- *managedResources*—The set of resources that are manually specified or manually generated for the build
- *unmanagedResources*—The set of files found in the resource directory

Unlike the sources settings, resources don't use filters. All files found in the resource directory will be available at runtime. Let's take a look at where the resource directory is:

```
> show resourceDirectory
[info] <project-dir>/src/main/resources
```

So far, the default project tree for sbt—at least the parts we've inspected—looks like this:

```
<project-dir>
    build.sbt
    project/
        build.properties
    src/
        main/
            scala/
            java/
            resources/
```

Those familiar with Maven may recognize this convention, because it's borrowed from their ecosystem.

Note that for our own project, we have only the src/main/scala directory. Although sbt will use the default directories if they exist, there's no need to create them if you aren't using them.

4.2.2 *Testing sources*

Besides these main sources, many projects contain other kinds of source files. The most prominent ones are the *test source files*, which contain code to test your software but will never enter production. Typical examples include unit tests written using a testing library like ScalaTest, ScalaCheck, or JUnit. Of course, there can also be *test resources*, files that won't be compiled but are needed at the time of test execution as is.

As you may recall from section 3.4, sbt has the ability to mirror keys into alternative namespaces, called configurations. To delineate the different dimensions of sources, sbt places the *compile source file* settings into a configuration called `Compile` and the *test source file* settings into a configuration called `Test`. You can inspect the dependency tree for test sources by running the `inspect tree test:sources` command in the sbt shell:

```
> inspect tree test:sources
[info] test:sources = Task[scala.collection.Seq[java.io.File]]
...
```

We cut off the output, because it's not very readable in book format. Figure 4.4 shows a graphical representation of the output.

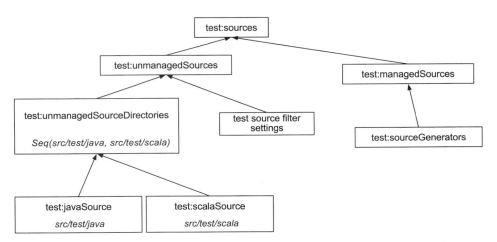

Figure 4.4 A more readable way to see the dependency tree for test sources obtained by running the `inspect tree test:sources` command in the sbt shell

You may notice that the `test:sources` task uses the exact same lookup as the `compile:sources` task. That's because under the covers, sbt is using the same set of settings to find your source files. sbt does this same thing with the resources task, creating settings for configuring testing resources under the `test:resources` task.

You have a few dimensions alongside which you have to structure your sources: programming language, production or test, real source or resource. The hierarchy in which you find source files now looks like the following:

```
<my-project>/
  src/
    main/
      java/
      resources/
      scala/
    test/
      java/
      resources/
      scala/
```

Although this layout is the current convention for most JVM-based projects, it may not be the convention you'd like. Let's look at how you can alter the source configuration settings to create your own conventions.

4.2.3   *Custom organization of sources*

To start configuring the default source directories sbt uses, you read the `inspect tree` results and alter the settings you desire.

Think before you act!

As mentioned earlier, the standard organization of sources has become a well-established convention among Scala and Java developers. Any deviation may lead to confusion, so it's a good idea to help reduce that confusion through documentation or else question whether changing the defaults is truly necessary.

The lowest setting in the tree, `sourceDirectory`, which has type `File` in the `Global` configuration scope (*), is defined to be src/. By default it depends on another setting of type `File`: `baseDirectory`, which points to the base directory of your project. `source-Directory` points to a new src child directory underneath the project's baseDirectory.

Conceptually, this is sbt's default `sourceDirectory` configuration:

```
sourceDirectory := new File(baseDirectory.value, "src")
```

If you want to change the root directory for the sources to, let's say, sources/, then add the following line to your build definition:

```
sourceDirectory := new File(baseDirectory.value, "sources")
```

Now the project hierarchy tree looks like the following:

```
<base directory>/
    sources/
        main/
            java/
            scala/
            resources/
        test/
            java/
            scala/
            resources/
```

Next let's look at main/ and test/, which are underneath sources/. As you probably guessed, those two directories are defined in terms of settings that depend on the sourceDirectory setting. This is necessary to make main/ and test/ child directories of sources/ when you change the sourceDirectory setting. But what are those two settings for main/ and test/?

Interestingly, they're both sourceDirectory again but scoped to a different configuration:

```
sourceDirectory in Compile :=
  new File(sourceDirectory.value, "main")

sourceDirectory in Test :=
  new File(sourceDirectory.value, "test")
```

In this code, the sourceDirectory "slot" in the Compile and Test configurations is making use of the sourceDirectory "slot" from the master configuration.

> ### Chaining through configurations
> You just saw that the sourceDirectory in the Compile setting is defined against the master sourceDirectory setting. It's common in sbt to rely on chained settings so that less configuration is needed to customize a build.

If you want to change the directory for the main sources to, let's say, production/, then add the following line to your build definition:

```
sourceDirectory in Compile :=
  new File(sourceDirectory.value, "production")
```

This gives you the following directory layout:

```
<base directory>
    sources/
        production/
            java/
            scala/
            resources/
        test/
            java/
            scala/
            resources/
```

This is a pretty contrived example. It's more realistic to assume that instead of a single src/ directory with lots of children, the project should have a top-level src/ directory for the main sources and another top-level test/ directory for the test sources. You need to modify the settings appropriately:

```
sourceDirectory in Compile :=
  new File(baseDirectory.value, "src")

sourceDirectory in Test :=
  new File(baseDirectory.value, "test")
```

As you can see, you ignore the `sourceDirectory` setting in the `Global` configuration scope when defining `sourceDirectory` in the `Compile` and `Test` configurations.

Finally, you have java/, resources/, and scala/, which are underneath src/main/ and src/test/, respectively. These are defined via the following settings scoped to `Compile` and `Test`, respectively:

```
javaSource
resourceDirectory
scalaSource
```

You can customize your directories and source discovery as needed for the project. But what about the missing filter settings that we glossed over earlier? Let's look a bit into sbt's source filters.

4.2.4   *Filtering the source you want*

What we've covered so far should be enough for most typical Scala and Java projects. For many projects it's best to stick to the default organization of the sources. And if for some reason you have to customize that at the level shown previously, sbt makes that not only possible but even easy for you.

If you're not interested in these details right now, skip this section and move on to the next one.

In most projects, source code is exclusively created by you, the developer—that is, source files written with an IDE or any other editor. But sometimes you also want to have source code generated. sbt supports that through so-called managed sources. Later in this book we'll show you how to use sbt plugins to add source code generation. For now all you need to understand is that sources are distinguished into unmanaged—those you write—and managed—those that are generated.

For the unmanaged sources, sbt further applies filters to include and exclude source files. You've already seen the default directories where you put your Scala and Java sources. Using the filters, sbt determines which files from these directories should be treated as sources and which ones should be ignored. By default the `include-filter` setting is initialized with a filter that includes all *.scala and *.java files, and the `exclude-filter` setting excludes any hidden files—for example, those starting with a dot (.). Let's say you want to change that so that *.java files are no longer compiled but hidden files are. Open your build.sbt and add the following lines:

```
includeFilter in (Compile, unmanagedSources) := "*.scala"

excludeFilter in (Compile, unmanagedSources) := NothingFilter
```

As you can see, both filter settings are scoped to the `Compile` configuration and the `unmanagedSources` task. For the `includeFilter` you use a string that will be implicitly converted into a `NameFilter` using a glob pattern, which is convenient. For the `excludeFilter` you use the `NothingFilter`, which won't exclude anything at all, not even hidden files.

Multiple key scopes

Although we mentioned before that keys can be scoped using a configuration, it's also true that keys can be scoped by additional items, specifically project, configuration, and task. The project axis is often implicitly defined by the context of the setting—for example, by the location of the build.sbt file or the settings field of a particular project in Build.scala. If no scope is provided for configuration, the default configuration is used. If no scope is provided for task, then the key is available only when unscoped.

Exclude filters take precedence over include filters. The actual implementation runs the include filter first and then checks the exclude filter, leading to any excludes overriding the includes.

4.3 Depending on libraries

It's practically impossible these days to work on a project without relying on libraries or other projects. Even in chapter 2, we pulled in the specs2 library for writing tests in the preowned-kittens project. sbt provides a pretty robust way to specify dependencies, so figure 4.5 digs into it using the inspect tree compile:dependencyClasspath.

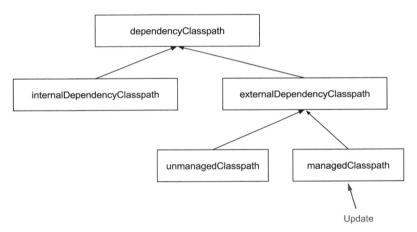

Figure 4.5 **sbt provides a robust way to specify dependencies, so let's dig into it using** `inspect tree compile:dependencyClasspath`.

The dependencies are split into two parts:

- *Internal dependencies*—These are the dependencies between projects defined in the current sbt build.
- *External dependencies*—These are dependencies that must be pulled from somewhere outside, via Ivy or the filesystem. Ivy is a dependency management library, discussed in detail in appendix A.

Whereas internal dependencies are calculated using the project `dependsOn` method, external dependencies are a bit more involved. They're further split into the following two components:

- *Unmanaged dependencies*—These are external dependencies sbt discovers from default locations.
- *Managed dependencies*—These are external dependencies you specify in the sbt build. These dependencies are resolved by the `update` task.

Let's dig deeper into how you can define external dependencies.

4.3.1   *Unmanaged dependencies*

To add a library as an unmanaged dependency, drop a jar archive into the lib/ directory of your project. For example, add the SLF4J API to the preowned-kittens build:

```
<my-project>/
  lib/
    slf4j-api-1.7.2.jar
```

sbt will put all libraries found in the lib/ directory on the project's `unmanagedClasspath`. The default directory where sbt looks for libraries is also configurable. You can do this by altering `unmanaged-base` of type `File`, but again, be aware that most sbt users will expect it to be named `lib/`.

Although it's convenient to drop jars into a project and begin using them as dependencies, this has long-term drawbacks. First and most important, many libraries have dependencies of their own; that is, you get transitive library dependencies. As a result, you have to download the additional libraries and put these into the lib/ directory, too. Second, there's no way to distinguish between various configurations—say, `Compile` and `Test`—for unmanaged dependencies. Therefore, test libraries, which belong to the `Test` configuration, would end up in your packaged main artifact. And finally, it can become hard to understand which libraries your project depends on. If you have more than 10 or so library dependencies, looking at a couple of weird filenames in the lib/ directory can get pretty confusing.

4.3.2   *Managed dependencies*

The recommended approach to library dependencies is using managed dependencies. If you've been using Maven, Gradle, or some other advanced build tool, the concept of declarative library management won't be new. sbt's managed dependencies are similar: you declare one or more library dependencies in the build definition, and sbt will download these from a repository and put these on the classpath when needed.

Although `managedDependencies` can be used to specify files/jars directly, it's recommended to directly use Ivy and the `update` task. Figure 4.6 shows what the `update` task depends on.

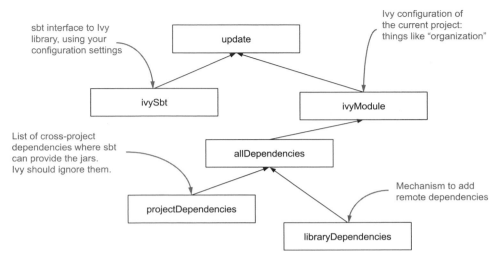

Figure 4.6 Determining what the update task depends on

The `update` task makes use of the configuration of Ivy for sbt and the configuration of the current project, called a *module* in Ivy. The `ivySbt` task pulls in all the global configuration of Ivy, like where to look for dependencies and what credentials to use. The `ivyModule` task pulls together all the configuration for the current project, like what its identifier (name) is, what dependencies it has, and what artifacts it will produce. For more information on the details of Ivy and what the various pieces mean, please read appendix A: "What you need to know about Ivy."

The most important setting to know about `IvySbt` is the `resolvers` setting. This is where you can specify how and where to find libraries. Although Ivy supports configurable lookup mechanisms, most projects make use of sbt's default, which is to load from a Maven repository. Now you can add a new location to pull your artifacts from:

```
resolvers += "Preowned Kitten Maven Repository" at "http://internal-
    repo.preowned-kittens.com"
```

Batteries included! a.k.a. default resolvers

sbt comes out of the box with a few configured repositories:

- Bintray's JCenter
- Maven Central
- Typesafe releases
- sbt community releases

These repositories contain a significant portion of JVM-related dependencies and are starting to see the addition of JavaScript dependencies. For simple projects, configuring new resolvers is most likely unnecessary.

This setting adds a new resolver to the configured Ivy resolvers. Resolvers are responsible for informing Ivy where and how to load libraries. The sbt default is to treat URLs as Maven repositories. This setting informs Ivy to look at the repository found at the URL http://internal-repo.preowned-kittens.com for jars.

Now that you have a location from where you'll pull artifacts, you can start configuring what artifacts to pull. As you'll recall from chapters 2 and 3, you had these dependencies configured:

```
libraryDependencies ++= Seq("junit" % "junit" % "4.11" % "test",
                            "org.specs2" % "specs2_2.9.1" % "1.10" % "test")
```

Here you add to the `libraryDependencies` setting two dependencies for JUnit and specs2. The `libraryDependencies` setting is defined as a collection of `ModuleID` values. `ModuleID` is an sbt abstraction to simplify the declaration of dependencies.

`ModuleID` consists of three mandatory values: `organization`, `name`, and `revision`. These are Ivy's variants of Maven's `groupId`, `artifactId`, and `version` attributes and are a way to uniquely identify a library. Usually you won't be directly creating `Module-IDs` and instead will use sbt's shortcuts, as shown previously.

In sbt, you can define a module ID using the `%` method against strings. Simply specify the organization, name, and revision separated by `%`. Here's an example of adding the `SLF4J API` and `Logback-Classic` dependencies:

```
libraryDependencies ++= Seq(
  "org.slf4j" % "slf4j-api" % "1.7.2",
  "ch.qos.logback" % "logback-classic" % "1.0.7"
)
```

As you can see, you're using strings to define `organization`, `name`, and `revision` of the two library dependencies. The individual strings are combined with the `%` operator, which is provided by sbt as an extension method to `String` and creates a `ModuleID` as a result.

When it comes to dependencies on Scala libraries, you need to pay special attention to binary compatibility. You have to use a version of the library that was compiled against the same or at least a binary-compatible version of Scala, like the one we're using for our project. Starting with Scala 2.9, all micro releases are binary-compatible—for example, 2.9.0, 2.9.1, and 2.9.2. Therefore, you can use a library compiled against Scala 2.9.1 and use Scala 2.9.2 for your project. But you couldn't use Scala 2.10.0 for your project, because you'd risk getting runtime errors.

For a library author, there are two ways of dealing with this issue: either ignore it and publish the library compiled against only one Scala version or cross-build the library against multiple Scala versions. Luckily, most library authors go for the second approach, which enables the library to be used by a broader audience. But what exactly do cross-built libraries look like? How are they identified by `organization`, `name`, and `revision`? sbt has established a de facto standard where the Scala version is encoded in the name of the library by name mangling. Actually, it's not the full Scala version that's added to the name but only the Scala binary version, which by default consists of the major and minor version numbers; for example, 2.10. Let's look at an example, replacing the SLF4J API from the previous example with ScalaLogging:

```
libraryDependencies ++= Seq(
  "com.typesafe" % "scalalogging-slf4j_2.10" % "0.4.0",
  "ch.qos.logback" % "logback-classic" % "1.0.7"
)
```

As you can see, the name of the API has been extended with an underscore and the Scala binary version 2.10. Although this works, it's not only cumbersome to write the names of library dependencies is this fashion, but also error-prone. Just guess what might happen if you updated the Scala version of the project to, let's say, Scala 2.11.0. You'd probably forget to update the Scala binary version in all the library dependencies and get nasty issues at compile or even at runtime.

Therefore, sbt offers a convenient and safe way to declare dependencies on cross-compiled Scala libraries. Instead of the % operator, you use the %% operator between the organization and name and omit adding the Scala binary version to the name:

```
libraryDependencies ++= Seq(
  "com.typesafe" %% "scalalogging-slf4j" % "0.4.0",
  "ch.qos.logback" % "logback-classic" % "1.0.7"
)
```

This is as easy as before, and sbt will automatically create a ModuleID, which has a name mangled with the Scala binary version.

4.3.3 *Managed dependencies and configurations*

Now that you understand how to declare library dependencies, let's take a look at executing more fine-grained control and scoping these to configurations. Configurations usually come with their own sources and classpath; for example, the Compile configuration uses the main sources, and the Test configuration the test sources. If you're using testing libraries like ScalaTest, ScalaCheck, or JUnit, which we strongly recommend, the test sources of your project will depend on these libraries:

```
import org.scalatest.WordSpec
import org.scalatest.matchers.MustMatchers

OwnerMatchingSpec extends WordSpec with MustMatchers {
  // Tests using ScalaCheck go here
}
```

As you can see in this example, the OwnerMatchingSpec class extends some classes and traits from the ScalaTest library. Therefore, ScalaTest and all its transient dependencies have to be on the classpath. But because these library dependencies are needed only to compile the test sources, it would be a bad idea to define them globally. Instead, you can add the proper configuration to a ModuleID:

```
libraryDependencies ++= Seq(
  "org.scalatest" %% "scalatest" % "2.0.M4-B2" % "test"
)
```

You append the name of the Test configuration to the library dependency, using an additional % operator to define the configuration. By default, all dependencies are put onto the default configuration, used for both running and compiling all code in your project. For more details on configurations, see appendix A, "What you need to know about Ivy."

Now that you can declare dependencies and sources for compilation, let's look at the configuration options you can use to package and deliver your software.

4.4   *Packaging your project*

Most software is written so that someone else will use it. The preowned-kittens project you're working on will be deployed on your internal testing web servers and to the Amazon cloud for production. But there's a transformation that must happen between raw output of the compiler and the web server before you can deploy your software. This is known as *packaging*.

The default sbt build is oriented around *open source JVM libraries*. This means that, by default, sbt will package your project as reusable jar files that can be published to Ivy or Maven repositories and consumed by others. Publishing to Ivy or Maven requires a few things:

- A jar file containing the library to share
- A jar file containing the source code of the shared library
- A jar file containing the documentation (Scaladoc or Javadoc) of the shared library
- A configuration file (pom.xml or ivy.xml) that identifies the project and where it came from

If you look at the default package task, using the inspect tree package command, you'll find a tree like the one in figure 4.7. You'll see that it builds only the first jar file, containing the library you want to share.

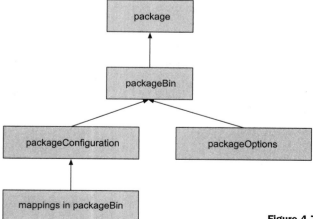

Figure 4.7   Default package task tree

The `package` task depends on the `packageBin` task, which generated the binary artifact (jar) for the project. The contents of this file are defined by the `mappings` in `packageBin` task.

The `mappings` task has the type `Seq[(File, String)]`, a list of files and string names. The files are the list of files to include in the resulting jar, and the names are the location within the jar to store the file.

For the `preowned-kittens` project, you'll want to include a licensing file in the resulting jar files. Although you could put this license in the src/main/resources directory and it would be automatically included by convention, you can manually specify a license file:

```
mappings in packageBin in Compile +=
  (baseDirectory.value / "LICENSE") -> "PREOWNED-KITTEN-LICENSE"
```

Here the file located in the base directory called LICENSE will wind up in the resulting jar file at its base directory with the name PREOWNED-KITTEN-LICENSE.

Although creating the project's binary artifacts is convenient, let's look at how sbt creates the other artifacts in the base build: the documentation and the source. Figure 4.8 shows what happens when you run the `inspect tree` command against the `publish` task to see what shows up. Although we won't list the output directly in the book (for space reasons), figure 4.8 shows the tree that's displayed.

NOTE The `publish` task's tree is rather complicated. This diagram simplifies the dependencies by ignoring extraneous tasks/settings.

Although the `package` task depends only on `packageBin`, publishing to Ivy will make use of `packageSrc` and `packageDoc` in addition to `packageBin`. Each of these three `publish*` tasks has similar `mappings` settings as those shown for the `packageBin` tasks.

The truly hard part in sharing a project with others is the most difficult thing in all of computer science: naming your project.

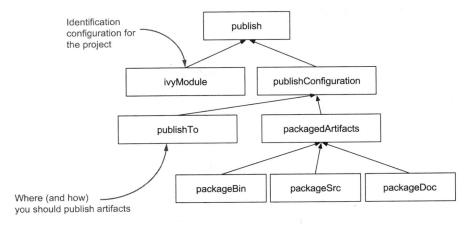

Figure 4.8 Running the `inspect tree` command against the `publish` task

4.4.1   *Identifying your project*

Every project in an sbt build should have a sensible name. Because this name will be used for artifacts created while packaging your project—for example, for jar files—you should use an expressive and sensible name. This can be defined via the name setting:

```
name := "preownedkittens-core"
```

Obviously, name is of type Setting[String]. For a multimodule build (that is, one with multiple projects) it's common practice to have a base name with a suffix for each particular project. In this example preowned-kittens is the base name and core the particular suffix. If you don't define the name, sbt will use default.

Closely related to the name is the organization setting, which helps identify your project:

```
organization := "org.lostkittens"
```

Again, this is a Setting[String] and it defaults to default. It's common practice to apply the reverse-domain-naming convention for the organization. This means that you take a URL you own or are entitled to use that either uniquely identifies your organization or even your project, and reverse it. That way, the risk for name clashes is minimized, which is important because the organization will be used alongside the name to resolve managed library dependencies.

In a multimodule build, the same organization is usually used for all the projects. Therefore, the organization is usually defined at the build level; that is, scoped to the build instead of the individual projects. For those of you who are familiar with Maven, name and organization are equivalent to artifactId and groupId from Maven.

Finally, each project should have an expressive version. There are various versioning strategies (for example, semantic versioning), but in the end it's completely up to you to decide about the version number. Well, not completely, because the version is used to resolve managed library dependencies. Because most Scala and Java libraries are published to Maven repositories, your version should stick to the Maven versioning scheme. This basically looks like the following:

```
major.minor.micro-qualifier
```

major, minor, and micro have to be numbers and qualifier has to be alphanumeric. Only major is mandatory; the others may follow one by one. For details see the Maven documentation.

In order to define your project's version, use the version setting:

```
version := "1.0.0"
```

Like name and organization, version is a Setting[String]. Its default is "0.1-SNAP-SHOT". Like organization, version is typically defined at the build level, so that all projects in a multimodule build have the same version value.

Now that you have sensible names and have configured the packaging to be exactly how you want it, you're ready to begin publishing your artifacts for consumption on

Maven or Ivy. Well, at least you know the basics of how to do that. A complete outline of deployment options is found in chapter 12, "Distributing your projects." This includes how to deploy any project, be it a library, server, command-line utility, or Windows application.

4.5 Summary

We've shown you the core build that sbt provides by default. It's both powerful and flexible in how it can be configured to the needs of any project. Although this configuration is possible, it's not always beneficial to override these default conventions into nonstandard preferences. For example, by moving the default source directory to somewhere other than src/main/scala, you may be introducing something that confuses newcomers to your project.

In this chapter you saw the conventional names for settings and tasks, as shown in table 4.1.

Table 4.1 Conventional setting and task names

Internal vs. external	*Internal* refers to something sbt will find or create. *External* refers to something obtained outside sbt, like using Ivy to resolve artifacts.
Managed vs. unmanaged	*Managed* refers to something that's directly specified in the sbt build, like Ivy dependencies. *Unmanaged* refers to something that's automatically discovered by convention, like source files.
Include and exclude filters	All tasks that discover files on the filesystem support both an include and an exclude filter, configured on the task scope axis.

We also outlined the major tasks involved with a project's development lifecycle and how to configure those tasks, specifically the following:

- `update`—Resolve external dependencies. Call directly only when forcing dependency resolution.
- `compile`—Compile your code.
- `package`—Build a distributable jar of your project.
- `publish`—Push your project into Ivy for other projects to depend on it. See chapter 12 for complete details on publishing.

In sbt all tasks form dependency trees that you can introspect by means of the `inspect tree`, `show`, and `help` commands. We walked through the default conventions in this chapter, but you could do the same on any sbt build, not just the default one.

This chapter didn't cover the arts of running and writing tests in sbt. That's the topic of the next chapter: testing your code.

Part 3

Working with sbt

In Part 3, we'll help expand your knowledge of sbt. First, we'll explore some of the testing solutions for your Scala and Java development. Then we'll delve into how you can use sbt to manipulate files and external processes. In Chapter 7, we'll give you some pointers on how to interact with the user in the sbt console. You'll learn how to use code that other people have written. Finally, we'll cover some tips and tricks for debugging your build.

This chapter covers

- Configuring your build to use specs2
- Learning how to run JUnit tests
- Incorporating external libraries and code into your testing
- Using the ScalaCheck library to improve your testing experience
- Incorporating Selenium HTML tests using the ScalaTest Selenium DSL

In the previous chapters, you set up your `preowned-kittens` project and learned about the default build. Obviously, you're quality conscious, so you want to do as much testing as possible. In this chapter you'll learn how to use the power and interactivity of sbt to make the development and testing cycle a pleasant experience. You're also eclectic in your choice of testing frameworks, so we'll show you how to set up four: specs2, ScalaCheck, JUnit, and ScalaTest. Each has its strengths and weaknesses; thus you can use each of these frameworks for testing different aspects of the project. We'll show you how to configure each framework separately.

You also want to demonstrate to potential customers that you'll take good care of their kittens and that they can trust you. How can you show this? Well, you'll

include on your site a report of the tests that you've run as part of the development
cycle. This will help persuade potential clients. To generate the reports, you'll have to
fork your tests to run them in a different JVM from sbt. Because there isn't a built-in
solution for reporting with JUnit, you'll incorporate our custom code into the build to
get the reports you want.

5.1   Configuring specs2 with sbt

You'll recall from chapter 2 that you have a set of specs2 specifications for your testing:

```
object LogicSpec extends Specification {
  "The 'matchLikelihood' method" should {
    "be 100% when all attributes match" in {
      val tabby = Kitten(1, Set("male", "tabby"))
      val prefs = BuyerPreferences(Set("male", "tabby"))
      Logic.matchLikelihood(tabby, prefs) must beGreaterThan(0.999)
    }
    "be 0% when no attributes match" in {
      val tabby = Kitten(1, Set("male", "tabby"))
      val prefs = BuyerPreferences(Set("female", "calico"))
      val result = Logic.matchLikelihood(tabby, prefs)
      result must beLessThan(0.001)
    }
  }
}
```

All that you need for sbt to compile and run these tests is the following in build.sbt:

```
libraryDependencies += "org.specs2" %% "specs2" % "1.14" % "test"
```

If you run sbt test, you'll get the following output:

```
[info] LogicSpec
[info]
[info] The 'matchLikelihood' method should
[info] + be 100% when all attributes match
[info] + be 0% when no attributes match
[info]
[info]
[info] Total for specification LogicSpec
[info] Finished in 11 ms
[info] 3 examples, 0 failure, 0 error
[info]
[info] Passed: Total 3, Failed 0, Errors 0, Passed 4
[success] Total time: 1 s, completed 11-Jan-2015 21:26:40
```

Already you're doing well as far as the build itself is concerned. But sbt isn't just a
build tool; it can help with the development process as well. Let's start at the beginning by looking in depth at three tasks: test, testOnly, and testQuick. From the
command line, you can run any one of these tasks:

```
$ sbt test
$ sbt testOnly org.preownedkittens.LogicSpec
$ sbt testQuick
```

test runs all of the tests that sbt can find. testOnly runs only those tests specified on the command line. You can have wildcards in there; for instance:

```
$ sbt testOnly *Logic*
```

This will run all of the tests that contain the string "Logic." Finally, testQuick runs all of the tests that (1) failed in the previous run, (2) haven't yet been run, or (3) depend on code that has changed.

You can use sbt to improve the development experience by writing your tests, running just those tests from the command line, and then changing the code so that the tests pass, rerunning the tests after every save.

This works well, but you can do even better. If you prefix an sbt command with ~, sbt will wait in a loop, looking for changed files. If it detects a changed file, it will rerun the task, along with all of its dependencies. This works through the command line as well as the console. Let's see. Start the sbt console and then type ~test, as shown in the following listing.

Listing 5.1   Running the ~test task

```
$ sbt
[info] Loading project definition from .../chapter5/project
[info] Set current project to preowned-kittens (in build ...)
> ~test
[info] LogicSpec                                       ◁────── Runs tests continuously
[info]
[info] The 'matchLikelihood' method should
[info] + be 100% when all attributes match
[info] + be 0% when no attributes match               ◁────── Results of tests
[info]
[info] Total for specification LogicSpec
[info] Finished in 15 ms
[info] 2 examples, 0 failure, 0 error
[info]                                                         Waiting for
[info] Passed: Total 2, Failed 0, Errors 0, Passed 2           file changes
[success] Total time: 2 s, completed 15-May-2015 09:45:35
1. Waiting for source changes... (press enter to interrupt) ◁─┘
```

You can see that it has run the tests, and then, on the last line, it's waiting for you to change the source code. If you save one of the source files again, it will rerun all of the tests. This is extremely useful when you're in the middle of a code/test cycle, because you get immediate feedback from your tests without having to run them each time.

Now, running all of the tests may take some time, so you may wish to run only a subset. You can do this with testOnly, in exactly the same manner, as shown in the next listing.

Listing 5.2   Running the ~testOnly task

```
> ~testOnly *Logic*                   ◁────── Run only *Logic* tests
[info] LogicSpec
[info]
```

```
[info] The 'matchLikelihood' method should
[info] + be 100% when all attributes match
[info] + be 0% when no attributes match
[info]
[info] Total for specification LogicSpec
[info] Finished in 14 ms
[info] 2 examples, 0 failure, 0 error
[info]
[info] Passed: Total 2, Failed 0, Errors 0, Passed 2
[success] Total time: 2 s, completed 15-May-2015 09:48:42
1. Waiting for source changes... (press enter to interrupt)
```

In addition to using wildcards, you can autocomplete the test names by using the Tab key. If you enter

```
> ~testOnly org<TAB>
```

then sbt will autocomplete the test name to the full name of the test:

```
> ~testOnly org.preownedkittens.LogicSpec
```

Testing tasks

There are three main testing tasks: `test`, `testOnly`, and `testQuick`.

`test` runs all of the tests sbt can find in your project.

`testOnly <testname1>` runs only the test(s) specified on the command line. You can use wildcards, (*) and if you're running in the sbt console, you can use autocomplete by pressing <TAB>.

`testQuick` runs the tests that have previously failed, that haven't already been run, or that depend on code that has been recompiled. You can also specify a test.

5.1.1   *Reports and forking tests*

Now, as part of your site, you want to incorporate your test reports so that the kitten owners will have more confidence in the site.

specs2 can generate an HTML report of the tests you've run, so you'll use that as a basis of your reports. First you need to generate the HTML; this is done by specifying the `html` option to specs2 in build.sbt:

```
testOptions in Test += Tests.Argument("html")
```

specs2 uses pegdown, an HTML generator library, to generate the HTML, so for this to work you need to add another dependency, `"org.pegdown" % "pegdown" % "1.0.2"`. Note that you're adding a test configuration:

```
libraryDependencies += "org.specs2" %% "specs2" % "1.14" % "test"

libraryDependencies += "org.pegdown" % "pegdown" % "1.0.2" % "test"
```

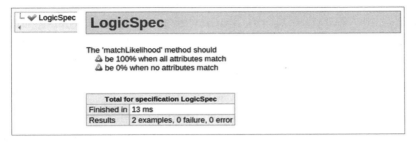

Figure 5.1   The HTML for the target/specs2-reports/LogicSpec.html report

When you reload and run the tests again, this produces a nice HTML report in target/specs2-reports/LogicSpec.html, along with the images and CSS required; see figure 5.1.

> **Remember to reload when changing build definition**
> Whenever you change the build.sbt file (or indeed any of the other files that contribute to the sbt build definition), you need to reload to get the changes recognized by sbt:
>
> ```
> > reload
> [info] Loading project definition from /home/mfarwell/code/sbt/sbt-in-
>            action-examples/chapter5/project
> [info] Set current project to preowned-kittens (in build file:/home/
> mfarwell/code/sbt/sbt-in-action-examples/chapter5/)
> ```

These files will now be generated each time you run the tests because by default the tests are run as part of the build. In real life, you'd publish these somewhere as part of your build.

To include them as part of your website, you want to change the output directory so that you can pick them up later when you build the final site to deploy. To change the output directory of specs2, you can specify a Java system property

```
-Dspecs2.outDir=<directory>
```

and it will create the files in there. You could achieve this by adding a custom task called `System.setProperty("specs2.outDir", "/something")`, which is executed before the test, and then a `System.clearProperty("specs2.outDir")` after. This solution is fairly complex and changes the running sbt environment. Although this doesn't matter in this use case, it's still not very nice. For a better solution, you should run the tests in a different instance of the JVM, and then you can specify parameters to that JVM. In sbt, this is called *forking* the JVM. You can do this for various tasks, such as compiling and testing. And obviously running the application forks the JVM. In sbt, you can use the `javaOptions` setting to specify the options to the new JVM:

```
javaOptions in Test += "-Dspecs2.outDir=target/generated/test-reports"
```

This will create a specific directory, named generated, to put your generated files in so that everything is in one place. You'll use this again later for other generated files. Note that you're putting the generated files in the target directory so that it will be cleaned up when you execute a clean. javaOptions can be applied to the test and run tasks, and you can specify anything you're able to on the Java command line; for instance:

```
javaOptions in run += "-Xmx2048m" // we need lots of heap space
```

If you specify the run scope, then this will apply to both the run and run-main tasks (run-main allows you to select the class to run, whereas run selects the class for you). But javaOptions won't work without forking:

```
fork in Test := true
```

> ### Forking your JVM
> When you specify javaOptions, you must set fork to be true for it to be taken into account. If you don't, you'll be pulling your hair out when it doesn't work. fork doesn't always need to be true for all tasks. In the previous case you're setting it only for the testing tasks. One task that you don't need to fork for is compilation. sbt does the necessary steps for these to work correctly, and you don't need to fork to compile.

Again, the fork setting can apply to the run, run-main, and test tasks, with run and run-main sharing the same setting (run).

There's one more thing you need to watch out for here: you shouldn't be hard-coding target in your -D string; this is bad practice, because this value can change. target is the directory where sbt puts all of its work, but this isn't fixed; it's actually a setting. If you hard-coded target, someone could change it like this:

```
target := file(baseDirectory.value / "foobar")
```

Then sbt clean wouldn't clean up your generated files. To make sure you always use the correct value, use the value of the target setting:

```
javaOptions in Test += "-Dspecs2.outDir=" + (target.value / "generated/test-
    reports").getAbsolutePath
```

The target.value actually returns a file (not a String). A file has a method called /, which appends the argument to the name of the file and produces another file. Because the current working directory isn't necessarily the base directory, either, call getAbsolutePath to avoid problems with relative paths.

What have you done? You wanted to generate HTML reports for your tests, so you configured specs2 to do that. The default output directory wasn't good enough, so you changed it to target/generated/test-reports by forking your JVM for the tests and setting the system property for the output directory. Now, for each subproject using this setting, its target directory will have the generated specs2 tests.

Forking processes

Most of the time you don't need to fork, but there are four main reasons why you may want to fork:

- *New JVM requires different parameters*—If you want to change the memory used by the new JVM or change the JVM itself, you'll need to fork. A common use case is to add a `-D` option, as you've done.
- `System.exit()`—If your code calls `System.exit()`, this normally shuts down the JVM. Most of the time sbt copes with this, but there are certain situations where it doesn't.
- *Threads*—If your code creates a lot of new threads, and these threads are not tidied before the main method returns, then this can cause problems. For instance, a GUI using Swing creates a number of threads. In general, these don't terminate until the JVM itself terminates.
- *Class loading*—If you're using class loaders, or if you're deserializing for any reason, this can cause issues. Note that it may not be you who is doing the class loading but a library that you're using, such as scalate. Scalate is a template engine that creates HTML from a template. It does this by creating Scala files and then compiling and loading the classes. This can cause problems with PermGen in some JVMs.

5.1.2 Digging deeper: other options for forking

sbt provides other options when you're forking your processes. Note that for these options to work, you need to have `fork := true`.

CHANGING THE JVM

You can also specify a Java installation by using the `javaHome` setting. This is the directory in which the Java installation is found:

```
javaHome := file("/path/to/jre")
```

This doesn't change sbt itself. You can also specify the configuration for the `run` and/or `test` tasks.

CHANGING THE WORKING DIRECTORY

When a task forks, you can set the working directory for the forked JVM:

```
baseDirectory := file("/working/directory")
baseDirectory in (Compile,run) := file("/working/directory")
```

Note, again, that this doesn't affect sbt itself, just the new JVM. Again, you can specify the configuration for the `run` and `test` tasks for different configurations.

INPUT AND OUTPUT

When you fork a process, you can change where the output goes to and where input is read from. You do this using the `outputStrategy` setting:

```
outputStrategy := Some(CustomOutput(new java.io.FileOutputStream("/tmp/
    run.log")))
```

By default, all standard output is logged to the sbt console at the Info level, and all standard errors are logged at the Error level. There are any number of options for output. Here's how to send all output (standard out and error) to sbt standard out (not the logger):

```
outputStrategy := Some(StdoutOutput)
```

Finally, if you want your task to wire the standard input of the new process into the standard input for sbt—for example, if you want to ask a question of the user—you can use `connectInput`:

```
connectInput in run := true
```

5.2   *JUnit and using custom code*

The preowned-kittens.com website wasn't actually a new project when you inherited it. Initially it was written in Java, but the process was taking so long that the original kittens became cats. But as a leftover from the first version, you inherited a number of legacy tests that were written in Java, using the JUnit testing framework. So as not to waste that effort, you decided to keep these tests around and run them against the new Scala code.

You'll recall from chapter 2 that sbt can compile Java, so all you have to do is include the files in the correct places in the source tree, which are src/main/java and src/test/java. You need to link these tests into your build. You do this by adding two dependencies into your build. The first is JUnit itself:

```
libraryDependencies += "junit" % "junit" % "4.11" % "test"
```

As an example test, use the file shown in the following listing.

> **Listing 5.3   Failing JUnit test**

```
package org.preownedkittens;

import org.junit.*;
import scala.collection.immutable.*;

public class LogicJavaTest {
    @Test
    public void testKitten() {
        Kitten kitten = new Kitten(1, new HashSet());
        Assert.assertEquals(1,
    kitten.attributes().size());                          ◁————————❶ This fails!
    }
}
```

Add this in, run sbt test, and all of your tests will pass. Which they shouldn't, because you have a failing test ❶. In fact, sbt isn't even running the Java test. Why? As you've seen, sbt "knows" how to run certain test frameworks out of the box. But how does it know this? sbt defines a `test-interface`, which allows sbt (1) to find the list of classes to run as tests, and (2) to run those tests. JUnit doesn't know about this interface.

> ### The test-interface of sbt
> sbt supports, by default, ScalaTest, ScalaCheck, and specs2. This is because all of those test frameworks include in their jars a class that implements the sbt `test-interface` classes. JUnit does not, because it's not a Scala testing framework; it's a Java one.

In order to run your JUnit tests, you need to define an sbt `test-interface` for JUnit. Fortunately, someone has already done it for you, and all you need to do is add it to the dependencies for your project. It's called `junit-interface`:

```
libraryDependencies += "junit" % "junit" % "4.11" % "test" // already added
libraryDependencies += "com.novocode" % "junit-interface" % "0.11" % "test"
```

Now when you run your tests, they fail as expected:

```
$ sbt "testOnly org.preownedkittens.LogicJavaTest"
[info] Loading project definition from ...
[info] Set current project to preowned-kittens ...
[info] Test run started
[info] Test org.preownedkittens.LogicJavaTest.testKitten started
[error] Test org.preownedkittens.LogicJavaTest.testKitten failed:
    expected:<1> but was:<0>, took 0.045 sec
[info] Test run finished: 1 failed, 0 ignored, 1 total, 0.053s
[error] Failed: Total 1, Failed 1, Errors 0, Passed 0
[error] Failed tests:
[error]     org.preownedkittens.LogicJavaTest
[error] (analytics/test:testOnly) sbt.TestsFailedException: Tests
    unsuccessful
[error] Total time: 1 s, completed 14-Jan-2015 23:32:02
```

Correct the test, and everybody is happy. You've now incorporated your JUnit tests into your build.

5.2.1 Report generation with JUnit

You've generated HTML reports with specs2, but can you do this with JUnit? There isn't an easy way to have your reports, like in specs2. But the previous project owners produced reports from their JUnit tests, using a `RunListener` class that they defined. A `RunListener` is a JUnit-defined class with a defined set of methods that are called when tests start, finish, or fail. It looks like this:

```
public class RunListener {
    public void testRunStarted(Description description) throws Exception { }
    public void testRunFinished(Result result) throws Exception { }
    public void testStarted(Description description) throws Exception { }
    public void testFinished(Description description) throws Exception { }
    public void testFailure(Failure failure) throws Exception { }
```

```
    public void testAssumptionFailure(Failure failure) { }
    public void testIgnored(Description description) throws Exception { }
}
```

Each of these methods is called on a specific event. For instance, testStarted is called before each JUnit test method, and testRunFinished is called once, at the end of all tests.

This is the Java class that was defined, which gives you a basic HTML report:

```java
package com.preownedkittens.sbt;

import org.junit.*;
import java.io.*;
import org.junit.runner.*;
import org.junit.runner.notification.*;

public class JUnitListener extends RunListener {
    private PrintWriter pw;
    private boolean testFailed;
    private String outputFile = System.getProperty("junit.output.file");

    public void testRunStarted(Description description) throws Exception {
        pw = new PrintWriter(new FileWriter(outputFile));
        pw.println("<html><head><title>JUnit report</title></head><body>");
    }
    public void testRunFinished(Result result) throws Exception {
        pw.println("</body></html>");
        pw.close();
    }
    public void testStarted(Description description) throws Exception {
        pw.print("<p> Test " + description.getDisplayName() + " ");
        testFailed = false;

    }
    public void testFinished(Description description) throws Exception {
        if (!testFailed) {
            pw.print("OK");
        }
        pw.println("</p>");
    }
    public void testFailure(Failure failure) throws Exception {
        testFailed = true;
        pw.print("FAILED!");
    }
    public void testAssumptionFailure(Failure failure) {
        pw.print("ASSUMPTION FAILURE");
    }
    public void testIgnored(Description description) throws Exception {
        pw.print("IGNORED");
    }
}
```

This isn't going to win any prizes for prettiness, but it does the job. It produces an HTML page like the one shown in figure 5.2.

Test testKitten(org.usedkittens.LogicJavaTest) FAILED!   **Figure 5.2 JUnit HTML report**

Let's find a place to store this output. You need to be able to specify this `RunListener` to `junit-interface`. Most of the implementation details of the previous class are irrelevant here, but we need to cover two things. The first is how to tell the `RunListener` which file to output to, which is done through a system property:

```
private String outputFile = System.getProperty("junit.output.file");
```

As with specs2, this means that you need to add a `"-Djunit.output.file= " + (target .value / "generated/junit.html")` to your build.sbt and fork the tests as before:

```
javaOptions in Test += "-Djunit.output.file=" + (target.value / "generated/
    junit.html").getAbsolutePath
fork in Test := true
```

In your build.sbt, the `fork` setting is already `true` for your build, so you don't need to do it twice.

---

sbt settings are immutable

When we're talking about settings, the most recently defined setting wins. If you specify the same setting twice, the value that was defined last will be the one that's used. This can be confusing for those expecting a more line-by-line flow, where line x is executed, and then that value used in line $x + 1$; for example:

```
name := "preowned-kittens"
organization := name.value + " Inc"
name := "This is the one"
```

The final value of the `organization` setting is "This is the one Inc". Note that we aren't recommending that you specify a setting twice. As you can see, it can get very confusing. It's good practice to specify a setting only once.

Additionally, you need to specify the `RunListener` class to `junit-interface`. This needs to be done through adding entries to `testOptions`, the same as before when you were using specs2:

```
testOptions += Tests.Argument("--run-
    listener=com.preownedkittens.sbt.JUnitListener")
```

Now everything should work. But, as you may have spotted, there's a problem with using `testOptions` again. You now have these two lines in the build.sbt file:

```
testOptions += Tests.Argument("html")
testOptions += Tests.Argument("--run-
    listener=com.preownedkittens.sbt.JUnitListener")
```

The problem here is that you're adding two parameters to `testOptions`, but they're for two different testing libraries! You need to be able to differentiate between the testing libraries, sending only the specs2 options to specs2, and the `junit-interface` parameters to JUnit. Fortunately, sbt provides a way to do this—a delimiter for testing library options, which it calls a test framework:

```
testOptions += Tests.Argument(TestFrameworks.Specs2, "html")
testOptions += Tests.Argument(TestFrameworks.JUnit, "--run-
    listener=com.preownedkittens.sbt.JUnitListener")
```

sbt test frameworks

sbt defines five `TestFrameworks`:

```
val ScalaCheck = new
        TestFramework("org.scalacheck.ScalaCheckFramework")
val ScalaTest = new
        TestFramework("org.scalatest.tools.ScalaTestFramework")
val Specs = new TestFramework("org.specs.runner.SpecsFramework")
val Specs2 = new TestFramework("org.specs2.runner.SpecsFramework")
val JUnit = new TestFramework("com.novocode.junit.JUnitFramework")
```

These are defined by sbt and can be used out of the box. But if you use a test framework that isn't defined here, you can define and create your own.

Now rerun your tests, and you'll get the target/generated/junit.html generated along with the target/generated/test-reports/* that you had for specs2.

5.3   *ScalaCheck*

ScalaCheck is a test framework that's designed for property-based testing. The main difference between a more traditional unit-testing framework and a property-based framework is that with a traditional framework, you have to provide the data with which to test your classes. With a property-based framework, it provides the data. You tell it what sort of data you want, and then it generates a set of data and runs the tests. You need to provide some code that asserts that a combination of data is correct. Let's look at an example. In chapter 2, you created a specs2 test to test the buyer-kitten-matching algorithm. It looked like this:

```
object LogicSpec extends Specification {
  "The 'matchLikelihood' method" should {
    "be 100% when all attributes match" in {
      val tabby = Kitten(1, Set("male", "tabby"))
      val prefs = BuyerPreferences(Set("male", "tabby"))
      Logic.matchLikelihood(tabby, prefs) must beGreaterThan(0.999)
    }
    ... // elided to save space
  }
}
```

These are good tests, but using only four test cases to cover the logic in this test seems a bit light. To up your confidence in the algorithm a bit, you can add tests for the same method using ScalaCheck, as shown in the next listing.

Listing 5.4   ScalaCheck property testers

```
package org.preownedkittens

import org.scalacheck.Properties
import org.scalacheck.Prop.forAll
import org.scalacheck._

object LogicSpecification extends Properties("Logic") {
  val allAttributes = Array("Harlequin","Tortoiseshell","Siamese",
                 "Alien","Rough","Tom","Sad","Overweight")

  val genKitten: Gen[Kitten] = for {
    attributes <- Gen.containerOf[Set,String](Gen.oneOf(allAttributes))
  } yield Kitten(1, attributes)

  val genBuyerPreferences: Gen[BuyerPreferences] = (for {
    attributes <- Gen.containerOf[Set,String](Gen.oneOf(allAttributes))
  } yield BuyerPreferences(attributes))

  def matches(x: String, a: Kitten) =
        if (a.attributes.contains(x)) 1.0 else 0.0

  property("matchLikelihood") = forAll(genKitten, genBuyerPreferences)
  ((a: Kitten, b: BuyerPreferences) => {
    if (b.attributes.size == 0) true
    else {
      val num = b.attributes.map{matches(_, a)}.sum
      num / b.attributes.size - Logic.matchLikelihood(a, b) < 0.001
    }
  })
}
```

① Generator for kittens

② Generator for buyer preferences

③ Property tester

The methods `genKitten` **①** and `genBuyerPreferences` **②** are the data generators. The work is done by **③**, the property tester. This takes the two generators for the case classes you created and produces a partial function. This is called 100 times with 100 generated values. These are random values. The assertion in the `property` function is true if the implemented version agrees with the test version. If the generated values don't meet the assertion, the test fails.

If the test does fail, you'd normally take the failing instance and put it into another test format, such as specs2 or JUnit. This cycle is an example of how you could use the interactivity of sbt to help you pass the tests. Each time you run a ScalaCheck test, the data generated is different, so you could have the following development cycle:

- Add the property-based tests for a method.
- In sbt interactive mode, run `test` and look for failing tests.
- For each failing test, add the failing data to a specs2 test. Fix the bug and rerun the ScalaCheck test.
- If there aren't any failing tests, rerun ScalaCheck a couple of times to make sure.
- Stop when bored.

To achieve this, you can use the `~test` feature of sbt. This executes all of the tests each time one of the source files is changed. Try it:

```
$ sbt
> ~test
[info] > ARG_0: Kitten(1,List(Rough, Rough, Overweight))
[info] > ARG_1: BuyerPreferences(List(Alien, Tortoiseshell, Sad, Rough))
[info] ! Logic.matchLikelihood: Falsified after 15 passed tests.
[info] Test run finished: 1 failed, 0 ignored, 1 total, 0.0s
....
[error] Failed: : Total 9, Failed 5, Errors 0, Passed 4, Skipped 0
[error] Failed tests:
[error]          org.preownedkittens.LogicSpecification
[error] (test:test) sbt.TestsFailedException: Tests unsuccessful
[error] Total time: 3 s, completed 24 mars 2013 17:56:29
1. Waiting for source changes... (press enter to interrupt)
```

We cut down the output here to make things readable. This is showing you that the method `matchLikelihood` is failing with the following data:

```
[info] > ARG_0: Kitten(id,List(Rough, Rough, Overweight))
[info] > ARG_1: BuyerPreferences(List(Alien, Tortoiseshell, Sad, Rough))
```

You've told ScalaCheck to use your attribute strings. This shows that you have a `Kitten` with three attributes and `BuyerPreferences` with four attributes. There's one immediate problem with the data that you're passing in: there are two `Rough` attributes. It doesn't make sense to have duplicated attributes in a `Kitten` (or indeed `BuyerPreferences`). This means that the data model is probably wrong. This shouldn't be a `List[String]` but instead a `Set[String]`. You have to fix your model, changing the `List` into a `Set`. Add a new test to your `LogicSpec` that gives multiple duplicate attributes to the `Kitten` and to the `BuyerPreference` class to make sure it doesn't happen again:

```
"be 100% when all attributes match (with duplicates)" in {
  val tabby = Kitten(1, Set("male", "tabby", "male"))
  val prefs = BuyerPreferences(Set("male", "tabby", "tabby"))
  Logic.matchLikelihood(tabby, prefs) must beGreaterThan(0.999)
}
```

Once the new model.scala and logic.scala are saved, the tests get rerun automatically because you're doing `~test`. Here's the output, again cut down:

```
> test
[info] ! Logic.matchLikelihood: Falsified after 7 passed tests.
[info] > ARG_0: Kitten(id,Set(Rough))
[info] > ARG_1: BuyerPreferences(Set(Harlequin, Rough))
[error] Failed: : Total 9, Failed 5, Errors 0, Passed 4, Skipped 0
[error] Failed tests:
[error]          org.preownedkittens.LogicSpecification
[error] (test:test) sbt.TestsFailedException: Tests unsuccessful
[error] Total time: 3 s, completed 24 mars 2013 19:36:39
```

There's still a problem. There are no duplicates, but the algorithm is wrong some-where. The problem is actually in the definition of `Logic.matchLikelihood`:

```scala
object Logic {
  /** Determines the match likelihood and returns % match. */
  def matchLikelihood(kitten: Kitten, buyer: BuyerPreferences): Double = {
    val matches = buyer.attributes.toList map { attribute =>
      kitten.attributes contains attribute
    }
    val nums = matches map { b => if(b) 1 else 0 } // (a)
    nums.sum / nums.size      // (b)
  }
}
```

The problem is the integer division at (b), which will always be either 1 or 0. Between chapter 2 and chapter 4 someone has introduced a regression at (a). These should be doubles, not integers. You must add a test to `LogicSpec`, using the test case provided by ScalaCheck:

```scala
"be 66% when two from three attributes match" in {
  val tabby = Kitten(1, Set("female", "calico", "overweight"))
  val prefs = BuyerPreferences(Set("female", "calico", "thin"))
  val result = Logic.matchLikelihood(tabby, prefs)
  result must beBetween(0.666, 0.667)
}
```

When the test is run, it fails:

```
[info] Compiling 1 Scala source to C:\code\sbt\sbt-in-action-
    examples\chapter5\target\scala-2.10\test-classes...
...
[error] Failed tests:
[error]          org.preownedkittens.LogicSpecification
[error]          org.preownedkittens.LogicSpec
[error] (test:test) sbt.TestsFailedException: Tests unsuccessful
[error] Total time: 5 s, completed 24 mars 2013 20:03:15
```

And now you can fix the problem:

```scala
val nums = matches map { b => if(b) 1.0 else 0.0 } // (b)
```

This demonstrates some of the power of sbt as a development environment, in con-junction with the right kind of tests. Note that your tests are still not complete, but this gives you more confidence that you're going in the right direction. One more thing that could be added to your ScalaCheck tests is to use real attributes rather than auto-generated ones. This would increase the chances of finding problems with your logic with realistic data.

Another thing you can do is to augment the number of times that the property is tested. By default, ScalaCheck uses 100 different combinations. Because ScalaCheck isn't guaranteed to find all of your problems, it's probably a good idea to up the num-ber and see if anything breaks. You can do this in one of two ways: through `test-Options` or on the command line. First, `testOptions`:

```scala
testOptions += Tests.Argument(TestFrameworks.ScalaCheck, "-s", "5000")
```

The -s is the minimum number of successful tests needed to have a passing test. This will run the test with 5000 sets of data.

Alternatively, if you're using the test or testOnly task, you can specify this on the command line:

```
> ~testOnly org.preownedkittens.LogicSpecification -- -s 5000
```

The -- means that this is the end of the tests to run, and you're starting the options to pass to the test framework.

5.4   *Integration testing*

In this section you'll add integration tests to your build, which will be run at a different time than the unit tests that were written in the previous sections. We'll use the ScalaTest Selenium DSL to illustrate this, and, as we've done with the others, we'll incorporate the ScalaTest HTML reports.

5.4.1   *ScalaTest and Selenium*

Another commonly used Scala testing framework is ScalaTest. ScalaTest implements a number of different styles of testing, including specification-style testing like specs2, unit testing like JUnit, and even behavior-driven development-style testing. Which style you use depends on what you want to test and what stage of your project that you're at.

One of the recently added features of ScalaTest is the Selenium DSL (domain-specific language). Selenium is a tool that aids the testing of websites. It's available for a number of languages, including Java/Scala, Ruby, Python, and the .NET languages. Selenium works by starting a browser via what it calls a web driver and interacting with it, telling it to click this button or enter some text into this or that field. It can drive Microsoft Internet Explorer, Mozilla Firefox, and Google Chrome browsers, among others. One of the advantages of using Selenium is that you're interacting with the system as a user would interact; you're performing the same actions as an end user. The disadvantage is that you need to test the full stack, from the browser to the database. You need all of the pieces. For this reason, Selenium tests are generally considered to be integration tests.

You'll use the FlatSpec classes of ScalaTest. ScalaTest integrates Selenium through an internal DSL, so you're actually writing Scala code, but it turns out to be much more readable than normal Scala. This is mostly easier to write, and it can be useful when you're explaining the tests to a third party who doesn't know the code intimately. Let's see an example:

```
"Home page" should "redirect to kitten list" in {
    go to "http://localhost:9000"
    currentUrl should startWith ("http://localhost:9000/kittens")
}
```

The goal of the DSL is to make the code more readable and understandable, and this is a simple test, but there's quite a bit going on in this example. You can read the aim of the test by reading the first line. If the user goes to the bare URL (without the /kittens), then the user is redirected to the page http://localhost:9000/kittens. The first thing to note is that the example code is pure Scala, so you can do anything you normally would be able to in code; it just looks a bit more readable. Line 1 is pretty much plain text, which aids the description of the test. Line 2 opens the bare URL http://localhost:9000, the default page for the site, and then, when that action has been completed by the browser, it checks that the current URL is actually /kittens (line 3), so the website has redirected the user to this page. When you run this test, you get output like the following from sbt:

```
[info] SeleniumSpec:
[info] Home page
[info] - should redirect to kitten list
```

An aside about your site: it has three pages. The initial page looks like figure 5.3, which is a list of all kittens that you currently have on your books along with a form that allows the user to select three attributes that they want from a kitten.

When visitors click the Find Me A Kitten button, another page shows all of the kittens that match their selected attributes, and they can click the Purchase button, which adds the kitten to the basket.[1] See figure 5.4.

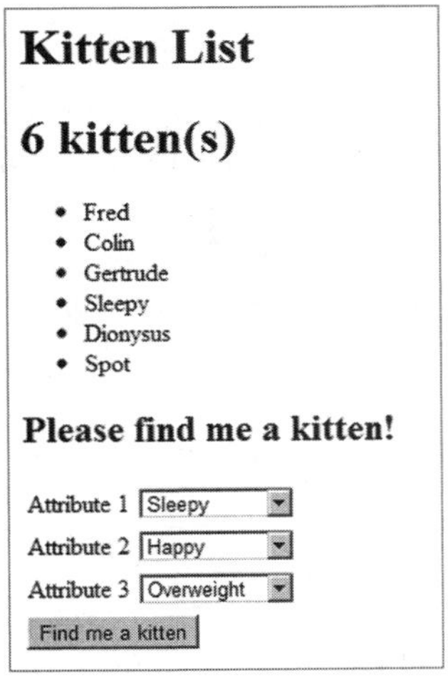

Figure 5.3 The initial page for your preowned-kittens site

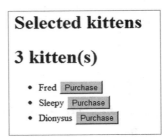

Figure 5.4 Visitors to your site make their selections for purchase.

---

[1] Shopping basket, not cat basket.

You're using the Play Framework for your site, and you've added a `main` method to run it,[2] so you can use `sbt run` to make the site available:

```
$ sbt run
[info] Loading project definition from ...
[info] Set current project to preowned-kittens ...
[info] Running Global
[info] play - database [default] connected at jdbc:h2:mem:play
[info] play - Application started (Prod)
[info] play - Listening for HTTP on /0:0:0:0:0:0:0:0:9000
```

For now, you can run the site in one window and the tests from another. You'll have a better solution to this in chapter 6.

You can add another more in-depth test:

```
it should "show three dropdown lists of attributes in sorted order" in {     ◁─┐
    def select(name: String) =
findAll(xpath("//select[@name='" + name + "']/option")).                  Description ❶
map { _.text }.toList
    def assertListCompleteAndIsSorted(list: Seq[String]) = {              ◁─┐
      list.size should be(20)
      list.sorted should be(list)                                          Assertion
    }                                                                       utility
                                                                            method ❸
    go to homePage + "/kittens"

    assertListCompleteAndIsSorted(select("select1"))
    assertListCompleteAndIsSorted(select("select2"))
    assertListCompleteAndIsSorted(select("select3"))
  }
```

Drop-down utility method ❷ (margin annotation pointing to `map { _.text }.toList`)

We don't need to go into too much detail here, but you can see that line 1 contains the description ❶, except that you don't have to say Home page again. You can just say it. You define two utility methods, one to select the text from the drop-down lists ❷, and one to make some assertions that they contain the default value and that they are sorted ❸. The test itself goes to the `/kittens` page and then asserts that all of the lists are correct and present. The output now looks like this:

```
[info] SeleniumSpec:
[info] Home page
[info] - should redirect to kitten list
[info] - should show three dropdown lists of attributes in sorted order
```

5.4.2 *Challenges of integration testing*

What challenges does this present to the build? The first, most obvious one is that in order to run your tests, you need a website that's up and running. This means that before you run your tests, you'll have to actually build the site: you'll have to package the website in some manner, and you'll have to start the website so that you can interact with it. Normally, integration tests use realistic data, so you may need a database and also may need to clean up the database before each test run.

---

[2] You can download the code from the GitHub repository.

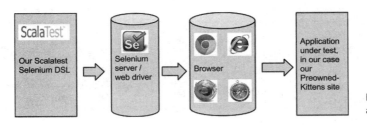

Figure 5.5 The Selenium architecture

This implies that the integration tests can't be run at the same time as all of your other tests. Usually, when you're developing, you want feedback as quickly as possible, so it's worth running the unit tests before you start worrying about starting servers or any other expensive operations. It's also conceptually a good idea to separate the two sets of tests because you'll end up with a cleaner build. We'll talk about starting the server and the packaging in chapters 6 and 8.

Another thing you need to take into account is how Selenium works. It's not quite as simple as starting a browser and forgetting it. The architecture actually looks more like figure 5.5.

The ScalaTest Selenium DSL drives the Selenium server. The Selenium server in turn drives the browser. There's a specific driver for each browser. The browser interacts directly with the site under test.

Most of the time it's easier to use Firefox as a target, because Selenium has a built-in server for Firefox. But we'll use Google Chrome in our examples, so you'll need to tell Selenium where your Chrome driver is and, importantly, start up the Chrome driver server before the tests begin and shut it down after the tests have finished. Because the startup and shutdown of the Chrome server is expensive, you can't do it for each test, so it's better that you do it only once, before all the tests, and then shut it down at the end. Again, more about this in chapter 6.

Finally (as if all this wasn't enough), one of the advantages of Selenium is its multi-browser capability; it can handle Firefox, Chrome, Internet Explorer, and other browsers. Therefore, you want to write your tests in such a way that you can easily switch the browser that you're testing against. And you'll want to run tests against all browsers each night. But this will be a pain if you have to do this every time you build locally, so you'll want an option in your build to run the full suite of browser tests on the continuous integration server only at night.

That's quite a list. Let's get started.

5.4.3 Adding integration tests to sbt

sbt has a built-in configuration for integration tests. To use it, you add the integration test settings to your top-level build, changing the `PreownedKittenProject` method:

```
def PreownedKittenProject(name: String): Project = (
  Project(name, file(name))
    .settings( Defaults.itSettings : _*)
    .settings(
```

❶ Adds integration test settings

```
    libraryDependencies += "org.specs2" %% "specs2" % "1.14" % "test",
    javacOptions in Compile ++= Seq("-target", "1.6", "-source", "1.6"),
    resolvers ++= Seq(
      "Typesafe Repository" at "http://repo.typesafe.com/typesafe/releases/",
      "teamon.eu Repo" at "http://repo.teamon.eu/"
    )
  )
  .configs(IntegrationTest)                              ❷ Adds integration
)                                                          test configuration
```

This adds the predefined integration test configuration ❷ to your project. From now on, you can use the name it to refer to this configuration; for instance, when you want to add a dependency to your build. ❶ adds the compilation, testing, and packaging tasks, as well as the settings that apply to these tasks, to the IntegrationTest configuration. You can also use this in your build.sbt file.

By default, this configuration uses the directory src/it, so it will look for Scala sources in src/it/scala, and resources in src/it/resources. It compiles classes to target/it-classes.

Now you can add the relevant dependencies to your build[3] in build.sbt:

```
libraryDependencies += "org.scalatest" %% "scalatest" % "2.0" % "it"
libraryDependencies += "org.seleniumhq.selenium" % "selenium-java" % "2.31.0"
    % "it"
```

Note that you're using the it configuration here, not test. If you wanted to use Scala-Test for both the test and it configurations, you could say

```
libraryDependencies += "org.scalatest" %% "scalatest" % "2.0" % "it,test"
```

Next add your tests into src/it/scala/SeleniumSpec.scala:

```
class SeleniumSpec extends FlatSpec with ShouldMatchers with BeforeAndAfter
    with BeforeAndAfterAll with HtmlUnit {
  val homePage: String = "http://localhost:9000"

  "Home page" should "redirect to kitten list" in {
    go to "http://localhost:9000"
    currentUrl should startWith ("http://localhost:9000/kittens")
  }

  it should "show three dropdown lists of attributes in sorted order" in {
    def select(name: String) = findAll(xpath("//select[@name='" + name + "']/
      option")).
map { _.text }.toList
    def assertListCompleteAndIsSorted(list: Seq[String]) = {
      list.size should be(20)
      list.sorted should be(list)
    }

    go to homePage + "/kittens"
```

---

[3] Be careful about using the correct version of Selenium for your browser. You may need to change the Selenium dependency version here.

```
        assertListCompleteAndIsSorted(select("select1"))
        assertListCompleteAndIsSorted(select("select2"))
        assertListCompleteAndIsSorted(select("select3"))
    }
}
```

Now you can run it. As I said before, you need to tell Selenium where to find the web driver for Chrome, which you do with a `System` property. Currently this is stored in src/it/resources and is part of your source tree. In build.sbt, you add a `-D` for chromedriver:

```
javaOptions in IntegrationTest += "-Dwebdriver.chrome.driver=" +
(baseDirectory.value / "src/it/resources/chromedriver.exe").getAbsolutePath
```

Of course, this works only on Windows systems. To enable people who work with Linux-based systems, including Mac OS, to run your tests as well, you can add a method that uses a Java system property to detect if you're running Windows and run the correct server accordingly:

```
def chromeDriver = if (System.getProperty("os.name").startsWith("Windows"))
"chromedriver.exe" else "chromedriver"

javaOptions in IntegrationTest += "-Dwebdriver.chrome.driver="
+ (baseDirectory.value / "src/it/resources" / chromeDriver).getAbsolutePath
```

Those running on other systems will have to find their own versions of the chromedriver and modify their builds accordingly.[4] Note that you're using `baseDirectory` similarly to how you used `target` before. You'll also need to ensure that Chrome is installed on your local machine.

You can now run the tests. For the integration test configuration, the `test` and `testOnly` tasks are available but have to be prefixed by `it`:

```
> it:test
[info] SeleniumSpec:
[info] Home page
[info] - redirect to kitten list
[info] - show three dropdown lists of attributes in sorted order
[info] Passed: : Total 2, Failed 0, Errors 0, Passed 2, Skipped 0
[success] Total time: 32 s, completed 7 avr. 2013 22:23:23
```

You can also use the autorun feature of sbt as usual: `~it:test`.

As you can see, this is quite a lot of setup for the tests that you have, but if you had more tests, it would become more worth it. If you were playing along at home, you would have noticed a few things when you executed the tests.

The first, most obvious, is that the tests are quite slow to execute, at least compared to the normal unit test cycle. This becomes especially painful if you're using the add test/develop cycle that you used in the previous section.

---

[4] We've put the relevant drivers into the GitHub repository, or you can download them yourself by searching the internet for Selenium Chrome driver.

Second, you can actually interact with the browser started by the tests during the tests. You can close it. This, not surprisingly, causes the tests to fail.

Third, for the Windows users among you, when you run this on a Windows machine, you get a UAC warning from Windows every time you start the chromeserver. UAC stands for User Account Control. Basically, it's warning you that you're about to do something that requires administrator privileges. It's generally a bad idea to disable these kinds of security checks, but they do interrupt the workflow because you have to click on the warning to allow the tests to continue.

This means that these tests as they're written aren't necessarily a good fit for your interactive test/code cycle. It also slows down the development of these tests.

But there is a partial solution to these problems. As I said before, Selenium supports the Google Chrome, Mozilla Firefox, and Microsoft Internet Explorer browsers, but it also supports another "browser" called Apache HtmlUnit, which acts like a browser but isn't interactive. It does all the things that a browser does: downloads the HTML pages, downloads the JavaScript, and even executes the JavaScript, but it doesn't require any external process. It's much quicker and simpler to use, but you have the disadvantage of not testing directly through a browser, so you could develop your tests using the HtmlUnit interface and run the full set of tests in your build during the night using the full browser.

I find that using the HtmlUnit interface allows me to develop integration tests more quickly and easily than using the full browser tests. But for JavaScript-heavy applications, this doesn't work as well.

Finally, you need a nice HTML solution for your reports. Fortunately, ScalaTest has a very nice solution; all you need to do is add an -h option to your testOptions in build.sbt:

```
testOptions += Tests.Argument(TestFrameworks.ScalaTest, "-h",
(target.value / "html-test-report").getAbsolutePath)
```

You use the test framework delimiter to ensure that these options apply only to Scala-Test. Note that ScalaTest uses pegdown as well, so you need to add pegdown to the dependencies for the integration tests. You can do this in one of two ways. If the versions were the same, you could add the it configuration to the existing dependency that you put in for specs2:

```
libraryDependencies += "org.pegdown" % "pegdown" % "1.0.2" % "test,it"
```

But in this case you want to use a different version (1.1.0), so you can add a new line with the it configuration, and this won't cause any problems or clashes:

```
libraryDependencies += "org.pegdown" % "pegdown" % "1.1.0" % "it"
```

Now running the tests produces the HTML output for ScalaTest that looks like figure 5.6.

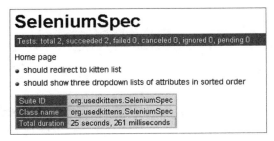

Figure 5.6 The HTML output after running your tests

5.5 Summary

In sbt, you can easily incorporate multiple styles of testing. Most Scala testing frameworks are supported natively through the sbt `test-interface`. You can also easily add options specific to one testing framework. You can add relatively complex tasks to your build fairly easily, and you can generate some nice reports on your tests for inclusion in your site.

Finally, through use of ~ you can have a better development experience because you get immediate feedback through your tests.

I think your kittens will be impressed.

But the job isn't finished yet. You still need to package the generated HTML files for inclusion, and you still need a mechanism for running your Selenium integration tests on the build server. You'll need to add some specific tasks to your build for that. We'll look at this in chapter 6.

The IO and
Process libraries

This chapter covers

- Creating sbt tasks that run external processes
- Manipulating files with sbt's IO library
- Logging information with sbt's task loggers
- Managing the task dependency graph
- Forking Java processes

So far you're up and running with sbt and you have a basic build, along with tests to make sure that your code works. But you still have a couple of issues with your build. Your integration tests aren't quite as slick as you'd like—you still need to start the preowned-kittens application manually. To be fully integrated in your build, you should start the server before running the tests and stop it afterward. You'll start other processes as well. But before that, you have the problem of packaging. Normally, when you package using sbt, it will create a jar containing just your classes. But you want to package the application into a runnable jar so that it can be deployed to another server for system testing and eventually production. For this you'll use the built-in sbt IO library. This way, you're testing what you'll eventually deploy.

In this chapter, you'll mainly work in the website/build.sbt file, unless otherwise stated.

6.1 *Packaging using processes*

In chapter 3 you saw an example of how to use the sbt Process library, the task that retrieved the Git head revision hash:

```
val gitHeadCommitSha = taskKey[String]("Determines the current git commit
  SHA")
gitHeadCommitSha := Process("git rev-parse HEAD").lines.head
```

You can see from this that it's simple to define and run a new process from sbt. Can you do your packaging in the same way? The answer is yes, but with a pretty important warning that we'll come to. To package your build into a single jar, you need to take all of the classes that you've defined, along with all of the classes in your dependencies; these you write into a single big jar, which you can deploy and run from the command line. This is one approach of many that you can take (for instance, a single jar with the dependencies listed in the MANIFEST.MF or using a plugin).

One approach to do this is to copy all of the relevant files into a directory and then create a jar with these files. The first thing you need to do is to define a target directory to copy into:

```
val dependentJarDirectory = settingKey[File]("location of the unpacked
  dependent jars")
dependentJarDirectory := target.value / "dependent-jars"
```

Here, you define a directory called dependent-jars into which you'll copy everything. Note that the directory is inside your target directory, so it will be cleaned when you do an sbt clean; this is good practice when generating files.

---

sbt cross-compiling

If you've looked into the target directory in an sbt project, you'll have noticed that the classes directory (where sbt puts your compiled classes) isn't directly underneath target, which is where it would be in a Maven build. The directory structure is target/scala-2.10/classes and target/scala-2.10/test-classes and so on. Maven would be target/classes. sbt adds the scala-2.10 so that you can easily compile against multiple Scala versions; for instance, 2.9 and 2.10. To do this, you add the following setting into your build.sbt:

```
crossScalaVersions := Seq("2.8.2", "2.9.2", "2.10.0")
```

Now if you use +package (with the + before the command), sbt will compile against every version of Scala that you've specified and you'll produce three extra jars. In your build, you're only worried about one version of Scala, 2.10, so you don't mind dependent-jars being directly underneath target. If you were cross-compiling against multiple versions, you'd need target/scala-2.10/dependent-jars. And the same would go for the results files you created in chapter 5 when you were testing.

Next you need a task to create the directory:

```
val createDependentJarDirectory =
    taskKey[File]("create the dependent-jars directory")

createDependentJarDirectory := {
 Process(s"mkdir ${dependentJarDirectory.value}") !         ⟵── **Executes the command**
 dependentJarDirectory.value
}
```

You define the process using a `Process()` method. You're using a slightly different syntax from the Git command you used previously; you add a `!` to the end of the command. This has the same effect as the lines method: it executes the command, but `!` throws the output away. But you aren't interested in it, so you don't mind.

Combining processes and output

You don't need to restrict yourself to one process per task. There are lots of ways of combining processes (too many to list here), but here are a few examples:

- `a #&& b`   Execute a. If a is successful (zero exit code), execute b and return the exit code of b. If a fails (non-zero exit code), then b is not executed and the exit code of a is returned. Possible use: if a process is running, kill it.
- `a #|| b`   Execute a. If a is successful (zero exit code), don't execute b and return the exit code of a. If a fails (non-zero exit code), then b is executed and the exit code of b is returned. Possible use: if a directory does not exist, create it.
- `a #| b`   Execute a and b, piping the output of a to the input of b. This allows you to use a command such as `grep` or to sort easily from your build.

Also, you have options for what you can do with the output; you can redirect it to a file using `#>`:

```
url("http://databinder.net/dispatch/About") #> file("About.html") !
```

This retrieves the contents of a web page and saves it to a file. Or you can use a combination of the previous commands:

```
url("http://databinder.net/dispatch/About") #> "grep JSON" #>>
        file("About_JSON") !
```

This reads a URL, runs the `grep` command on the output (which searches for any lines that contain JSON), and appends those lines to the About_JSON file.

So far, so good. Now you have to take the contents of your dependencies and copy them into this directory. But how do you know what your dependencies are? Well, you could use the setting `libraryDependencies`. This contains a list of your dependencies. But this isn't actually useful in this case—you need the physical location of the files so that you can unpack them. You'll use the runtime classpath; this contains the location of the jars that you'll use. The classpath is a sequence of either jars or directories, so you'll need to cope with both. If you have a jar, you can extract all of the files within using the `unzip` command; after all, a jar is just a zip file. If it's a directory, you need to recursively copy the directory. In the following example, you'll use the Windows `xcopy` command. If you're running on a Unix-based system, this won't work, and we'll get to a better solution later. You'll define the method:

```
def unpack(target: File, f: File) = {
  if (f.isDirectory) Process(s"xcopy /E /Y ${f.getAbsolutePath}
${target.getAbsolutePath}") !
  else Process(s"unzip -n -qq -d ${target.getAbsolutePath}
${f.getAbsolutePath}") !
}
```

Don't worry for now about all of the options to `unzip` and `xcopy`. You also need a task that calls this method:

```
val unpackJars = taskKey[Seq[_]]("unpacks a dependent jars into
  target/dependent-jars")

unpackJars := {
  Build.data((dependencyClasspath in Runtime).value).map ( f =>
  unpack(dependentJarDirectory.value, f))
}
```

When you run this, it works—maybe. If you're following along and it doesn't work for you, again, don't worry. Also, be warned that it's very slow; on my machine it takes about 90 seconds:

```
> createDependentJarDirectory                         ◁──────┐ Creates the
[success] Total time: 0 s, completed 15-May-2015 11:33:33    │ directory

> unpackJars                                          ◁─────── Unpacks the jars
[info] ... lots of output
67 File(s) copied
[success] Total time: 79 s, completed 15-May-2015 11:33:52
```

You've now copied all of the classes you need into a directory. But you'll have seen the basic flaw in what you've done, especially if you're not using Windows. This is because the previous code is specific to the machine on which you're running the build.[1] In fact, for most builds, this code would be unacceptable. Taking the example of the copy, you're using `xcopy`, which is a command available only on Windows systems. The `unzip` command may not be available, and it may not have the same behavior or command-line parameters. As you'll recall from chapter 1, avoiding this kind of operating system dependency was one of the reasons Apache Ant was created in the first place, because `make` was too operating-system specific.

---

[1] It doesn't work if you run it twice, and it's slow. But I promise we'll get to these as well.

> ### Consider alternatives to command-line processes
>
> It's important to consider the machines on which the build will be run if you're calling out to the command line to execute a process. This obviously includes the continuous integration system. For a project that's restricted to a well-defined team (a personal project that no one else will use or a company team that uses only Windows machines), then it may be acceptable to push to the command line.
>
> Also, if you're guaranteed to have access to the command-line tool in question, running this command using `Process` may be acceptable, even if the operating systems differ. For our Git example, it would be reasonable to assume that the end developer has Git installed if the project was held in a Git repository. I think it's fairly safe to assume that you'll have a JVM installed as well, though it may not be where you expect it to be. Later on you'll see the best way to use these. For a real project, you'll have to use your judgment; there are often better alternatives than pushing to the command line. But then again, you may not have an alternative. It's your call.

6.2   *Packaging using the sbt.IO library*

How do you get around this operating system problem? There are a couple of options. The first is to write your own file-manipulation methods or to use a library that's designed for file handling, such as Apache Commons IO. But in sbt, you generally don't need to do this, because sbt has a lot of built-in methods available by default in the sbt.IO package, and these are designed to be OS independent. Let's start with the createDependentJarDirectory task:

```
createDependentJarDirectory := {
  sbt.IO.createDirectory(dependentJarDirectory.value)
  dependentJarDirectory.value
}
```

This is fairly self-explanatory: it creates the directory, if it doesn't exist already. And for the more complex unpack method, you use two methods, sbt.IO.copyDirectory and sbt.IO.unzip, which do what you'd expect:

```
val excludes = List("meta-inf", "license", "play.plugins",      ⟵┐  Don't copy
➥"reference.conf")                                                 │  these files.

def unpackFilter(target: File) = new NameFilter {
 def accept(name: String) = {
   !excludes.exists(x => name.toLowerCase().startsWith(x)) &&    ⟵  Exclude files
     !file(target.getAbsolutePath + "/" + name).exists              that match
 }                                                                   excludes or
}                                                                    exist already.

def unpack(target: File, f: File, log: Logger) = {                   Unpack
 log.debug("unpacking " + f.getName)                                 using
 if (f.isDirectory) sbt.IO.copyDirectory(f, target)                  sbt.IO.
 else sbt.IO.unzip(f, target, filter = unpackFilter(target))    ⟵┘
}
```

A NameFilter is a standard Java java.io.FileFilter, so the unpackFilter filters out those files that you don't want (in this case, meta-inf and license files) and also makes sure that the first file on the classpath is prioritized. If foo/Bar.class appears twice on the classpath, then only the first will be taken. This should work over multiple runs, and it's a much better solution, because it avoids operating system–specific solutions. But it's still not optimal, as you'll see in a minute.

Finally, you need to tie this together into a single jar. Here you could reasonably use the jar command, because this is part of the Java JDK distribution, and we're sure that you will have that. But using sbt.IO is concise and does the job, so stick with that. You need a task that will create the single jar (sometimes called an uber jar):

```
val createUberJar = taskKey[File]("create jar which we will run")

createUberJar := {
  val output = target.value / "build.jar"
  create (dependentJarDirectory.value, output);
  output
}
```

Note that you're returning the file you just created. This is good practice, because you can subsequently use the value in a dependent task; you'll see more about that later. To build the jar file, you can use the sbt.IO.zip method. This requires a list of files and final name for the file (how it will appear in the zip). To retrieve the list of files (everything under dependent-jar), you can use one of the path finder methods, **. This gives you a recursive list of all of the files in a directory that match a pattern. Here's the create method that you'll use:

```
def create(dir: File, buildJar: File) = {                    ❶ Recursively gets
 val files = (dir ** "*").get.filter(d => d != dir)            all files except
 val filesWithPath = files.map(x =>                            top-level dir
➥(x, x.relativeTo(dir).get.getPath))
 sbt.IO.zip(filesWithPath, buildJar)                         ❷ Maps files to a
}                                                               new directory
```

This method requires some explanation. First, you get a list of all of the files within the dir directory ❶. The ** gives a recursive list. This is the same as the previous example using the FileFilter but much more succinctly put. Conceptually, ** is similar to Apache Ant globbing (matching files based on wildcards). You want all of the files within the dependent-jars directory, except for the top-level directory itself. files is a sequence of files: Seq[File]. But sbt.IO.zip requires a seq of pairs of File and String, Seq[(File, String)] where the String is the name within the zip; for instance, (file("/foobar/sbt-in-action-examples/target/dependent-jars/com/foo/bar/Foo.class"), "com/foo/bar/Foo.class").

For each file that's returned by the **, you need to retrieve the path name relative to the dependent-jars directory. You achieve this with the relativeTo(dir) ❷ method, which returns an Option[File]. Finally, you call the sbt.IO.zip method to create the jar, remembering that a jar file and a zip file have the same structure; it's the name that differs.

There's one final thing you have to do: add some definition files. Your application uses the Play framework, and it needs three more files:

- *play.plugins*—List of plugins that the Play framework needs
- *reference.conf*—Configuration parameters for the Play framework. Normally, these are picked up from the classpath from each individual jar dependency, but since the build is in one single jar, you have to have a single merged copy.
- *META-INF/MANIFEST.MF*—This file contains the Java main class—so `java -jar build.jar` will work.

These files were explicitly excluded from the unpack because there were multiple versions of them in the various jars. They could be automatically merged or generated as part of the build, but for now, they're contained in the directory website/src/main/uber, so you can pick them up from there.[2] You need to modify the `createUberJar` task and the create method—you add another parameter:

```
createUberJar := {
  val output = target.value / "build.jar"
  create (dependentJarDirectory.value, (baseDirectory.value / "src/main/
    uber"), output);
  output
}
def create(depDir: File, extraDir: File, buildJar: File) = {
  def files(dir: File) = {
    val fs = (dir ** "*").get.filter(d => d != dir)
    fs.map(x => (x, x.relativeTo(dir).get.getPath))
  }
  sbt.IO.zip(files(depDir) ++ files(extraDir), buildJar)
}
```

Once the task is executed, you can run the application from the command line using a simple `java` command (outside of sbt):

```
$ java -jar target/build.jar
[info] play - Application started (Prod)
[info] play - Listening for HTTP on /0:0:0:0:0:0:0:0:9000
```

6.3   *More mappings*

You can now package your application, but you have two problems: the solution you have is slow because of too much copying, and it's incorrect. The incorrectness comes from an attempt to speed up the `unpackJars` task. A class isn't copied into dependent-jars if it already exists there. If you recompile a class, it won't be updated in the uber jar because it already exists. You could update only the files that have changed, but trying to work this out is complex: the compilation will have changed files, deleted files, and created new files. The upshot is that you can't trust the contents of the dependent-jars directory, so you'll have to clean the dependent-jars directory every time you compile. So much for optimization. But there is a cleaner way. You can take the view that in your

---

[2] These are available in the GitHub repository.

build the external dependencies are relatively stable—they won't change often—so it's not really a problem if you have to do a `clean` if you update them. The solution has two parts: you use the dependent-jars directory as a cache for the files extracted from your external dependencies (and only the external dependencies), which means you only have to extract them once, and copy the compiled classes directly from the project jars each time.

First, you need a way to identify the external dependencies rather than the project jars. To do this, you can use a simple test. If the jar is below the base directory of the project, then it's not an external dependency. To test this, use the method `sbt.IO.relativize`, which returns an `Option[String]` that has `isDefined = true` if the file is below the base directory:

```
def isLocal(f: File, base: File) = sbt.IO.relativize(base, f).isDefined
```

Then, you'll need a method `unpackJarSeq`. This takes a sequence of files and unpacks the jars into the target directory. It also takes a parameter `local`; this is `true` if you want to only unpack files local to the project, and false if only external dependencies:

```
def unpackJarSeq(files: Seq[File], target: File, base: File, local:
Boolean) = {
  files.filter(f => (local == isLocal(f, base))).map(f => unpack(target,
f))
}
```

In your `unpackJars` task, you need to unpack only the jars from the external dependencies—`local = true`. You also need to specify the base directory. Note that if you use `baseDirectory.value`, this will give you the baseDirectory of the website project—you need the base directory of the entire build, so you use `(baseDirectory in ThisBuild).value`:

```
unpackJars := {
  val dir = createDependentJarDirectory.value
  val bd = (baseDirectory in ThisBuild).value
  val classpathJars = Build.data((dependencyClasspath in Runtime).value)
  unpackJarSeq(classpathJars, dir, bd, false)
}
```

Now when you run the `unpackJars` task, you should get only the contents of external dependencies in the dependent-jars directory.

Finally, you need to add this logic into your `createUberJar` task. Using the jars local to the project, you unpack them to a temporary directory and then use this directory in the create method. You can use the `sbt.IO.withTemporaryDirectory` method to create a temporary directory, which will be automatically cleaned up after use. The final task looks like this:

```
createUberJar := {
  val bd = (baseDirectory in ThisBuild).value
  val output = target.value / "build.jar"
  val classpathJars = Build.data((dependencyClasspath in Runtime).value)
  sbt.IO.withTemporaryDirectory ( td => {
```

```
      unpackJarSeq(classpathJars, td, bd, true)
      create (dependentJarDirectory.value, td, (baseDirectory.value /
      "src/main/uber"), output)
    })
    output
}
def create(depDir: File, localDir: File, extraDir: File,
      buildJar: File) = {
  def files(dir: File) = {
    val fs = (dir ** "*").get.filter(d => d != dir)
    fs.map(x => (x, x.relativeTo(dir).get.getPath))
  }
  sbt.IO.zip(files(localDir) ++ files(depDir) ++ files(extraDir),
      buildJar)
}
```

Now when you run `createUberJar`, the build will create the jar correctly, and, importantly, running `createUberJar` will be quick and relatively robust after a compile.

We hope that we've shown you how easy it is to create a build that does relatively complex things with sbt. But the solution still isn't good enough for some use cases. For this particular problem (packaging to a single jar), there exist a number of pre-packaged solutions. We'll look at these when we talk about plugins in chapter 8, "Using plugins and external libraries."

6.4   *Task dependencies*

Now, unless you like typing, you'll have noticed that this solution isn't optimal; every time you want to build the jar, you need to manually run `createDependentJar-Directory`, then `unpackJars`, and then `createUberJar`. This is also error prone because you'll likely forget to do one of the items and have to start again from the beginning. You need to chain your tasks together so that you can just call `createUber-Jar`, and it will do the rest. You'll do this using task dependencies.

How do you declare that one task depends on another? This is simple: you can define the inputs to a task by simply referencing the value inside the task. And you've already done something similar in your `createDependentJars` task: you used the value of `dependentJarDirectory`. `dependentJarDirectory` in a setting, but the same principle applies to tasks. If you want `createUberJar` to depend on `unpackJars`, you must reference the value; you don't necessarily have to use it:

This value is solely to declare a dependency on another task. The result of calling the task is ignored.

```
createUberJar := {
  val ignored = unpackJars.value          ⟵
  val bd = (baseDirectory in ThisBuild).value
  val output = target.value / "build.jar"
  val classpathJars = Build.data((dependencyClasspath in Runtime).value)
  ...
```

It's as simple as that. When the build.sbt is being compiled, sbt will read these dependencies and construct a dependency tree to determine which task can be executed when.

As we've mentioned before, sbt executes tasks in parallel if it can, so you need to think carefully about task dependencies. You have createUberJar, which depends on unpackJars. If you were naively to add createDependentJarDirectory to your dependencies for createUberJar, it's possible that you'd end up with builds sometimes failing because the directory wouldn't exist when you tried to unpack the jars into it. unpackJars should have the dependency on createDependentJars-Directory. If necessary, you can declare the dependency in both tasks; the task will be executed only once. You'll complete the dependency tree for your build later, after you've done the task for running the jar.

The other task dependency you want is that unpackJars should depend on createDependentJarDirectory, so change that task as well:

```
unpackJars := {
  val dir = createDependentJarDirectory.value
  val bd = (baseDirectory in ThisBuild).value
  val classpathJars = Build.data((dependencyClasspath in Runtime).value)
  unpackJarSeq(classpathJars, dir, bd, false)
}
```

Now when you call createUberJar, it will create the directory and unpack the jars before creating the jar. Much nicer.

6.5 Logging using the sbt logger

Sometimes it's useful to know what's going on in a task, especially if the task fails. sbt provides a standard logging framework, called Streams, to enable you to add output to trace the build. Adding this to your tasks is easy: you use streams.value.log. This is a reference to the streams task, which provides per task logging and I/O via a Streams instance. Using this has a number of advantages over a simple println.

There are various levels of logging that you can use: debug, warn, error, or info. Modify your unpackJars task and unpack method to log some output:

```
unpackJars := {
  val dir = createDependentJarDirectory.value
  val log = streams.value.log
  val bd = (baseDirectory in ThisBuild).value
  val classpathJars = Build.data((dependencyClasspath in Runtime).value)
  unpackJarSeq(classpathJars, dir, bd, false, log)
}
def unpack(target: File, f: File, log: Logger) = {
  log.debug("unpacking " + f.getName)
  if (f.isDirectory) sbt.IO.copyDirectory(f, target)
  sbt.IO.unzip(f, target, unpackFilter(target))
}
```

Note that you have to pass streams.value.log from the task to the method; you can't reference it in the unpack method.

> ## sbt and Scala macros: using the values of other tasks
>
> sbt 0.13 uses Scala macros to help reduce the amount of boilerplate that you need when referencing other tasks. Before version 0.13, you had to use a strange form that made things hard to understand. Let's compare two definitions of a task that concatenates the value of the target setting with `"out.zip"`:
>
> **0.12 (AND BEFORE)**
>
> ```
> zipPath <<= target map {
>   (t: File) => t / "out.zip"
> }
> ```
>
> **0.13**
>
> ```
> zipPath := target.value / "out.zip"
> ```
>
> As you can see, the 0.13 version is a lot simpler. To achieve this, sbt uses Scala macros. Macros allow sbt to analyze code at compile time, which means that it can convert the second form internally into the first form whenever it sees it. It does this automatically, and you don't need to worry about it, except for one thing: sbt only does this in task and setting definitions, not in methods defined in the build.sbt file. This means that if you try to use `target.value` in a method, it won't work. You can see this by defining an `appendTarget` method that uses the setting `target.value`:
>
> ```
> def appendTarget(s: String) = target.value / s
> ```
>
> sbt will output something like the following:
>
> ```
> chapter6/build.sbt:144: error: `value` can only be used within a task or
>             setting macro, such as :=, +=, ++=, Def.task, or
>             Def.setting.
> ```
>
> What consequences does this have, concretely? If you're using the value of a task or setting in a method, you have to pass it in as a parameter.

You rerun the redefined task, and nothing extra seems to happen; no extra output appears:

```
> createUberJar
[success] Total time: 11 s, completed 08-Nov-2013 23:24:53
```

Has it actually logged anything? The answer is yes. When executing a task, sbt writes log output to a file and, depending on the log level, to the screen as well. You use debug; by default this only gets written to the file. All of the output is still available. You can use the `last` command to make it appear:

```
> last
...
[debug] unpacking javax.servlet-api-3.0.1.jar
[debug] unpacking bonecp-0.7.1.RELEASE.jar
[debug] unpacking h2-1.3.168.jar
[debug] unpacking tyrex-1.0.1.jar
[debug] unpacking scalate-core_2.10-1.6.1.jar
[debug] unpacking scalate-util_2.10-1.6.1.jar
[debug] unpacking scala-compiler-2.10.0.jar
[success] Total time: 11 s, completed 23-Sep-2013 16:33:58
```

You can also specify which previous command is a parameter to `last`, such as this:

```
> last compile
```

This will give the output of the previous `compile` command.

This is particularly useful if a command fails; you can always ask for the complete output post-execution. By default, sbt displays only the warn and error levels on the console. You can change this for a particular task, configuration, or project or globally. To do this, use the `logLevel` setting:

```
set logLevel in unpackJars := Level.Debug
```

This will show all of the log messages (and a few more besides) on the console when you rerun the task. To set the global level, use (`logLevel in Global`):

```
set logLevel in Global:= Level.Warn
```

6.6 *Running your build using fork*

Now that you have a jar, you can create the task that runs the jar. When you defined the tasks that created the jar, you didn't want to use the external `unzip` command, because you were unsure that everyone who runs the build would have it. In this case, you can be absolutely certain that they'll have Java installed on their machines. You can't run sbt without it. The first and most obvious thing that you can try is to run the `java` process using the `Process` method:

```
val runUberJar = taskKey[Int]("run the uber jar")
runUberJar := {
  val uberJar = createUberJar.value
  Process("java -jar " + uberJar.getAbsolutePath) !
}
```

Note that you're ensuring that you're using the output of `createUberJar` in your task. This adds a dependency between `runUberJar` and `createUberJar`. When you run this task, it works, but it assumes that `java` is on the path of your shell (it has to be available, but there's no guarantee that it's on the path of your shell, or even that the `java` that is on your path is the same one that you're using for sbt). You should replace the `java` with the `javaHome` setting:

```
runUberJar := {
  val uberJar = createUberJar.value
  Process((javaHome.value / "bin" / "java").getAbsolutePath +
          " -jar " + uberJar.getAbsolutePath) !
}
```

This improves things but is still not perfect, because you can do better. sbt (from 0.13 onward) has a better solution; it has an API specifically for running `java`: the Fork API. This is the general style:

```
val options = ForkOptions(...)
val arguments: Seq[String] = ...
val mainClass: String = ...
val exitCode: Int = Fork.java(options, mainClass +: arguments)    ◁──┐  Runs
                                                                      the java
                                                                      process
```

In this case, it becomes a lot simpler:

```
runUberJar := {
  val uberJar = createUberJar.value
  val options = ForkOptions()
  val arguments = Seq("-jar", uberJar.getAbsolutePath)
  Fork.java(options, arguments)
}
```

This works. It runs the application:

```
> runUberJar
[info] play - Application started (Prod)
[info] play - Listening for HTTP on /0:0:0:0:0:0:0:0:9000
```

6.7   *Linking everything together: dependencies*

You now have your two tasks: the task(s) that will build the jar and the task that can execute the jar. You need to tie it all together with your integration tests. To recap, when you run the `it:test` command that you used in chapter 5, you'd like to have the server up and running, with the database prefilled with the data that you defined.

The first thing that you need to think about is dependencies. You'll see when you run `it:test` that if the sources in src/main/scala have changed, they'll automatically get recompiled, so you already have a dependency on the `compile` task in `it:test`. This is good. But by default there's no dependency between `it:test` and the `test` task. This means that when you run `it:test`, the `test` task isn't run. You need to make a decision: do you want `it:test` to depend on the outcome of `test`?

Remember that if you do add a dependency, `it:test` won't run if `test` doesn't succeed. The answer to this question isn't easy. If you have the same things tested in both sets of tests and you run them both, then you'll get double the errors. If you run `it:test` only if `test` succeeds, each build will take longer. In this case, you might take the view that the `test` task doesn't take much time, so you'll run `it:test` only if `test` has succeeded. You need to say that your `it:test` depends on `test`. But you didn't define either of these tasks; they were predefined, so you can't change them. But you can replace them. You want to replace the task with another task that does exactly the same thing but with an extra dependency. You can do this by reassigning the (`test in IntegrationTest`) to a new value that includes both (`test in Test`) and (`test in IntegrationTest`), which will be the old value of this task. Add the following to website/build.sbt:

```
(test in IntegrationTest) := {
  val x = (test in Test).value  // Here we run the tests
  (test in IntegrationTest).value
}
```

Then, when you run the `it:test` task, you'll see that your unit tests aren't executed. sbt seems to have ignored what you did! The reason is simple: when you specified (`test in Test`), you implicitly specified the website project, which doesn't contain

Replacing an already defined value

When you replace a task (or a setting) that was defined elsewhere, you need to be careful: the build definition is built up line by line into an immutable data structure, and this is then executed. It's not executed line by line. This sometimes has surprising results if you're expecting the script to be executed line by line. Let's look at an example. You define three tasks, t1, t2, and t3, which print t1, t2, and t3. t2 and t3 also depend on t1. Then, at (a) you add a line that contains a redefinition of t1. Now, what happens when you execute t2?

```
val t1 = taskKey[Unit]("t1")

val t2 = taskKey[Unit]("t2")

val t3 = taskKey[Unit]("t3")

t1 := { println("t1") }                              ◁────────   Redefines
                                                                 task tl
t2 := { val x = t1.value; println("t2") }

t1 := { println("another t1") }

t3 := { val x = t1.value; println("t3") }
```

t2 and t3 depend on t1. But which t1? When you redefine t1, the other definition gets forgotten. When you execute t2, you get the following output:

```
> t2
another t1                                      ◁─────────   Not tl!
t2
[success] Total time: 0 s, completed 15-May-2015 11:52:39
```

You might expect t2 to print t1 then t2, but in fact, the task t2 will eventually refer to the definition at (a). This can be a source of confusion. We'll speak more about this in chapter 9.

any unit tests. You need to put this task redefinition at the global level, not just in the website project. Add the following lines to the parent `build.sbt`:

```
def PreownedKittenProject(name: String): Project = (
  ...
  .configs(IntegrationTest)
  .settings(
    (test in IntegrationTest) := {
      val x = (test in Test).value
      (test in IntegrationTest).value
    }
  )
)
```

Then you can run `it:test`. You'll see that your unit tests are run before the integration tests:

```
> it:test
[info] + Logic.matchLikelihood: OK, passed 500 tests.
[info] + Logic.matchLikelihood: OK, passed 500 tests.         ◁────────   Runs unit
[info] Test run started                                                   tests
```

```
[info] Test org.preownedkittens.LogicJavaTest.testKitten started
[info] Test run finished: 0 failed, 0 ignored, 1 total, 0.006s
[info] Passed: Total 6, Failed 0, Errors 0, Passed 6
[info] SeleniumSpec:
[info] Home page
[info] - should redirect to kitten list
[info] - should show three dropdown lists of attributes in sorted order
[info] Run completed in 15 seconds, 41 milliseconds.
[info] Total number of tests run: 2
[info] Suites: completed 1, aborted 0
[info] Tests: succeeded 2, failed 0, canceled 0, ignored 0, pending 0
[info] All tests passed.
[success] Total time: 23 s, completed 17-May-2015 11:37:41
```

Runs
integration
tests

Next you need to make sure that the server is running when you run your tests. Again, you need to make a decision on dependencies. You could make your `createUberJar` depend on your unit tests, or you could make it depend on `compile`. If you depend on the unit tests, this will take longer. If you depend on `compile`, you'd actually save time because sbt would execute your unit tests at the same time that it was creating your uber jar. You could add the dependency to `runUberJar`:

```
(test in IntegrationTest) := {
  val x= (test in Test).value  // Here we run the unit tests
  val y = runUberJar.value // run in parallel with the unit tests
  (test in IntegrationTest).value
}
```

6.8   *Linking everything together: processes*

There are still two problems with this solution. First, if you run `it:test` here, sbt won't return to the command prompt. It won't even run the integration tests. Why? The following line contains the problem:

```
Fork.java(options, arguments)
```

If you look at the Scaladoc for this method, you'll see the problem:

> *Forks the configured process, waits for it to complete, and returns the exit code.*

It waits for the process to complete. You're correctly running your server, but you've told it to wait for the `java` process to exit before running your integration tests. And it won't exit. Your build grinds to a halt. The method `Fork.java.fork` is the solution to this problem. This forks a process but doesn't wait for the process to exit. The return type (`Process`) has a method `destroy()`, which allows you to kill the process. You could try that, remembering to change the type of the task:

```
val runUberJar = taskKey[Int]("run the uber jar")

runUberJar := {
    val uberJar = createUberJar.value
    val options = ForkOptions()
    val arguments = Seq("-jar", uberJar.getAbsolutePath)       Uses
    Fork.java.fork(options, arguments)              Fork.java.fork
}
```

This is the naive (wrong) implementation of (test in IntegrationTest). You run the unit tests, run the uber jar, run the integration tests, destroy the uber jar process, and return the results of the integration tests. This seems like a reasonable approach, but it won't work:

```
(test in IntegrationTest) := {
 val x = (test in Test).value              ⟵——————— Runs unit tests
 val y = runUberJar.value                  ⟵——————— Runs the jar
 val z = (test in IntegrationTest).value   ⟵——————— Runs integration tests
 y.destroy()                               ⟵——————— Shuts down the jar
 z
}
```

If you run this, your integration tests will fail:

```
> it:test
...
[info] Home page
[info] - should redirect to kitten list *** FAILED ***         Failing
[info] - should show three dropdown lists of attributes         tests
⮕in sorted order *** FAILED ***
[info] Run completed in 15 seconds, 41 milliseconds.
[info] Total number of tests run: 2
[info] Suites: completed 1, aborted 0
[info] Tests: succeeded 0, failed 2, canceled 0, ignored 0, pending 0
[info] *** 2 TESTS FAILED ***
```

Why? Well, as we've said, sbt runs its tasks in parallel by default. This means that when you declare that task A depends on tasks B and C, B and C get run in parallel. sbt is taking your definition of the (test in IntegrationTest) task and running the run-UberJar, (test in Test) and (test in IntegrationTest) in parallel. It does run uberJar, but the integration tests finish before the application is up and running, so the tests naturally fail. How do you ensure that dependent tasks are run in the correct order? Well, you'll have to wait for chapter 9 to find that out.

Fortunately for this problem, there's an easier method, because you can define Tests.Setup and Tests.Cleanup in IntegrationTest. These are testOptions that you can specify, similarly to all of the testOptions that you used in chapter 5. Tests.Setup is run before the tests, and Tests.Cleanup is run after the tests. This is a common idiom in testing: a setup method and a teardown method. First you need to define a little bit of pure Scala code, which you'll put into project/UberJar-Runner.scala:

```
import sbt._

trait UberJarRunner {                ⟵——① Defines a trait
 def start(): Unit
 def stop(): Unit
}                                              ② Stores the
                                                 process
class MyUberJarRunner(uberJar: File) extends UberJarRunner {   reference
 var p: Option[Process] = None           ⟵—┘
```

```
def start(): Unit = {
  p = Some(Fork.java.fork(ForkOptions(),
        Seq("-cp", uberJar.getAbsolutePath, "Global")))     ❸ Runs the
}                                                                uber jar
def stop(): Unit = p foreach (_.destroy())        ❹ Destroys the process
}
```

You define a reusable trait UberJarRunner ❶. You then create a class that implements this trait and in the start() method runs the uberJar to which you pass a file ❸. This contains the same code as you saw in the previous runUberJar task. It stores the process handle in a field p ❷. Finally, the stop() method calls the destroy() method on your process ❹. You can then define a task in build.sbt that creates a new instance of this class:

```
val uberJarRunner = taskKey[UberJarRunner]("run the uber jar")
uberJarRunner := new MyUberJarRunner(createUberJar.value)
```

This can then be used in the Setup/Cleanup methods, as follows:

```
testOptions in IntegrationTest += Tests.Setup { () =>
    uberJarRunner.value.start() }
testOptions in IntegrationTest += Tests.Cleanup { _ =>
    uberJarRunner.value.stop() }
```

And finally, you can define your (test in IntegrationTest) task:

```
(test in IntegrationTest) := {
  val x = (test in Test).value
  (test in IntegrationTest).value
}
```

You don't need a dependency on the createUberJar task from (test in Integration) because you've already mentioned it in (testOptions in IntegrationTest). Now Setup and Cleanup are called in the appropriate place. And your tests pass. Once again, woohoo!

```
> it:test
[info] + Logic.matchLikelihood: OK, passed 500 tests.          Runs
[info] + Logic.matchLikelihood: OK, passed 500 tests.          unit
[info] Test run started                                        tests
[info] Test org.preownedkittens.LogicJavaTest.testKitten started
[info] Test run finished: 0 failed, 0 ignored, 1 total, 0.006s
[info] Passed: Total 6, Failed 0, Errors 0, Passed 6           Starts
[info] play - database [default] connected at jdbc:h2:mem:play application
[info] play - Application started (Prod)
[info] play - Listening for HTTP on /0:0:0:0:0:0:0:0:9000      Runs
[info] SeleniumSpec:                                           integration
[info] Home page                                               tests
[info] - should redirect to kitten list
[info] - should show three dropdown lists of attributes in sorted order
[info] Run completed in 15 seconds, 41 milliseconds.
[info] Total number of tests run: 2
[info] Suites: completed 1, aborted 0
[info] Tests: succeeded 2, failed 0, canceled 0, ignored 0, pending 0
[info] All tests passed.
[success] Total time: 23 s, completed 17-May-2015 11:37:41
```

6.9 *Summary*

sbt allows you to run external processes easily, and you can combine them in a shell-like manner. But sbt also provides sbt.IO, a powerful and rich library for process and file manipulation, which allows you to do complex tasks relatively easily.

sbt runs its tasks in parallel, so you need to be careful when thinking about dependencies. It's usually a good idea to be explicit about them.

You can run Java processes using the `sbt.Fork` class; you can wait for the task to finish or not, as you wish.

You can use `Tests.Setup`/`Tests.Cleanup` to execute code before and after your tests.

Accepting user input

This chapter covers

- Interacting with the build user
- Customizing automation for development
- Autocompleting parser combinators

In the previous chapters, we focused on how to use sbt to automate the development tasks for the `preowned-kittens` project. Although this is vitally important, sometimes automation can cause friction in development. For example, if the developers create a ton of slow-running unit tests, it can hurt developer productivity. sbt counters this lost productivity through customized automation, like the `testOnly` task.

As you may recall from chapter 4, the `testOnly` task takes user input and declares a filter for which unit tests to run. sbt provides a generalized mechanism for users to customize automation via *input tasks*.

In sbt, an input task is any task that can accept additional user input before execution. This input is limited to what a user can type in the console or pass in via the command line. But the interaction between the user and the build tool can be highly customized, as you'll see in this chapter. In particular, input tasks can provide context-sensitive help via tab completion to users of the build console.

> **Greasing the developer experience**
>
> You should always balance automation with developer productivity. In sbt, the easiest things to configure are the automation tasks and settings. Input tasks require a bit more background to design and implement, but they represent the first step in bridging the productivity-to-automation gap. Although most projects may not require the creation of new input tasks, knowing how to add a few here and there can really "grease the build" for a team. The default build of sbt itself has only a 25:1 ratio of regular tasks to input tasks. But these input tasks greatly help the testing and development of projects. Just a few can go a long way.

Let's start off by examining your project and determining an ideal place to inject some input tasks to help improve productivity. The preowned-kittens web project is using a local embedded database to speed up developer testing. This database stores information about users and kittens. For version 1 of the website, you'll use a relational database and the Play framework's built-in database "evolutions." These evolutions define the schema of a database and are responsible for upgrading or downgrading the database schema as needed.

During development, the team is using an embedded database, Apache Derby, to run the application. Derby is like a full-blown relational database server, but it runs right in the same JVM as the application. Although this has simplified the time it takes a new developer to start working on the preowned-kittens project, Derby is lacking some convenience features that are usually accompanied by a full-featured RDBMS server.

In particular, you'd like a set of tools where developers can

- Look at data inside the Derby database
- Debug/test database evolution scripts

In Play, a database evolution script is a numbered SQL script file that's run at startup to ensure the database schema matches what the code expects. For example, the preowned-kittens project has a database evolution script that will ensure the KITTENS table exists and has the columns needed for the website project to run.

When developing a new database evolution script, you'd like to dump your live production database into your local Derby and try out your migration queries to ensure things come to a consistent state. You'd also like to avoid the normal "bookkeeping" of migration scripts, so that you can rerun your queries in the event of failure, and having the database in an inconsistent state is okay, because you can restore from a production drop.

As an example, let's look at the following workflow. You need to create a table in your database that tracks the temperament of the kitten using some new analytics you've added. You'd like to download the existing kitten database (or a portion of it) and load it into your local Derby database. Then, you want to test out the SQL queries needed to add a field to the database and fill that field with default values. Finally, you'd like to test your application with this new database evolution script and ensure that it works.

The development flow for the database queries is to use a local database SQL console and copy-paste out of your migration script into the database SQL console. Although this isn't terrible, you'd like to avoid the copy-paste/retry loop for fixing up queries. Also, you want to run directly against the migration files to ensure you haven't mistyped some syntax. Finally, you'd still like the ability to run queries against the database in the same place you're testing the migration script.

As a first cut at usage, you want to add the necessary tasks so that you can just type

```
> dbQuery select * from preowned_kittens;
```

and see the results. For running the migration scripts, you want to type

```
> dbEvolutionTest up 1
```

and have the `1.sql` "up" evolution script run.

Let's see if you can alter your build to help developers be more productive.

7.1   *Accepting user input with input tasks*

To run queries against the local embedded database, you'll create a simple input task. But first you need a mechanism to make queries into the database. You'll create a simple abstraction that you can reuse for all database tasks inside your build. Open the project/databasehelper.scala file and add the following API:

project/databasehelper.scala
```
import sbt.Logger
trait DatabaseHelper {
  def runQuery(sql: String, log: Logger): Unit
}
```

> ### Using build libraries
>
> In sbt, any .scala file in the project/directory can be used as a library in your build. sbt will automatically include all of its libraries and the project plugins for use when compiling library .scala files. This is an excellent way to develop more-advanced code for your build than is practical in build.sbt.
>
> As a rule of thumb, if you're doing something advanced and coding-intensive, use a .scala file. If it's configuration or build wiring, put it in the .sbt file.

Next, you'll add a quick implementation of the interface that sbt can instantiate. The details of wiring into JDBC aren't included in this book, but you can copy the implementation out of the source code examples for the book. The important piece is that you have a constructor of this interface for the Apache Derby database, which looks like the following:

project/derby.scala

```
import sbt._
import sbt.Keys._
object derby {
  def apply(cp: Classpath, db: File): DatabaseHelper =
    new DerbyDatabaseHelper(cp, db)
}
```

The `derby` object can construct a database helper given a classpath that contains the Derby JDBC driver and the location of the database. The `DerbyDatabaseHelper` class can be found in the example code for the book but is left out as an exercise for the reader to implement. We felt the details of JDBC, and in particular Apache Derby, were beyond the scope of this book. But now that you have a means of constructing the `DatabaseHelper` class, you can wire its construction into your website/dbtest.sbt:

website/dbtest.sbt

```
val dbLocation = settingKey[File]("The location of the testing database.")

dbLocation := target.value / "database"

val dbHelper = taskKey[DatabaseHelper]("A helper to access testing
    database.")

dbHelper := derby((fullClasspath in Compile).value, dbLocation.value)
```

The `dbLocation` key stores the directory where Derby will store its database files. This directory, in Derby, is effectively the entire database. You then use this location setting, along with the classpath of the project, to construct the database helper. Here you're using a feature of Scala. Any object that has an `apply` method can be used as if it were a method. In other words, `derby(...)` is the same as `derby.apply(...)`.

> ### Classpath crazy!
> The previous code to access the Derby database is pulling the database driver from the compile classpath. This means that it uses the database driver defined in your `libraryDependencies` for the project.
>
> When sbt is compiling your .sbt file, it doesn't know that you've asked for this library, which is why you can't depend on it directly. Instead, you wait for the `update` task to resolve the library and pull the jar from the the `fullClasspath` task. You must construct a classloader and dynamically access the JDBC driver from the dependencies of the project. This code is all included in the example project but omitted here for space.

Now that the database helper is available, you'll make use of it to create the `runQuery` input task. To create the input task, first you must create a key for the input task, similar to a task key. Because you don't currently plan to use the result of the query task, you'll define it to not return anything interesting (`Unit`):

```
val dbQuery = inputKey[Unit]("Runs a query against the database and prints
    the result")
```

Now that you have a key to define the input task, you need a parser for the user input. SQL queries are arbitrarily long sets of characters, so you'll define your parser to accept anything and group it all into a string:

```
val queryParser: Parser[String] = {
  import complete.DefaultParsers._
  token(any.* map (_.mkString))
}
```

For now, don't focus on the mechanism of defining parsers, because those are covered in section 7.2. The important thing to note is that a query parser parses what the user types and returns a String as the result. You can make use of this in the input task definition via the parsed method shown here:

```
dbQuery := {
  val query = queryParser.parsed
  val db = dbHelper.value
  val log = streams.value.log
  db.runQuery(query, log)
}
```

Obtains the database helper defined earlier

Parses user input using the query parser, and returns a String. The user input is implicitly passed in by sbt.

This defines the dbQuery input task as parsing input data, obtaining a handle on the database and logger, and then running the query and dumping results to the logger. Take a look at some output from using this within sbt (after reloading the new build definition):

```
> dbQuery CREATE TABLE preowned_kittens (name VARCHAR(255))
[success] Total time: 1 s, completed Jun 18, 2013 2:58:40 PM

> dbQuery INSERT INTO preowned_kittens VALUES ('Fluffy')
[success] Total time: 1 s, completed Jun 18, 2013 2:59:16 PM
> dbQuery INSERT INTO preowned_kittens VALUES ('Blaze')
[success] Total time: 1 s, completed Jun 18, 2013 2:59:22 PM
> dbQuery INSERT INTO preowned_kittens VALUES ('Muffins')
[success] Total time: 1 s, completed Jun 18, 2013 2:59:30 PM

> dbQuery select * from preowned_kittens
[info] -=== Query [ select * from preowned_kittens...] results ===-
[info]                               NAME
[info] -----------------------------------------------------------------
[info]                              Fluffy
[info]                              Blaze
[info]                             Muffins
[success] Total time: 1 s, completed Jun 18, 2013 3:00:14 PM
```

In the previous session, you used the query functionality to create a new table and insert some kittens before querying it. This code shows the kittens loaded into your production database (please, let us have more users soon). This input task gives you a rather simple way to interact with the local testing database right inside your build tool, which is what you needed to be able to check consistency of the database after running your evolution scripts.

Another nice thing about input tasks, as with regular tasks, is that sbt will automatically catch nonfatal errors and turn them into task failure rather than crashing the build. To try this out, issue an invalid query and see what happens:

```
> dbQuery CREATE TABLE owners ((
[trace] Stack trace suppressed: run last *:dbQuery for the full output.
[error] (*:dbQuery) java.sql.SQLSyntaxErrorException: Syntax error:
    Encountered "(" at line 1, column 23.
[error] Total time: 1 s, completed Jun 18, 2013 3:03:12 PM
```

Here sbt catches the error and notifies you that the task has failed. Another nicety is that the JDBC driver for the Apache Derby database issues helpful SQL syntax error messages right in the exception.

Now you have a nice interface for the user to execute queries, and most of the work is done by the Apache Derby driver. Even the error messages on SQL error messages are quite good, all with a few lines of code.

Next you'll expand your database debugging environment in the build to include loading .sql files and pushing them into the database. You'll do this with a new input task called dbRunScript, which will take in a file instead of a raw query. You'd like the file you parse to be a valid filename, so you need to define a parser for filenames first.

7.2   *Defining an interface with parsers*

Remember the parser defined in section 7.1 for reading in a SQL query? Let's look at it again:

```
val queryParser: Parser[String] = {
  import complete.DefaultParsers._
  token(any.* map (_.mkString))
}
```

Parsers are able to take an input stream and attempt to see if that string matches their expectations. If it does, the parser return a value, denoted in its type. For example, the query parser has the type Parser[String], denoting that if it successfully parses a query, it will return a String.

The sbt completion library provides a core set of parsers within the DefaultParsers object that you can use to build up more-complex parsers. The queryParser uses the any parser, which is defined to accept any one character of input and return it as a result. The type of the any parser is Parser[Char], because it just returns the value it parsed. This parser then has the * method applied to it. This method converts the underlying parser to a new parser that accepts the underlying parser zero or more times (similar to regular expression usage). The new any.* parser has type Parser[Seq [Char]], denoting that it returns a sequence of results from the underlying any parser; see figure 7.1.

The final piece of the queryParser is the map (_.mkString) method call. The map method is used to take the result of a parser, if it parsed successfully, and convert it into another return value. If the parser failed to parse the value, an error message is

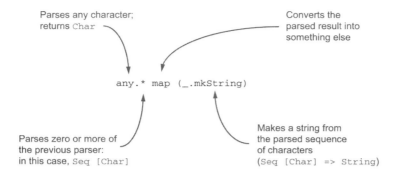

Figure 7.1   Examining a parser combinator

returned instead and the map is not run. In the `queryParser` case, the `map` method calls `mkString` on a `Seq[Char]` to convert the parsed set of characters into a unified `String` when the parser successfully parses a string.

> ## Combinators everywhere
> The notion of combinators is common throughout the Scala ecosystem and the functional programming world. Many libraries provide a set of minimal components that can be combined to produce more-complex systems, similar to GUI programming in most OO settings. Combinators happen to be a more elegant way to define custom parsers.

sbt defines a robust set of parsers and combinators for use when defining input tasks. Advanced parsers are generated by creating simple parsers and applying the combinator methods (like `map`, `*`) to these simple parsers. Table 7.1 shows a few examples.

Table 7.1   Default parsers

DefaultParser.\<name>	Meaning	Result Type
any	Parses any single character	Char
Bool	Parses a `true` or `false` string	Boolean
Digit	Any single number, 0–9	Char
IntBasic	A valid positive or negative integer, like 100 or –2345	Int
StringBasic	A string literal, like "Hello", or "F\"oo"	String
Space	A group of whitespace characters	Seq[Char]
NotSpace	A nonwhitespace character	String
ID	A valid identifier, like hi-five1	String

These parsers are all included in sbt's completion library. You can use them by importing sbt.complete.DefaultParsers._. The completion library also defines a pair of methods to make new parsers, as shown in table 7.2.

Table 7.2 Default parsers

DefaultParser.<name>	Meaning	Result Type
literal(c: Char)	Parse a particular character	Char
literal(s: String)	Parses a complete string	String

These form the core set of parsers that you can combine to create more-complex parsers. You can use these with the core set of combinators to produce more-meaningful parsers. Table 7.3 shows the commonly used combinators that sbt provides.

Table 7.3 Combinators

Method	Meaning	Parser Example	Example Input	Example Result
<parser>.*	Parses zero or more times.	any.*	H i	Seq('H', ' ', 'i')Seq()
<parser>.+	Parses once or more.	Digit.+	123	Seq('1','2','3')
repsep(<parser>, <sep>)	Parses something more than once, with a given separator.	repsep(NotSpace, ",")	Hi,You,Guys Hi	Seq("Hi", "You", "Guys") Seq("Hi")
<parser>.?	Attempts to parse something, but continues even on failure.	Digit.?	H 9	None Some('9')
<p1> | <p2>	Attempts to use parser 1, but tries parser 2 if parser 1 fails.	Digit | Char	H 9	'H' 9
<p1> ~ <p2>	Parses the first thing, and then the second, returning a tuple containing the two parsed items.	Digit ~ Char	9H	(9, "H")
<p1> ~> <p2>	Parses the first thing and then the second. Ignores the result from the first parser, and just returns the second parser.	Space ~> Char	' H'	"H"

Now you'll use these parsers to create a testing environment for Play's database evolutions.

Before we dig into how to create a debugging environment for database evolutions, let's first discuss what they are. Database evolutions are a mechanism to define a series of database DDL scripts (and queries) that are run upon startup to ensure that the database being used is in synch with the current project. Each script is given a number, which denotes the order in which they're run. These scripts can also be used to "back down" a database from a later version to an earlier version; for example, when switching from a development branch to a bug-fix branch.

Let's take a quick gander at what an evolution script for the Play web framework looks like (this example is taken from the Play documentation):

conf/evolutions/1.sql

```
# Users schema

# --- !Ups

CREATE TABLE preowned_kittens (name VARCHAR(255));

# --- !Downs

DROP TABLE preowned_kittens;
```

Each script consists of two areas, an ups and a downs. The ups area is used to define queries that run when migrating an older database to this version. The downs area is used to migrate a new database away from this version.

Although these scripts are powerful, it can be difficult to debug them via copy-paste. It would be better to be able to execute the ups and downs of a migration in a direct fashion. Ideally, right inside the sbt prompt you'd be able to write

```
sbt>  dbEvolutionScriptTest ups 1
```

and watch the evolution script run, while seeing any failures that happen. You don't want the entire evolution engine to run, just the script you're working on, for testing. This is definitely not something you want to run in your CI server, but it can dramatically help development of new evolutions. You'd also like to be able to test your downs, via a similar mechanism:

```
sbt>  dbEvolutionScriptTest downs 1
```

This is where the input tasks and parsers can help you. In the next section you'll define a new dbEvolutionScriptTest input task that will perform these queries and help you identify issues quickly.

7.3   *Defining a database evolution parser*

You need to define a parser to handle your desired syntax. First, you'll create a new library file for the build where you can write your parsers and functions in pure Scala. Create the following file:

project/databaseevolutiontesting.scala

```
import sbt._
import sbt.complete._
import DefaultParsers._
```

```
object DatabaseEvolutionTesting {
}
```

This file will be compiled by sbt and made available to definitions inside your website/ dbtest.sbt. This file imports the complete library and all of sbt's default parsers. Figure 7.2 shows a parser that can handle the syntax ups 1.

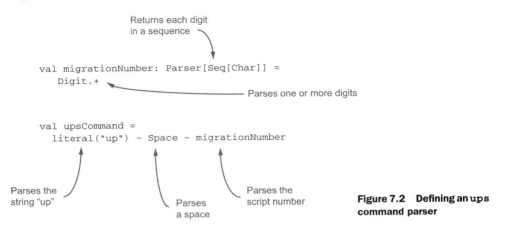

Figure 7.2   Defining an ups command parser

Here you define a parser to handle migration script numbers. Then you combine this with a literal parser to be able to parse the string "up 1". But once you parse it, you don't get back a useful result from determining that a string was "up 1". In fact, the result of the upsCommand parser currently is ((String, Seq[Char]), Seq[Char]). You'd like for the parser to return an object that helps you run the command. To do this, you need to use the map method on Parser to return a more useful value after a successful parse.

First change the migrationNumber parser to return a String instead of a Seq[Char]. The resulting parser is shown in figure 7.3.

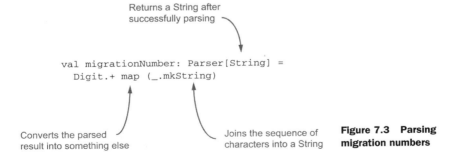

Figure 7.3   Parsing migration numbers

Next you'd like to *ignore* portions of the parser in your output. For example, you want spaces to be between the "up/down" command and the script number, but you don't need to retain knowledge of the space. The parser combinator library provides a ~>

combinator for you, which will allow you to ignore the parser on the left side of the arrow. You can use this to define a more useful upCommand parser, as shown here:

Creates a class to store what you parse

```
case class UpCommand(migrationNumber: String)
```
Parser should return the utility class

```
val upsCommand: Parser[UpCommand] = {
  val base: Parser[String] =
    literal("up") ~> Space ~> migrationNumber

  base map { num => UpCommand(num) }
}
```

Ignore the "up" and space strings; only keep the migration number.

After parsing the migration number, returns a new UpCommand instance with the migration number

This snippet shows how to parse an "up" command string and return the UpCommand class. You can define the "down" parser similarly:

```
case class DownCommand(migrationNumber: String)

val downCmd: Parser[DownCommand] =
    "down" ~> Space ~> migrationNumber map {
        num => DownCommand(num)
    }
```

Now you need to complete the parser for the evolution testing task. You'd like a parser that can detect if the user entered the up command or the down command. To do this, you can use the | combinator:

```
val evolutionTestParser: Parser[Any] =
    upCmd | downCmd
```

Now you have a fully-fledged parser that returns the command a user entered. But the type that it returns is a bit ugly (Any) because UpCommand and DownCommand don't share any similarities. You'll create a common superclass for these two to denote their relationship and improve the return value, as shown in the next listing.

Listing 7.1 Superclass

```
sealed trait EvolutionTestCommand {
   def migrationNumber: String
}

case class UpCommand(migrationNumber: String)
  extends EvolutionTestCommand

case class DownCommand(migrationNumber: String)
  extends EvolutionTestCommand

val evolutionTestParser: Parser[EvolutionTestCommand] =
    upCmd | downCmd
```

Now the evolution test parser directly returns an evolution test command. You can use this to directly define an evolution testing command. The following listing shows the definition.

Listing 7.2 The evolution test input task

```
val dbEvolutionTest = inputKey[Unit]("Tests a database evolution")


dbEvolutionTest := {
  val cmd: EvolutionTestCommand =
      DatabaseEvolutionTesting.evolutionTestParser.parsed
  val db = dbHelper.value
  val log = streams.value.log
  DatabaseEvolutionTesting.runCommand(cmd, db, log)
}
```

◁— **Runs the parser you defined on the remaining text in the sbt console**

◁— **Calls a function that can run the evolution script using the database helper**

The full solution is shown in the following listing.

Listing 7.3 Full evolution testing example

Evolution testing website/dbtest.sbt file

```
val dbEvolutionTest = inputKey[Unit]("Tests a database evolution")

DatabaseEvolutionTesting.evolutionsDirectoryDefaultSetting

dbEvolutionTest := {
  val cmd = DatabaseEvolutionTesting.parser.parsed
  val db = dbHelper.value
  val log = streams.value.log
  DatabaseEvolutionTesting.runCommand(cmd, db, log)
}
```

Evolution testing project/databasemigrationtesting.scala file

```
import sbt._
import sbt.complete._
import DefaultParsers._
import sbt.Project.Initialize
import sbt.Keys._


object DatabaseEvolutionTesting {

  sealed trait Command {
    def script: File
  }
  case class TestUp(script: File) extends Command {
    override def toString = s"UPS - ${script.getAbsolutePath}"
  }
  case class TestDown(script: File) extends Command {
    override def toString = s"DOWNS - ${script.getAbsolutePath}"
  }
  val evolutionsDirectory = settingKey[File]("location of evolutions
    scripts.")
  val evolutionsDirectoryDefaultSetting: Setting[_] =
    evolutionsDirectory := {
      (resourceDirectory in Compile).value / "evolutions/default"
    }
  val parser: Initialize[Parser[Command]] =
```

```
    Def.setting {
      commandParser(baseDirectory.value / "conf/evolutions")
    }
  def availableScripts(dir: File): Set[String] = {
   val scripts = IO.listFiles(dir, "*.sql")
   val scriptNumbers =
      for {
        script <- scripts
        filename = script.getName
        if filename matches "\\d+\\.sql"
      } yield filename.dropRight(4)
    scriptNumbers.toSet
}
def scriptNameParser(baseDirectory: File): Parser[File] = {
    val samples = IO.listFiles(baseDirectory, "\\d+.sql")
    val migrations: Set[String] = samples.map(_.getName dropRight 4).toSet
    val scriptName =
      token(Digit.+ map (_.mkString), "migration
     script").examples(migrations, true)
    scriptName map { name =>
      baseDirectory / s"$name.sql"
    }
  }
  def commandParser(baseDirectory: File): Parser[Command] = {
    val scriptName: Parser[File] = scriptNameParser(baseDirectory)
    val upCmd: Parser[TestUp] =
        literal("up") ~> Space ~> scriptName map TestUp.apply
    val downCmd =
      "down" ~> Space ~> scriptName map TestDown.apply
    Space ~> (upCmd | downCmd)
  }
  def runCommand(cmd: Command, db: DatabaseHelper, log: Logger): Unit = {
    log.info(s"Testing $cmd")
    val commands = getCommands(cmd)
    for(sql <- commands) {
      log.info("Executing query = [" + sql + "]")
      db.runQuery(sql, log)
    }
  }
  // Here is the implementation of the mechanism to rip apart db-evolution
      scripts.
  // Ideally, this would just use Play's DbEvolution classes directly.
  val upsMatcher = "\\s*#[\\s]*\\-*\\s*\\!Ups.*"
  val downsMatcher = "\\s*#[\\s]*\\-*\\s*\\!Downs.*"
  def isComment(line: String): Boolean = line.trim startsWith "#"
  def getCommands(cmd: Command): Seq[String] = {
    val lines = IO.readLines(cmd.script)
    val cmdLines =
      cmd match {
        case _: TestUp => getUpLines(lines)
        case _: TestDown => getDownLines(lines)
      }
    cmdLines.map(_.trim).mkString("
     ").split(";").map(_.trim).filterNot(_.isEmpty)
  }
```

```
    def getUpLines(lines: List[String]): List[String] =
      lines dropWhile { line =>
        !(line matches upsMatcher)
      } takeWhile { line =>
        !(line matches downsMatcher)
      } filterNot isComment
    def getDownLines(lines: List[String]): List[String] =
      lines dropWhile { line =>
        !(line matches downsMatcher)
      } filterNot isComment
}
```

Here you use the `EvolutionTestCommand` to parse the correct migration file and read in individual SQL statements for the ups or downs portion of the file. Then you take each of those SQL statements and run them using the database helper you defined earlier.

Now you can try out the command inside sbt after reloading the build definition:

```
> dbEvolutionTest down 2
[error] Expected 'down'
[error] dbEvolutionTest down 2
[error]                 ^
>
```

Here you can see that you immediately receive an error: `Expected 'down'`. The carat is pointing at the space between the `dbEvolutionTest` string and the `down` word. This is because by default, sbt input tasks return the entire string after an input task name to the input task parser. For example, the following will work:

```
> dbEvolutionTestdown 2
[info] Testing DOWNS - /home/jsuereth/projects/sbt-in-action/sbt-in-action-
      examples/chapter7/conf/evolutions/2.sql
[info] Executing query = [DROP TABLE owners]
[success] Total time: 1 s, completed Jul 12, 2013 9:40:02 AM
>
```

But this doesn't quite fit the goal you had for your interface. You'll adapt the parser to require one space before parsing the command:

```
val evolutionTestParser: Parser[EvolutionTestCommand] =
  Space ~> (upCmd | downCmd)
```

Now you can reload your build and try the new parser:

```
> dbEvolutionTest up 2
[info] Testing UPS - /home/jsuereth/projects/sbt-in-action/sbt-in-action-
      examples/chapter7/conf/evolutions/2.sql
[info] Executing query = [CREATE TABLE owners (name VARCHAR(255))]
[success] Total time: 2 s, completed Jul 12, 2013 9:41:54 AM
```

This is great! Now users can directly test migration scripts against the database. But you can make things even nicer. Right now, you accept input for any number when specifying which migration to run. You could actually determine the full list of possibilities by looking in the directory and providing an autocomplete option to the user so they can both tab-complete their command and see which migration numbers are available for testing.

7.4 *Helping the user with autocomplete*

The sbt console comes with baked-in autocomplete options when typing commands. For users to see what possible things they can type, they hit Tab, and sbt will attempt to provide possible completions. sbt even comes with completions for the dbEvoution-Test input task you just defined. Figure 7.4 shows what the user now sees when pressing Tab.

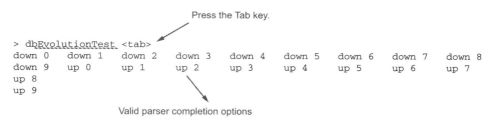

```
                                Press the Tab key.

> dbEvolutionTest <tab>
down 0    down 1    down 2    down 3    down 4    down 5    down 6    down 7    down 8
down 9    up 0      up 1      up 2      up 3      up 4      up 5      up 6      up 7
up  8
up  9
                    Valid parser completion options
```

Figure 7.4   Tab autocompletion

There are two issues with this autocompletion. First, you aren't sure what the numbers mean, and second, it's listing every possible number you could type, rather than the numbers that have associated migration scripts. You'll take care of the first issue. Go back to project/DatabaseEvolutionTesting.scala and adapt the migrationNumber parser so it knows what it's meant to parse. The result is as follows:

```
val migrationNumber: Parser[String] =
    token(Digit.+ map (_.mkString), "<Migration Script Number>")
```

Token takes a parser and attached meaning/completion options.   **This is the "meaning" you attach to this particular parser.**

Here you use sbt's token method to take an existing parser and give it a label for the user. Here's what happens to autocompletion when using tokens:

```
> dbEvolutionTest <tab>
down    up                              ⟵———————— sbt notifies you of possible commands.

> dbEvolutionTest up <tab>
<Migration Script Number>               ⟵———————— sbt tells you to enter a script number.
```

Now you're giving slightly better feedback to the user from tab completion. sbt will inform them of the next thing they must enter. But you can improve this further by restricting input to only the migration scripts that you know are available.

To restrict what migration scripts the user can enter, you use the examples method defined on token. This method takes a set of possible values and a flag telling the parser whether or not this is the complete set of allowed values. The next snippet modifies the migrationNumber parser to use the examples method:

```
val migrationNumber: Parser[String] =  {
  val base =
      token(Digit.+ map (_.mkString),
            "<Migration Script Number>")
 base.examples(Set("1", "2"), true)
}
```

The set of options shown in autocomplete

Only allows the user to enter one of the example values

With this change, you restrict the migrationNumber to be either 1 or 2. You can see this in action in the sbt console:

```
> dbEvolutionTest up <tab>
1    2
```

This is a bit nicer, but the list of available scripts is hardcoded. You'd like to dynamically generate the list of available scripts by reading the filesystem. Following is a method that will look inside a directory for <number>.sql files and return all the available script numbers:

```
def availableScripts(dir: File): Set[String] = {
 val scripts = IO.listFiles(dir, "*.sql")
 val scriptNumbers =
    for {
       script <- scripts
       filename = script.getName
       if filename matches \\d+\\.sql
    } yield filename.dropRight(4)
  scriptNumbers.toSet
}
```

Filters all files that match the glob expression

Further filters files so they are numerically named

Removes ".sql" from the filename

Next you need to have access to the build settings so that you can figure out where the evolution scripts are. Then you can use the availableScripts function to generate your list of script numbers for the parser. Here's how to use a bit of advanced sbt and rewrite your parsers for this one definition:

```
val evolutionTestParser: Initialize[Parser[Command]] =
 Def.setting {

 val evolutionsDirectory: File =
   baseDirectory.value / "conf/evolutions"

 val numbers: Set[String] =
   availableScripts(evolutionsDirectory)
```

Defines an initializer of a parser—the same kind of initializer stored in setttings

This method allows you to define an initializer that uses settings.

Here you can access the setting for the base directory.

```
val migrationNumber: Parser[String] =
  token( Digit.+ map (_.mkString),
         "<Migration Script Number>"
       ).examples(numbers, true)
...
}
```

| Passes the actual script
names to migrationNumber

The rest of the parser
setup is unchanged.

This is directly using sbt's initializer. As we stated in chapter 3, all settings in sbt are key-initializer pairs. When directly assigning an initializer to a setting, you can write

```
<key> := <initializer>.
```

But if you'd like to directly write an initializer, you'd write

```
val <name>: Initialize[<Some Type>] = Def.setting { <initializer> }
```

This allows you to construct reusable portions of initialization for use in later build definitions. Or for input tasks, it allows you to define parsers using build settings. Initialize and the core APIs of sbt are discussed in more detail in chapter 10, "Getting dirty with your build."

For input tasks, Initialize[Parser[_]] is usable in the same fashion as a regular Parser[_], so your input task definition is unchanged:

```
dbEvolutionTest := {
  val cmd: EvolutionTestCommand =
      DatabaseEvolutionTesting.evolutionTestParser.parsed

  val db = dbHelper.value
  val log = streams.value.log
  DatabaseEvolutionTesting.runCommand(cmd, db, log)
}
```

Let's take a look at the resulting tab completion:

```
> dbEvolutionTest up <tab>
1   2   3
```

Now only the three scripts that exist show up in autocompletion! You now have an interactive development environment for testing database evolution scripts.

7.5   *Summary*

In this chapter you learned the core concepts for developing better interactivity in your builds. You explored sbt's parser combinator library including

- How to create new parsers by combining existing parsers
- How to add names/meaning to parsers using the token method
- How to supply completion values via the examples method
- How to use settings in parsers using Initialize and Def.setting

When it comes to input tasks, the sky's the limit in terms of what you can add. As with all powerful tools, the recommendation here is to be conservative. Remember to automate your build before adding conveniences. Input tasks are great in terms of flexibility, but the automated parts of a build shouldn't require input, or they fail to be automatic. By using input tasks, you can adapt and use the automated portions of the build to add some great power and convenience for developers.

Next we'll look into how you can make use of sbt plugins to use the great automation and interaction that others have already designed for sbt.

Using plugins and
external libraries

This chapter covers

- Using plugins to check code style
- Using plugins to restart the application
- Alternatives to creating the uber jar by hand
- The build project
- Using external libraries in your build
- Adding user-level plugins
- Adding local credentials

One of the advantages of using Scala in general and sbt in particular is that you can easily reuse existing libraries from both the Scala and Java ecosystems. In this chapter we'll look at how you can reuse existing libraries from within your build code, both indirectly, using sbt plugins, and directly, using the Apache Velocity templating library.

Those who have an Apache Maven, Gradle, or Apache Ant background will be well versed in the idea of plugins (with Ant, they're called tasks). sbt plugins are similar conceptually to a Maven or Gradle plugin or a Ant task; they're code that's executed directly in your build.

For basic usage, sbt is pretty similar. We'll look at including a plugin—Scalastyle—in your build. Scalastyle checks code for style issues and certain common bugs. You'll integrate it into your build by using the existing Scalastyle sbt plugin, and then you'll generate an HTML report of the problems raised by Scalastyle from the results of the `scalastyle` task.

We'll look at different solutions to some of the packaging tasks that you created in chapter 7 when you built your jar: the `onejar` plugin and the `sbt-assembly` plugin. We'll look at the advantages and disadvantages of these plugins compared to the code you created in chapter 7.

It's good practice to sign your jars, so you'll use another plugin, the PGP plugin, to do this as well.

Finally, we'll look at other places apart from your project directories where sbt looks for plugins and settings: the user-level plugins and settings.

8.1 Using plugins to check your code

One of the focuses of your preowned-kittens website is quality, and you'd like to use a style checker as part of the development cycle. The one you'll use is called Scalastyle, a style checker for the Scala language. It reads your code and points out different errors, such as usage of tabs, too many methods in a class, and common programming errors (for example, not implementing `equals` and `hashCode` in the same class). You'll integrate this into your build using the existing Scalastyle sbt plugin.

To do this, you'll add the plugin as a dependency of the build project. You've already come across the build project in chapter 3, but it's worth a recap.

As you saw in chapter 3, an sbt project can have multiple submodules, which live in the directory underneath the project root. These submodules can have sub-submodules beneath them, and so on. But there's one special directory in an sbt build; this is the /project directory. We call this the build project because it contains definitions that apply to the build itself and not the artifact that sbt is building. When sbt is trying to construct your project definition, it reads the .sbt and .scala files files in /project, which forms the build definition for the build project itself. It then uses this to help read the .sbt files in the root directory. It compiles everything that it finds, and this gives you your build definition. sbt then runs this build and creates your artifact, your jar, or whatever.

Note that the /project directory is itself a recursive structure, so you can have sub-modules of your build project in there as well if you have a complex enough build.

One consequence of compiling your build definition is that your project build doesn't need to rely on predefined plugins. If you find a library that's useful, you can call it directly from your Build.scala in the project directory. We'll cover more about this in section 8.4. The second, more subtle implication is that the code that appears in the build.scala or project/plugins.sbt needs to be compatible with the current sbt version.

If you can include a jar as a dependency, what's the difference between this and a plugin? A plugin is a jar that contains settings or tasks. The jar contains a definition file that sbt reads to work out what settings and tasks are available. We'll cover creating a plugin in chapter 11, "Defining a plugin." By including this jar as a dependency in your project build, you're making these settings and tasks available in your build. You can include them as part of your build or run the tasks in the console.

It's possible (indeed, probable) that the plugin itself has dependencies on other jars and maybe other plugins, in which case the settings and tasks brought in by dependencies will also be available in your build.

To include a plugin in your build, you need to add the following lines to project/plugins.sbt:

```
addSbtPlugin("org.scalastyle" %% "scalastyle-sbt-plugin" % "0.5.0")

resolvers += "sonatype-releases" at "https://oss.sonatype.org/content/
    repositories/releases/"
```

The name of the file (in this case, /project/plugins.sbt) doesn't matter, as long as it's within the /project directory and the file suffix is .sbt. As you can see, this is similar to the mechanism that you used for declaring dependencies in the main build, except that you're calling this method `addSbtPlugin`, a shortcut method that simplifies the inclusion of plugins. It adds the dependency on the specified plugin (which will include the sbt version) and then tells sbt to initialize the plugin (more on this in a minute). The other line, an extra resolver, is there because this particular plugin isn't published to the standard set of repositories that sbt knows about by default. Note that any resolvers specified for the project build don't apply to the normal build. If you have a repository that contains both plugins and dependencies of your artifact, you'll need to include it in both project/plugins.sbt and build.sbt.

For the Scalastyle plugin, you also need to declare some settings in the build.sbt for it to work:

```
org.scalastyle.sbt.ScalastylePlugin.Settings
```

Then you can actually run the task:

```
$ sbt scalastyle
...
[info] Resolving org.fusesource.jansi#jansi;1.4 ...
[info] downloading http://repo1.maven.org/maven2/org/scalastyle/scalastyle-
    sbt-plugin_2.10_0.13/0.5.0/scalastyle-sbt-plugin-0.5.0.jar ...
[info]   [SUCCESSFUL ] org.scalastyle#scalastyle-sbt-plugin;0.5.0!scalastyle-
    sbt-plugin.jar (908ms)
[info] downloading http://repo1.maven.org/maven2/org/scalastyle/
    scalastyle_2.10/0.5.0/scalastyle_2.10-0.5.0.jar ...
[info]   [SUCCESSFUL ]
    org.scalastyle#scalastyle_2.10;0.5.0!scalastyle_2.10.jar (1231ms)
[info] Done updating.
[trace] Stack trace suppressed: run 'last *:scalastyle' for the full output.
[error](*:scalastyle) not exists: scalastyle-config.xml
[error] Total time: 0 s, completed 14-Jan-2014 22:33:51
```

This fails due to lack of configuration; it's looking for a file called scalastyle-config.xml, which doesn't exist (yet). We'll return to this in a minute, but there's something more subtle to look at. Even though by now you're used to the idea of dependencies in sbt, it's worth taking some time to explain what's going on here because the dependency management for the build project is slightly different from that of normal dependencies. You'll remember that you declared the following in project/plugins.sbt:

```
addSbtPlugin("org.scalastyle" %% "scalastyle-sbt-plugin" % "0.5.0")
```

sbt processes this and transforms it into the following URL:

```
http://repo1.maven.org/maven2/org/scalastyle/scalastyle-sbt-plugin_2.10_0.13/
    0.5.0/scalastyle-sbt-plugin-0.5.0.jar
```

You've encountered the %% operator before; you'll recall that it appends the Scala version onto the end of the name of the jar. For instance, in build.sbt you had

```
libraryDependencies += "org.specs2" %% "specs2" % "1.14"
```

This was resolved to (something like) this:

```
https://repo1.maven.org/maven2/org/specs2/specs2_2.10/1.14/specs2_2.10-1.14.jar
```

You can see that the URL contains both the Scala version (2.10) and the version of the library, 1.14. When the Scalastyle plugin is resolved, you have three version numbers:

```
.../org/scalastyle/scalastyle-sbt-plugin_2.10_0.13/0.4.0/scalastyle-sbt-plugin_2.10_0.13.0-0.4.0.jar
```

When sbt resolves the plugin, it appends both the Scala version and the sbt version. But the appended Scala version number is *not* the Scala version that you've declared in the build.sbt, but the version of Scala that's used by sbt.

> **For plugins, Scala version corresponds to sbt version**
>
> The Scala version used when resolving plugins for sbt (and added by default by the method `addSbtPlugin`) is the one used by sbt, not the one you've defined in build.sbt.
>
> Each version of sbt is compiled using a specific version of Scala; sbt 0.13 is compiled using Scala 2.10, 0.12 used 2.9, and so on. Each plugin needs to be compatible with these Scala versions. The Scalastyle plugin for sbt 0.12 needs to be compiled with 2.9, and the plugin for sbt 0.13 needs to be compatible with 2.10. This doesn't mean that sbt 0.13 can't compile Scala 2.9, but that the sbt plugins need to be compatible.
>
> For example, if you have the following build.sbt
>
> ```
> scalaVersion := "2.9.2"
> ```
>
> and you're running sbt version 0.13, the version appended by `addSbtPlugin` will be 2.10 and not 2.9.2 because sbt 0.13 uses version 2.10 of Scala. Similarly, if you're running sbt version 0.12 and you have `scalaVersion := "2.10"`, the version appended to the plugin will be 2.9.
>
> The following sbt versions correspond to these Scala versions:
>
> - sbt version 0.12.x uses Scala 2.9.x.
> - sbt version 0.13 uses Scala 2.10.
>
> Remember that from 2.10 onward, minor versions of Scala are binary-compatible, so any 0.13 version of sbt should work with the 2.10 version of the plugin.

To be able to run the `scalastyle` task, you need a configuration file. Fortunately, the Scalastyle plugin has a task that generates one, `scalastyleGenerateConfig`:

```
> scalastyleGenerateConfig
[success] created: C:\code\sbt\sbt-in-action-examples\chapter8\scalastyle-
    config.xml
[success] Total time: 0 s, completed 14-Jan-2014 23:07:15
```

Now you can run the `scalastyle` task:

```
> scalastyle
[info] Loading project definition from C:\code\sbt\sbt-in-action-
    examples\chapter8\project
[info] Set current project to preowned-kittens (in build file:/C:/code/sbt/
    sbt-in-action-examples/chapter8/)
warning file=C:\code\sbt\sbt-in-action-
    examples\chapter8\src\main\scala\database.scala message=Header does not
    match expected text line=1
... lots more errors
Processed 5 file(s)
Found 0 errors
Found 26 warnings
Finished in 5 ms
```

```
[success] created: C:\code\sbt\sbt-in-action-
    examples\chapter8\target\scalastyle-result.xml
[success] Total time: 1 s, completed 14-Jan-2014 23:10:36
```

You can see that with the default configuration you get 26 warnings and 0 errors. If you wished to include or exclude some rules or turn the warnings into errors, you could do this by editing the configuration file and rerunning the task.

In addition to the console output, you've created a scalastyle-result.xml file. This is an XML representation of the previous console output, suitable for processing other tools, such as Jenkins or SonarQube. You'll use this file to create your report later.

8.2   *Using the Revolver plugin to restart the application*

One way sbt helps to improve the developer experience is by helping with rapid development. Another example of this is the Revolver plugin from the Spray project. This plugin can automatically restart the application, as long as it can find a class with a main method. The command to do this is reStart. reStart first builds the application and then starts (or restarts) the application it's running. reStop stops the application if it's running. This isn't specific to the Spray project; it simply looks for a main method in your project. Try it out on your website application. First add in the top-level project project/plugins.sbt:

```
addSbtPlugin("io.spray" % "sbt-revolver" % "0.7.2")
```

Then add the settings to your website project:

```
Revolver.settings
```

There, that was simple. Now run sbt and change to the website project:

```
$ sbt
[info] Loading project definition from /home/mfarwell/code/sbt/sbt-in-action-
    examples/chapter8/project
[info] Set current project to preowned-kittens (in build file:/home/mfarwell/
    code/sbt/sbt-in-action-examples/chapter8/)
> project website
```

You can now run reStart, which will run your application, and you should get something like this:

```
> reStart
[info] Packaging /home/mfarwell/code/sbt/sbt-in-action-examples/chapter8/
    common/target/scala-2.10/common_2.10-1.0.jar ...
[info] Done packaging.
[info] Application website not yet started
[info] Starting application website in the background ...
website Starting Global.main()
[success] Total time: 1 s, completed 30-Sep-2014 15:36:54
website [info] play - database [default] connected at jdbc:h2:mem:play
website [info] play - Application started (Prod)
website [info] play - Listening for HTTP on /0:0:0:0:0:0:0:0:9000
>
```

The application has been started in the background, so you can still type commands into the sbt console. You can open your application using the browser, and you can stop the application using reStop:

```
> reStop
[info] Stopping application website (by killing the forked JVM) ...
[success] Total time: 0 s, completed 30-Sep-2014 15:38:58
website ... finished with exit code 143
```

The application is no longer running. This is already very useful. But, as you'll remember from chapter 5, you have the ~ command modifier. This runs a command every time the source tree changes. What happens if you try that?

```
> ~reStart
[info] Packaging /home/mfarwell/code/sbt/sbt-in-action-examples/chapter8/
    common/target/scala-2.10/common_2.10-1.0.jar ...
[info] Done packaging.
[info] Application website not yet started
[info] Starting application website in the background ...
website Starting Global.main()
[success] Total time: 0 s, completed 30-Sep-2014 15:41:00
1. Waiting for source changes... (press enter to interrupt)
website [info] play - database [default] connected at jdbc:h2:mem:play
website [info] play - Application started (Prod)
website [info] play - Listening for HTTP on /0:0:0:0:0:0:0:0:9000
```

Now change one of the source files, say something in common, and you'll get the following:

```
[info] Compiling 1 Scala source to /home/mfarwell/code/sbt/sbt-in-action-
    examples/chapter8/common/target/scala-2.10/classes...
[info] Packaging /home/mfarwell/code/sbt/sbt-in-action-examples/chapter8/
    common/target/scala-2.10/common_2.10-1.0.jar ...
[info] Done packaging.
[info] Compiling 1 Scala source to /home/mfarwell/code/sbt/sbt-in-action-
    examples/chapter8/analytics/target/scala-2.10/classes...
[info] Packaging /home/mfarwell/code/sbt/sbt-in-action-examples/chapter8/
    analytics/target/scala-2.10/analytics_2.10-1.0.jar ...
[info] Done packaging.
[info] Compiling 1 Scala source to /home/mfarwell/code/sbt/sbt-in-action-
    examples/chapter8/website/target/scala-2.10/classes...
[info] Packaging /home/mfarwell/code/sbt/sbt-in-action-examples/chapter8/
    website/target/scala-2.10/website_2.10-1.0.jar ...
[info] Done packaging.
[info] Stopping application website (by killing the forked JVM) ...
[info] Starting application website in the background ...
website ... finished with exit code 143
website Starting Global.main()
[success] Total time: 4 s, completed 30-Sep-2014 15:44:41
2. Waiting for source changes... (press enter to interrupt)
website [info] play - database [default] connected at jdbc:h2:mem:play
website [info] play - Application started (Prod)
website [info] play - Listening for HTTP on /0:0:0:0:0:0:0:0:9000
```

What happened? First, reStart has a dependency on the package task, so when you changed your file in common, sbt recompiled that and created that jar. This kicked off two more compilations in analytics and website because sbt knows that there are dependencies between these projects and common. Then it packaged these projects into jars. Finally, reStart stopped the currently running application and restarted it. This all happened without human intervention. If, like us, you're continuously waiting on restarts on web applications, this is great. It really speeds up development.

8.3 Creating your uber jar using the assembly plugin

Read over your compositions, and wherever you meet with a passage which you think is particularly fine, strike it out.

—Recalling "what an old tutor of a college
said to one of his pupils,"
Samuel Johnson, April 30, 1773

Now, a question: while reading chapter 6, were you thinking, "Surely someone must have created a single deployable jar before? There must be a better way." If you were thinking this, you were correct. There are indeed a number of plugins that do similar jobs. It's worth exploring this option. Indeed, normally you would have investigated this before creating all of the tasks that you did in chapter 6. We'll look at the assembly plugin. The assembly plugin creates a single uber jar, and it sounds similar to the job you did in chapter 6.

To include the assembly plugin, add the following line to project/plugins.sbt:

```
addSbtPlugin("com.eed3si9n" % "sbt-assembly" % "0.11.2")
```

Now add the following configuration to the top website/build.sbt:

```
import AssemblyKeys._

assemblySettings
```

Reload sbt, and then you can run the assembly task to create the jar:

```
> assembly
[info] Packaging /home/jsuereth/projects/sbt-in-action/chapter8/common/
    target/scala-2.10/common_2.10-1.0.jar ...
[info] Done packaging.
[info] Including from cache: website_2.10-1.0.jar
...
[info] Including from cache: javassist-3.16.1-GA.jar
[info] Checking every *.class/*.jar file's SHA-1.
[info] Merging files...
[warn] Merging 'META-INF/DEPENDENCIES' with strategy 'discard'
[warn] Merging 'META-INF/INDEX.LIST' with strategy 'discard'
[warn] Merging 'META-INF/MANIFEST.MF' with strategy 'discard'
[warn] Merging 'META-INF/services/java.sql.Driver' with strategy
    'filterDistinctLines'
[warn] Merging 'META-INF/spring.handlers' with strategy 'filterDistinctLines'
[warn] Merging 'META-INF/spring.schemas' with strategy 'filterDistinctLines'
```

```
[trace] Stack trace suppressed: run last website/*:assembly for the full
    output.
[error] (website/*:assembly) deduplicate: different file contents found in
    the following:
[error] /home/jsuereth/.ivy2/cache/org.springframework/spring-context/jars/
    spring-context-3.1.2.RELEASE.jar:META-INF/spring.tooling
[error] /home/jsuereth/.ivy2/cache/org.springframework/spring-beans/jars/
    spring-beans-3.1.2.RELEASE.jar:META-INF/spring.tooling
[error] Total time: 4 s, completed Jul 10, 2014 10:32:54 AM
```

Here you can see that the assembly plugin is complaining about duplicate files found in your jar dependencies. This is a common problem with most JVM software: jar files contain duplicate files, and merging them into a single jar requires some care in defining what to do when there are conflicts. Although the details of the Play framework and how its configuration files are used is outside the scope of the book, we outline how to fix these issues for the example project.

To fix these file conflicts, you need to add the following settings to website/build.sbt:

```
mergeStrategy in assembly <<= (mergeStrategy in assembly) { (old) =>
  {
    case "application.conf" => MergeStrategy.concat
    case "reference.conf" => MergeStrategy.concat
    case "META-INF/spring.tooling" => MergeStrategy.concat
    case "overview.html" => MergeStrategy.rename
    case x => old(x)
  }
}

excludedJars in assembly <<= (fullClasspath in assembly) map { cp =>
  cp filter { f =>
    (f.data.getName contains "commons-logging") ||
    (f.data.getName contains "sbt-link")
  }
}
```

The first setting defines how to handle duplicate files found in each of your dependencies. The important lines are defining that the typesafe config and Spring tooling config files are concatenated rather than discarded.

The second setting defines which jars should be excluded. In Java, it's common to *shade* other jars (or include their contents in your own). The sbt-link jar is also included in the play jar, and commons-logging is included in one of the SLF4J jars, so you remove both of these from the vision of the assembly plugin.

Also, to allow you to run the jar with java -jar, you need to specify the main class, Then the assembly plugin will generate the MANIFEST.MF correctly:

```
mainClass in assembly := Some("Global")
```

Now you can run the assembly tasks in the sbt console and get a new uber jar:

```
> assembly
[info] Including from cache: slf4j-api-1.6.6.jar
...
```

```
[info] Checking every *.class/*.jar file's SHA-1.
[info] Merging files...
...
[warn] Merging 'META-INF/spring.tooling' with strategy 'concat'
[warn] Merging 'play.plugins' with strategy 'concat'
[warn] Merging 'reference.conf' with strategy 'concat'
...
[info] SHA-1: d226c11d0f6499ebd63c6448e07e5940cf508265
[info] Packaging .../website/target/scala-2.10/website-assembly-1.0.jar ...
[info] Done packaging.
```

Well, it certainly seems simpler than the code you wrote previously. Now try to run the assembly jar from outside sbt:

```
$ java -jar website/target/scala-2.10/website-assembly-1.0.jar
[info] play - database [default] connected at jdbc:h2:mem:play
[info] play - Application started (Prod)
[info] play - Listening for HTTP on /0:0:0:0:0:0:0:0:9000
```

Again, you have a single jar that can run your application, but this time the assembly plugin gives you a lot of baked-in functionality, and configuring how to handle file conflicts between jars is much nicer than what you had before.

8.4   *Including a library in your plugin build*

You'll recall from chapter 1 that one of the major differences between sbt and Ant/Maven/Gradle is that sbt compiles its build files into .class files. This means that you can easily include pure Scala or Java code into the build. You've seen this a number of times in your build so far, and it means that you can use a library directly. This is great if there's no established plugin to do what you want. You've used libraries to a certain extent when you were defining tasks in your build.sbt, but you can use the full power of Scala and add pure Scala files to the /project directory.

> **When to use project/*.scala and when to use build.sbt**
>
> It is a debated point within the sbt community how much code should be in pure Scala and how much should be in the build.sbt file. This obviously depends on your project and team preferences—we can't answer this question for you. If you come from an Ant/Maven background, you'll probably be more used to a declarative approach, so you'll tend toward build.sbt. If you've been using Gradle, you'll be used to a mixed imperative/declarative approach. Some projects, such as Akka from Typesafe, take an extreme approach where the entire build is in pure Scala. But Akka is a very complex build. In general, both of the authors recommend starting off using the .sbt style files and, if necessary, using the .scala files. It's mainly a question of style. We're using the .scala file in this example to illustrate the difference, but it could just as easily be implemented in build.sbt.

Using the library dependencies defined in /project/plugins.sbt, you can import libraries into your build and then write code that exploits this library. You can then define tasks that use this code. To continue the quality theme, you'd like to include the output from Scalastyle in the build but as an HTML report. When you run the scalastyle task, you get XML output. You can transform this into HTML using a templating engine. For this example, you'll use Apache Velocity. Apache Velocity is a pure Java templating engine that can produce HTML output. You call the engine with a template HTML file and the output of scalastyle, and it will write the report.

You'll create a task called scalastyleReport. This will have a dependency on the Scalastyle plugin, which will generate the output XML. Your task will read this XML and call Apache Velocity using this as input.

To begin, create the task in build.sbt:

```
val scalastyleReport = taskKey[File]("runs Scalastyle and creates a report")

scalastyleReport := {
  // force the task dependency
  val result = org.scalastyle.sbt.PluginKeys.scalastyle.toTask("").value
  // TODO generate the report
  ??? // TODO unimplemented
}
```

At first glance, this looks strange.

First, the scalastyle task is referred to by its fully qualified name; you can find the location by looking at the documentation of the Scalastyle sbt plugin.

Second, scalastyle is not actually a taskKey; it's an inputKey. You'll remember from chapter 7 that they're slightly different. This means you can't call it directly. You have to transform it into a taskKey using the toTask method. You need to supply the parameters to the input task—the equivalent of the parameters that would be passed if you were calling this via the console. The scalastyle input task doesn't take any parameters, but if it did, you could pass them in here.

In this code, you have to make a decision about how to generate the Scalastyle output. You can either use the Scalastyle input task and then read the resulting XML, or you can call the Scalastyle core API directly, effectively duplicating what the Scalastyle sbt plugin does. Calling the task means you have to process the XML manually, but it will use the same settings that would be used if a developer ran the scalastyle task from the console, and you don't need to worry about using the correct parameters to the method. Also, Scalastyle produces XML output, which is Checkstyle compatible, so you're protecting yourself from API changes in the Scalastyle core libraries. You do still have a dependency on the API of the Scalastyle sbt plugin, but this is acceptable.

Next you need to add the dependency in Apache Velocity into your build. Remembering that it's a build project dependency, not a normal dependency, you need to add it to projects/plugins.sbt:

```
libraryDependencies ++= Seq(
  "org.apache.velocity" % "velocity" % "1.7"
)
```

This is resolved in the normal way. You can look at the dependencies for the plugin project by using the reload command and then show. The reload command changes the current project to the one specified:

```
> reload plugins
[info] Loading project definition from C:\code\sbt\sbt-in-action-
    examples\chapter8\project
> show library-dependencies
[info] List(org.scala-lang:scala-library:2.10.3:provided,
    org.scalastyle:scalastyle-sbt-plugin:0.5.0 (e:sbtVersion=0.13,
    e:scalaVersion=2.10), org.apache.velocity:velocity:1.7)
```

Finally, you create the method to generate the report, which will be pure Scala. Call the method `ScalastyleReport.report` and put it into projects/ScalastyleReport.scala:

```scala
import java.io._
import scala.xml._
import scala.collection.convert.WrapAsJava._
import org.apache.velocity.VelocityContext
import org.apache.velocity.app.Velocity

object ScalastyleReport {
  def report(outputDir: File, outputFile: String, templateFile: File,
reportXml: File): File = ??? // TODO
}
```

Note that you're passing in the output directory and file, the template file, and the XML produced by Scalastyle. Modify your task like this in build.sbt:

```scala
scalastyleReport := {
  val result = org.scalastyle.sbt.PluginKeys.scalastyle.toTask("").value
  val file = ScalastyleReport.report(target.value / "html-test-report",
                "scalastyle-report.html",
                baseDirectory.value / "project/scalastyle-report.html",
                target.value / "scalastyle-result.xml")
  println("created report " + file.getAbsolutePath)
  file
}
```

You're following the recommended style and returning the file you just created. Then you need to read the XML generated by Scalastyle:

projects/scalastylereport.scala

```scala
import scala.xml._
import scala.collection.convert.WrapAsJava._

case class ScalastyleError(name: String, line: String, level: String,
  message: String)

def report(outputDir: File, outputFile: String, templateFile: File,
reportXml: File): File = {
        // get text contents of an attribute
  def attr(node: Node, name: String) = (node \\ ("@" + name)).text

  val xml = XML.loadFile(reportXml)

  // get scalastyle errors from XML using the Scala built-in XML processing
  val errors = asJavaCollection((xml \\ "checkstyle" \\ "file").map(f => {
    val name = attr(f, "name")
    (f \\ "error").map { e =>
      val line = attr(e, "line")
      val severity = attr(e, "severity")
```

```
        val message = attr(e, "message")
        ScalastyleError(name, line, severity, message)
      }
    }).flatten)
```

You define a class `ScalastyleError` and then load it with text from the attributes of the XML. Note that you're forcing errors to be a Java collection with the `asJava-Collection` method, because Apache Velocity is a pure Java library and doesn't understand Scala collections. Now that you've read the XML, you need to call Velocity, first ensuring that the target directory exists:

```
    sbt.IO.createDirectory(outputDir)

    val context = new HashMap[String, Any]()
    context.put("results", errors)

    val sw = new StringWriter()
    val template = sbt.IO.read(templateFile)
    Velocity.evaluate(new VelocityContext(context), sw, "velocity", template)

    val reportFile = new File(outputDir, outputFile)
    sbt.IO.write(file, sw.toString())
    reportFile
  }
}
```

Note that you're reading the template file directly using `sbt.IO.read`. You then pass the collection of `ScalastyleError` to the Velocity template engine and write the resulting string to the output file using `sbt.IO.write`. We won't cover all of the capabilities of Velocity here; the template file is quite simple. It loops through the results using the `#foreach` construct and prints the filename, message level (warning, error, and so on), the message (what the problem is), and the line number of the problem:

```
<html>
<body>
 <h2>Scalastyle Results</h2>
  <table>
  <tr>
   <th>Name</th>
   <th>Level</th>
   <th>Message</th>
   <th>Line</th>
  </tr>
  #foreach( ${error} in ${results} )
  <tr>
   <td>${error.name()}</td>
   <td>${error.level()}</td>
   <td>${error.message()}</td>
   <td>${error.line()}</td>
  </tr>
  #end
 </table>
</body>
</html>
```

And after adding a bit of CSS,[1] you can run the scalastyleReport task:

```
> scalastyleReport
warning file=C:\code\sbt\sbt-in-action-
      examples\chapter8\src\main\scala\Global.scala message=Magic Number
      line=67 column=73
...
Processed 5 file(s)
Found 0 errors
Found 11 warnings
Found 0 infos
Finished in 21 ms
[success] created: sbt.SettingKey$$anon$4@10e728dd
created report C:\code\sbt\sbt-in-action-examples\chapter8\target\html-test-
      report\scalastyle-report.html
[success] Total time: 1 s, completed 03-Mar-2014 13:30:12
```

The task generates the HTML shown in figure 8.1.

Scalastyle Results

Name	Level	Message	Line
C:\code\sbt\sbt-in-action-examples\chapter8\src\main\scala\Global.scala	warning	Magic Number	67
C:\code\sbt\sbt-in-action-examples\chapter8\src\main\scala\Global.scala	warning	Public method must have explicit type	36
C:\code\sbt\sbt-in-action-examples\chapter8\src\main\scala\Global.scala	warning	Public method must have explicit type	41
C:\code\sbt\sbt-in-action-examples\chapter8\src\main\scala\Global.scala	warning	Public method must have explicit type	43
C:\code\sbt\sbt-in-action-examples\chapter8\src\main\scala\Global.scala	warning	Public method must have explicit type	53
C:\code\sbt\sbt-in-action-examples\chapter8\src\main\scala\Global.scala	warning	Public method must have explicit type	68
C:\code\sbt\sbt-in-action-examples\chapter8\src\main\scala\Global.scala	warning	Public method must have explicit type	69
C:\code\sbt\sbt-in-action-examples\chapter8\src\main\scala\ScalateIntegration.scala	warning	Method name does not match the regular expression '^[a-z][A-Za-z0-9]*$'	48
C:\code\sbt\sbt-in-action-examples\chapter8\src\main\scala\ScalateIntegration.scala	warning	Method name does not match the regular expression '^[a-z][A-Za-z0-9]*$'	52
C:\code\sbt\sbt-in-action-examples\chapter8\src\main\scala\ScalateIntegration.scala	warning	Public method must have explicit type	30
C:\code\sbt\sbt-in-action-examples\chapter8\src\main\scala\ScalateIntegration.scala	warning	Public method must have explicit type	34

Figure 8.1   Example Scalastyle-generated HTML

Using just a few lines of Scala, you've added a report based on one of your tasks using an external library, Apache Velocity.

8.5 Adding a plugin for use in all of your projects— signing your projects

Sometimes you need to add a plugin for settings that are applied globally to all of your projects. In this case you can add a plugin per user. One of the classic use cases for adding a plugin at the user level is signing artifacts. When you upload a jar or a war (an artifact) to a central repository, in general it's a good idea to sign it. When you sign it, you create a signature of the jar, which does two things: it verifies that the jar is as it was created and that the jar was created by those who are authorized to create it. When you download an artifact from the internet, you should check that the signature corresponds to the expected one. Some repositories such as Sonatype or Maven Central require that you sign artifacts to be able to upload to the site, at least for release versions of your artifacts.

---

[1] See the source code for this.

sbt looks for plugins and configuration in a number of places. For the majority of the time, you'll want all declarations of plugins and settings to be in directories and checked into your source control system. But there are times when this isn't appropriate. When you're publishing artifacts (jars or wars) to an Ivy or Maven repository, you clearly don't want the username and password of that repository in your build.sbt. Similarly, if you're signing your artifacts, you don't want private key information in your build files.

Declaring a user-level plugin is similar to declaring a plugin in your build. You add the required lines to an sbt file in $HOME/.sbt/0.13/; for instance, $HOME/.sbt/0.13/plugins/signing.sbt. This can contain exactly the same things as the files project/*.sbt. It must also follow the same rules as for normal .sbt files; for 0.13 it must be Scala 2.10, and so on. You aren't restricted to .sbt files; .scala files are equally valid. For instance, you can add the following to $HOME/.sbt/0.13/plugins/signing.sbt:

```
addSbtPlugin("com.typesafe.sbt" % "sbt-pgp" % "0.8.2")
```

This will add the PGP plugin to all that user's projects.

When user-level files conflict with project files

The rules that define how sbt resolves conflicts between user-level files and project files are complex. sbt will usually resolve to the latest version of the library in question. If there's a conflict, sbt should warn you, at least with version 0.13.7 or later. If there's a conflict you can't resolve, you can always remove the offending plugin from the user-level files.

After adding the plugin to the user-level files, you can publish a signed artifact using the `publish-local-signed` or `publish-signed` command:

```
> publish-local-signed
[info] Wrote C:\code\sbt\sbt-in-action-examples\chapter8\target\scala-
    2.10\preowned-kittens_2.10-1.0.pom
[info] :: delivering :: preowned-kittens#preowned-kittens_2.10;1.0 :: 1.0 ::
    release :: Mon Mar 03 15:27:42 CET 2014
[info]   delivering ivy file to C:\code\sbt\sbt-in-action-
    examples\chapter8\target\scala-2.10\ivy-1.0.xml
Please enter PGP passphrase (or ENTER to abort):
    *******************************
[info]   published preowned-kittens_2.10 to ...preowned-kittens_2.10-
    javadoc.jar
[info]   published preowned-kittens_2.10 to ...preowned-kittens_2.10-
    javadoc.jar.asc
[info]   published preowned-kittens_2.10 to ...preowned-kittens_2.10.jar.asc
[info]   published preowned-kittens_2.10 to ...preowned-kittens_2.10.pom.asc
[info]   published preowned-kittens_2.10 to ...preowned-kittens_2.10-
    sources.jar
[info]   published preowned-kittens_2.10 to ...preowned-kittens_2.10-
    sources.jar.asc
[info]   published preowned-kittens_2.10 to ...preowned-kittens_2.10.jar
```

```
[info]   published preowned-kittens_2.10 to ...preowned-kittens_2.10.pom
[info]   published ivy to C:\Users\mfarwell.NEXTHINK\.ivy2\local\preowned-
        kittens\preowned-kittens_2.10\1.0\ivys\ivy.xml
[success] Total time: 9 s, completed 03-Mar-2014 15:27:51
```

You will be prompted for your PGP passphrase[2] and then the jars will be created with corresponding .asc files, which contain the signatures of the jars.

8.6   *Adding local credentials for deployment*

The other thing that's usually stored at the user level is credentials, used when the artifacts are deployed to a remote repository. Normally, you add a `Credentials` object to the list in $HOME/.sbt/0.13/credentials.sbt:

```
credentials += Credentials("Sonatype Nexus Repository Manager",
                           "oss.sonatype.org",
                           "myusername",
                           "mypassword")
```

8.7   *Summary*

In this chapter, you learned how to incorporate sbt plugins and external libraries easily and quickly into your builds. You learned the core concepts of plugins including the following:

- sbt plugins use the Scala version corresponding to the version of sbt.
- You saw where the user can declare sbt plugins—per build or per user.
- You learned how to incorporate an external library in sbt.
- You learned how to define user-level settings.

Plugins are a great boon to a build; they use similar work done by others. There are hundreds to choose from. sbt makes it easy to use an existing plugin or library. When writing a build, you should default to using an existing plugin if one exists. But if it doesn't exist or it doesn't do quite what you want it to, you can create your own task.

Next we'll look at some of the tools available to help debug your build.

---

[2] We won't go into all of the details on how to create the keys that enable you to sign artifacts. You can follow the instructions in the sbt-pgp plugin at www.scala-sbt.org/sbt-pgp.

Debugging your build

This chapter covers

- Figuring out why your build won't compile
- Ensuring tasks will run when desired
- Correctly resolving dependencies

In this chapter we're going to look at a set of common failures in sbt and how to debug the underlying causes. The goal of this chapter is to learn how to debug sbt by understanding the initialization, loading, and execution of your build. Throughout the chapter, we'll dive a bit deeper into the core aspects of sbt, and you'll see the same concepts from chapter 3 in a new light.

Debugging in sbt takes on different aspects, depending on where in the lifecycle the failure is occurring, which correlates to the lifecycle of an sbt build. Let's take a look at a loose sketch of what sbt does when it loads your build file:

- Resolve sbt and any required plugins.
- Compile your build definition.
- Execute any requested tasks or commands.

Each of these phases pushes out different error messages. Because sbt uses a statically typed build definition language, you can catch a lot of errors in stages 1 and 2.

But some errors still happen when attempting to run tasks. Let's split these into three classes of errors:

- An error in the task definition
- Dependency resolution issues
- Task wiring issues

For now, you're going to ignore errors related to the task itself. Because sbt uses Scala code to define tasks, once you've ensured that all dependencies are resolved and the data is wired into the task at the right time, the rest is general program debugging for solving issues. Let's instead look at the other class of errors, which aren't seen as often in regular programming.

Dependency resolution issues show up as failures in the update task, general compilation failures due to the nonexistence of methods, or other library version incompatibilities. These can be hard to diagnose and fix because these are errors in the code defining the build, not in the source code of the project.

Somewhat related, task wiring issues usually show up in builds when trying to wire new functionality into existing tasks. For example, after wiring a task to automatically create source code from a Google protocol buffer message definition, you'll find that the code isn't getting compiled by the compile task.

All of these errors can be initially frustrating to investigate if you're not sure where to start looking. Let's start by looking at a few concrete examples of issues in build files and how to detect and fix the underlying cause. We'll do so by walking through the build lifecycle, starting with the bootup of sbt itself.

9.1 Running sbt

Although sbt is generally able to launch itself and begin running, there are a few moderately common errors/issues that can be solved before sbt even has a chance to look at your code; specifically, the following:

- Your computer needs to use an HTTP proxy to access the internet.
- Your build requires larger memory settings.

The easiest way to tell if you're having proxy issues is if you see a bunch of errors that look like this:

```
Getting org.scala-sbt sbt 0.13.0 ...

:: problems summary ::
:::: WARNINGS
        module not found: org.scala-sbt#sbt;0.13.0
```

If you see this type of issue, it means that the sbt launcher is unable to find sbt itself.

Either your computer has no internet connection or the launcher is unable to use it. If you're behind a proxy, you can fix this by setting the standard Java options on the command line:

```
sbt -Dhttp.proxyHost=192.168.2.131 -Dhttp.proxyPort=8080
```

The sbt launcher

When you install sbt, you're actually installing not the build tool itself but a utility that can find and execute other programs. This utility is called the sbt launcher. The sbt launcher will look at the current directory's project/build.properties file to determine which version of sbt it needs to download and use for a given build.

This means that as a user, you can always install the latest sbt but will still be able to build projects using an older version of sbt.

These settings are standard JVM settings, outlined in table 9.1.

Table 9.1   Standard JVM settings

Property	Value
http.proxyHost	Hostname or IP address of the proxy server
http.proxyPort	Port to use when connecting to the proxy server
http.proxyUser	User to use when connecting to the proxy
http.proxyPassword	The password to use to connect
http.nonProxyHosts	Hosts that you can access without proxy (usually your local artifact repository cache, like Nexus or Artifactory)

The other common startup issue is not having enough memory. Because sbt tries to load and keep as much information as possible in memory, it can use a lot, depending on the size of your projects. For small projects, memory usually isn't a concern. But for large multimodule projects, you may need to increase the amount of memory available for sbt so that your build can run efficiently and the important state remains active in cache.

Because sbt makes use of the JVM, you can use the standard Java memory options to configure sbt. Each sbt script honors a JAVA_OPTS environment variable you can specify with the options shown in table 9.2.

Table 9.2   Java memory options

Argument	Description
-Xmx<mem>	The maximum amount of memory to reserve for the JVM's heap
-Xms<mem>	The minimum amount of memory to reserve for the JVM's heap
-XX:MaxPermSize=<mem>	The amount of memory to reserve for the JVM to load in class files (your compiled code)
-XX:ReservedCodeCacheSize=<mem>	The amount of memory to reserve for the JVM optimizer to generate optimized native code

The default values for most sbt scripts are as follows:

```
-Xms1536m
-Xmx1536m
-XX:MaxPermSize=384m
-XX:ReservedCodeCacheSize=192m
```

Now that you've figured out how to ensure sbt starts up and runs smoothly, let's look into why your build may not be compiling.

9.2 *Making your build compile*

There are many reasons for your build not to compile, but there are a few that are more common, which we'll examine. These are

- Invalid blank line usage
- Attempting to use a task in a setting

The most common error when starting with build.sbt files is forgetting the golden rules of syntax in sbt:

- Any configuration setting/definition (values or methods) must be declared without any blank lines.
- There must be at least one blank line between each configuration setting/definition.

This shows up especially when using multiple projects with project-specific settings; for example:

```
val core = project.settings(  // The blank line is bad

  libraryDependencies += "org.scalacheck" %% "scalacheck" % "1.10"
)
```

Although this would be valid Scala code, due to the nature of how .sbt files are parsed, this was invalid sbt (prior to sbt 0.13.7). When you attempt to use this code in a build.sbt, sbt shows the following error:

```
$ sbt
[info] Loading global plugins from /home/jsuereth/.sbt/0.13/plugins
[info] Loading project definition from /home/jsuereth/projects/sbt-in-action/
    chapter9/bad-spaces/project
/home/jsuereth/projects/sbt-in-action/chapter9/bad-spaces/build.sbt:1: error:
    illegal start of simple expression
val core = project.settings(
    ^
[error] sbt.compiler.EvalException: Error parsing definition. Ensure that
    there are no blank lines within a definition.
[error] Use 'last' for the full log.
Project loading failed: (r)etry, (q)uit, (l)ast, or (i)gnore?
```

Here sbt is displaying the Scala compiler warning, as well as a suggestion that this issue may be due to an invalid blank line in the file. The blank line between the settings method call and the actual settings for the core project needs to be removed:

```
val core = project.settings(
    libraryDependencies += "org.scalacheck" %% "scalacheck" % "1.10"
)
```

Because of this restriction, and by design, any nontrivial code in your build should be placed into a .scala file in the project/ directory. In other words, once you start having complicated logic for your tasks or definitions, you should put that code into a .scala file and treat it as a library for your build. This allows you to take full advantage of the Scala language, as well as run unit tests against the code if so desired.

The next common error in sbt files is attempting to use tasks in setting definitions. A good example of this issue is, for example, if you wanted to include the Git head commit SHA in your version number. Pull the task to grab the current Git head commit from chapter 3:

```
val gitHeadCommitSha = taskKey[String]("Determines the current git commit
    SHA")

gitHeadCommitSha := Process("git rev-parse HEAD").lines.head
```

Now if you wanted to include this in the version of your artifacts, you might try to do the following:

```
version := "1.0-" + gitHeadCommitSha.value
```

But that would result in the following exception:

```
/home/jsuereth/projects/sbt-in-action/chapter9/build.sbt:23: error: A setting
    cannot depend on a task
version := "1.0" + gitHeadCommitSha.value
                 ^
[error] Type error in expression
```

This is because settings need to be fully initialized when sbt starts, whereas tasks are rerun every time you request them. This difference may not be apparent if you're always launching sbt from the shell (like sbt compile), but it starts to make a difference when using the sbt shell.

When sbt starts up, after loading and compiling all the build definition files it finds, it first tries to initialize all settings and reduce all tasks into sbt.Task[_] objects. These values are stored in a settings map that the engine will use throughout the execution. When running the sbt shell, this means that settings are not reevaluated after loading the build unless you explicitly request it via the reload command.

Basically, you have two levels of execution in sbt: settings, which are more seldom initialized, and tasks, which get rerun upon request. Settings can only be instantiated from other settings, whereas tasks can use either settings or the results of other tasks. What do you do if you want to use a task value in a setting?

There are two options here:

- Convert everything you want into tasks.
- Convert everything to use settings.

The first is relatively straightforward. Look for TaskKeys you can override instead of a setting, or adapt your setting/task design so that you're using tasks instead of settings. This works only if you're able to migrate from settings into tasks. For the Git SHA in the version number, you're unable to migrate sbt's core version setting to a task because that would require altering the core of sbt itself, something you're unable to do. Because of this, you need to read the gitHeadCommitSha upon build load. Because you'll be using a setting, you need to do all the error handling and reporting yourself to ensure a good experience.

Let's take a naive approach of converting the gitHeadCommitSha into a setting first. To do so, flip the key definition to be a settingKey and leave the rest of the code the same:

```
val gitHeadCommitSha = settingKey[String]("Determines the current git commit
    SHA")

gitHeadCommitSha := Process("git rev-parse HEAD").lines.head

version := "1.0-" + gitHeadCommitSha.value
```

This compiles and returns appropriately when the Git process returns successfully, as shown here:

```
$ sbt
[info] Loading global plugins from /home/jsuereth/.sbt/0.13/plugins
[info] Loading project definition from /home/jsuereth/projects/sbt-in-action/
    chapter9/settings-vs-tasks/project
version
[info] Set current project to settings-vs-tasks (in build file:/home/
    jsuereth/projects/sbt-in-action/chapter9/settings-vs-tasks/)
> version
[info] 1.0-2bb6d7bc051dd29a854d97c0ff120bdfae5e3375
```

But the error message upon load is much worse than normal task failure if you're not in a Git project yet:

```
$ sbt
Loading /usr/share/sbt/bin/sbt-launch-lib.bash
[info] Loading global plugins from /home/jsuereth/.sbt/0.13/plugins
[info] Loading project definition from /home/jsuereth/projects/tmp/foo/
    project
[info] Updating {file:/home/jsuereth/projects/tmp/foo/project/}foo-build...
[info] Resolving org.fusesource.jansi#jansi;1.4 ...
[info] Done updating.
fatal: Not a git repository (or any of the parent directories): .git
[error] Nonzero exit code: 128
[error] Use 'last' for the full log.
Project loading failed: (r)etry, (q)uit, (l)ast, or (i)gnore?
```

You need to harden the setting so that it doesn't crash if you can't find the current head commit. You'll modify things slightly so you can handle a case where Git isn't initialized yet:

```
val gitHeadCommitSha =                                          Setting now returns
  settingKey[Option[String]](                          ◄────┘  an optional string.
    "Determines the current git commit SHA")

gitHeadCommitSha := try {
  Some(Process("git rev-parse HEAD").lines.head)
} catch {                                                       On failure, return
  case _: Exception => None                            ◄────┘  an empty value.
}

version := "1.0-" +                                             If Git is uninitialized,
  gitHeadCommitSha.value.getOrElse("SNAPSHOT")         ◄────┘  use a default version.
```

This results in the following on startup:

```
$ sbt
Loading /usr/share/sbt/bin/sbt-launch-lib.bash
[info] Loading global plugins from /home/jsuereth/.sbt/0.13/plugins
[info] Loading project definition from /home/jsuereth/projects/tmp/foo/
      project
[info] Updating {file:/home/jsuereth/projects/tmp/foo/project/}foo-build...
[info] Resolving org.fusesource.jansi#jansi;1.4 ...
[info] Done updating.
fatal: Not a git repository (or any of the parent directories): .git
[info] Set current project to foo (in build file:/home/jsuereth/projects/tmp/
      foo/)
> version
[info] 1.0-SNAPSHOT
```

Now the build successfully starts and the backup version-naming scheme is used.

Settings are better used for configuration that's frequently accessed in a session, is relatively stable to compute, and doesn't change frequently. It's usually rare that you'll need (or want) to do something dangerous in settings, like touching the filesystem or running a process. Most of these actions are better handled in tasks, where errors are captured by sbt itself and can be handled or ignored as you require.

This brings us to the next possible issue with your build: getting tasks to run when you want them to.

9.3   *Ensuring tasks are run*

Given sbt's parallel nature, it can sometimes be hard to find the right place to put in custom functionality. The custom functionality needs to run at the right time in the build and in the correct order. Sometimes it's tricky to get both ordering and wiring correct for custom extensions. For example, let's look again at the integration testing extensions you added in chapter 6.

You wanted to ensure that you were running a live instance of the web application when running integration tests. First, you wanted to create a mechanism to start up your web application within the sbt build. Second, you wanted to add a new configuration for integrations tests where your server would start before the tests and stop after them. These integration tests use the same settings for normal unit tests, except with different source/target directories and the addition of starting/stopping the server.

When wiring new functionality into existing functionality, you need to first look at the flow of task executions throughout the build. If you want your task to run before another task, you either define that task to use yours or you add your task to a dependency of the other task.

> ### The task request
>
> So far, we've taken a naive view of sbt's task-execution system. In the sbt console, or command line, you can type in the name of a task or multiple tasks to execute. From here forward, we'll call these task requests. For a given task request, sbt will execute tasks in the task graph (via task dependencies) until it reaches the nodes that were requested. For any given request, a task is executed only once. But the task is re-executed upon any new request.
>
> This means that if you have a task that computes some object, all tasks that depend on it will share the same instance for their lifecycle. In chapter 6, you used this to share a `Service` object that could start and stop the web application by remembering the `Process` that was started.

The solution in chapter 6 was twofold:

- Create an object that will capture the state of whether or not the server is running. It also exposes a `start` method and a `stop` method.
- Hook the existing test tasks with a dependency on the controlling object. Here you can wire in the start and stop hooks.

Because for any given task request the object is created only once, any task that makes use of the `runUberJarService` gets the *same* object. This means that you can use tasks that expose services in your build, and these services can remember state for the duration of a task request. When adding in behavior, especially behavior that requires start/stop-like semantics, this is often the easiest and most efficient way to do so. Let's look at how the `runUberJarService` is used again:

```
testOptions in IntegrationTest += Tests.Setup { () =>
  uberJarRunner.value.start()
}

testOptions in IntegrationTest += Tests.Cleanup { _ =>
  uberJarRunner.value.stop()
}
```

Here the test arguments hook is used to attach the `start` and `stop` methods into the execution of the test suite. This is nice, because the test family of tasks defines these hook points for start/stop behavior. But what should you do if these hooks aren't provided?

In that case, you'll use a simple trick of the dependency system:

- Still define a task that exposes the service you need to start/stop semantics on.
- Create a new task to start the service and add this task as a dependency to one of the dependencies of the task you want to run.
- Modify the task you want to run to make sure it stops the service when it's finished.

This mechanism requires that the task you want to run has dependencies. For example, the `test` task has a `testOptions` dependency that you can hook your server startup to:

```
testOptions in IntegrationTest := {
    uberJarRunner.value.start()
    (testOptions in IntegrationTest).value
}

test in IntegrationTest <<=
  (test in IntegrationTest, uberJarRunner) apply { (testTask, runnerTask) =>
    for {
      runner <- runnerTask
      result <- testTask.andFinally(runner.stop())
    } yield result
  }
```

What these two settings are doing is ensuring the `uberJarRunner` is started in a prerequisite task to executing tests. Then you alter the `test` task itself to ensure that the server is stopped. This is a bit easier to view if you look at the dependency graph; see figure 9.1.

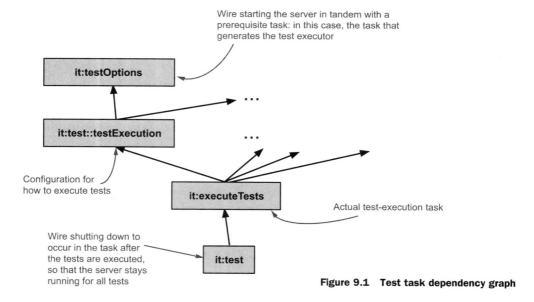

Figure 9.1   Test task dependency graph

Let's look back over the code that ensures the server is closed after the test task is completed:

```
test in IntegrationTest <<=
  (test in IntegrationTest, uberJarRunner) apply { (testTask, runnerTask) =>
    for {
      runner <- runnerTask
      result <- testTask.andFinally(runner.stop())
    } yield result
}
```

This code is a lot different from the API you've seen so far for sbt. In particular, you use the <<= method to define the key. This method allows you to work directly against the sbt.Task API rather than the higher-level asynchronous API, which is exactly what you need to control sequencing of operations. The apply method on the tuple of keys is how you can declare dependencies against existing sbt.Task[_] objects and use them to order operations. In this example, you draw the uberJarRunner out of its task and then call the andFinally method on the testTask to ensure that the runner is stopped when the testTask completes (either successfully or unsuccessfully). Finally, the whole block of code is in a for expression to ensure the resulting sbt.Task[_] that's returned will return the test results, if successful, or the error from the first failing task in the for expression.

> ### for expressions for sequential execution with tasks
> In Scala, the for expression is a simple way of encoding sequential execution of methods inside some context. For sbt, this means you can define sequential behavior inside an sbt.Task[_] object. The anatomy of a for expression is as follows:
>
> ```
> for {
>   value <- task1
>   value2 <- task2
> } yield calculateResult(value, value2)
> ```
>
> This for expression is used to construct a new Task[_] using existing tasks. Each line with <- is called an enumerator. The right side of an enumerator must be an expression that returns a task, whereas the left side is a variable name that will contain the result of that task. The for expression will execute each enumerator in the sequence defined. Finally, the expression after the yield is executed to return a result of the new task.

Although the mechanism of wiring into prerequisite and final tasks can work, it has a few drawbacks, in particular these:

- If someone tries to run the it:testOption task directly (rather than it:test), then the server will not be stopped.
- If there's an error in the it:executeTests task, the it:test task may not run, meaning that the server may not be stopped after it was started.

The better option in this instance is to directly wrap the executeTests task because it encapsulates the entire test execution in one stage. You can ensure your server is run before this stage and stopped after this stage directly. The code here is a bit simpler:

```
executeTests in IntegrationTest <<=
  (executeTests in IntegrationTest, uberJarRunner) apply {
    (testTask, runnerTask) =>
      for {
        runner <- runnerTask
        _ = runner.start()
        result <- testTask.andFinally(runner.stop())
      } yield result
  }
```

Once again, you use the <<= syntax to assign a value to the key so that you can work on the raw sbt.Task[_] level. In this case, you use the for expressions to do all the sequencing of operations on the resulting task, including starting the server, running the tests, and making sure the server is stopped regardless of whether the test task is a success or a failure.

> **More-versatile for expressions for sequential execution**
>
> In the previous for expression, you define an empty variable in the location where you want to start the runner:
>
> ```
> _ = runner.start()
> ```
>
> In normal Scala for expressions, helper variables may be declared anywhere after the first extractor. Here you're ensuring the runner is started and assigning the value to an empty variable (_). This is a mechanism of for expressions where you can chain together an action that's not an sbt.Task[_]. runner.start() is a method call with a return value. You're not pulling the return value of a task; you're assigning the return value directly.

When it comes to task sequencing, the for expression mechanism is the way to go. It's best to try to limit task sequencing (you need something to run before/after another task) to one task contained in one task key, so you can guarantee that resources are appropriately cleaned up. That is, when you need to ensure sequencing of operations, it becomes quite difficult to do so if you're using tasks defined in other key values. But in a pinch, attaching your code into task keys that happen before and after the desired task is an acceptable workaround.

Now let's move onto the next issue where a lot of debugging time is spent in sbt: dependency resolution.

9.4   *Resolving dependency conflicts*

The biggest cause of error in sbt build files usually has nothing to do with sbt itself but rather dependency management. sbt makes use of the Ivy dependency management tool. This means that failures to resolve Ivy artifacts may require you to dig into the Ivy-specific debugging information.

Resolution failures can be divided into two types of issues:

- Ivy can't find a given artifact.
- Ivy is resolving an undesired version of an artifact (or an undesired artifact).

9.4.1 Fixing resolution failures

Let's look into the issue of not being able to resolve an artifact. One thing that can surprise users is that sbt will run resolution more than once. When you download and install sbt, what you're installing is not the complete build tool but a launcher that will run sbt. This launcher is responsible for finding and downloading sbt. Therefore, the first place resolution can fail is in the launcher.

The sbt launcher is a generic application-launching program that can be used to resolve any Ivy/Maven artifact and run it. It uses its own configuration file for where to look for software. This set of repositories it looks in marks the default set of repositories that will be used in all your sbt builds. These are configured in the ${user.home}/.sbt/repositories file, if it exists, or the default sbt repositories if it does not.

Once sbt is resolved, along with all plugins, sbt will be able to boot into the sbt console. At this point, many tasks, including `compile`, `test`, and `package`, will require Ivy to resolve external dependencies declared by the project. This resolution will make use of any extra resolvers defined in your sbt build. If there is failure resolving at this point, it's from one of four things:

- The artifact doesn't exist (mistyped).
- The repository where the artifact is located isn't configured.
- The version of library you want isn't available for the Scala version you want, or an sbt plugin isn't available for the version of sbt you're using.
- The repository is configured with the wrong repository layout.

Let's look at an example failure and try to diagnose the cause:

```
> update
[info] Updating {file:/home/jsuereth/projects/sbt-in-action/chapter9/
➥bad-dep-plugin/}bad-dep-plugin...

[info] Resolving org.scala-lnag#scala-actors;2.10.3 ...        Artifact being
[warn]     module not found: org.scala-lnag#scala-actors;2.10.3   resolved

[warn] ==== local: tried                                      Checks artifact
[warn]     /home/jsuereth/.ivy2/local/org.scala-lnag/          and repository
➥scala-actors/2.10.3/ivys/ivy.xml                            for existence

[warn] ==== public: tried
[warn]     http://repo1.maven.org/maven2/org/scala-lnag/
➥scala-actors/2.10.3/scala-actors-2.10.3.pom
[info] Resolving org.fusesource.jansi#jansi;1.4 ...
```

```
[warn]        ::::::::::::::::::::::::::::::::::::::::::::::::::
[warn]        ::            UNRESOLVED DEPENDENCIES        ::
[warn]        ::::::::::::::::::::::::::::::::::::::::::::::::::
[warn]        :: org.scala-lnag#scala-actors;2.10.3: not found
[warn]        ::::::::::::::::::::::::::::::::::::::::::::::::::
```

Problem dependencies

```
[trace] Stack trace suppressed: run last *:update for the full output.
[error] (*:update) sbt.ResolveException: unresolved dependency:
↪org.scala-lnag#scala-actors;2.10.3: not found
[error] Total time: 1 s, completed Nov 9, 2013 10:31:50 AM
```

sbt informs you of two primary pieces of information that let you fix resolution bugs:

- What dependency it's trying to resolve
- Where it's looking for the artifact

In this failure, the first item (what's being resolved) is where the error is. In this case, the organization org.scala-lang was misspelled. But it may be hard to spot such a misspelling at first. The second step in debugging is to start looking at where Ivy was trying to resolve artifacts. The debugging output is repeated here:

```
[warn] ==== local: tried
[warn]    /home/jsuereth/.ivy2/local/org.scala-lnag/scala-actors/2.10.3/ivys/
      ivy.xml
```

This is the output for checking the local file repository. Ivy will create a report like this for each configured resolver in your build. Because this outputs the location it checks, you can use the local file browser or a web browser to check the location for the file. If you're using a repository manager, you can usually search for files with a given name to see where they may be located. If Ivy is unable to find a file, it's for one of the following reasons:

- The artifact doesn't exist.
- Ivy doesn't know where to look for the file.
- Ivy doesn't know how to look for the file.
- Ivy doesn't have permission to view the file.

In the event that an artifact doesn't exist, it could be because you're trying to use a version of software that hasn't yet been released, such as when you're integrating with another team. The solution here is to wait for the artifact to get published or ask the owner to publish you a version.

The second possible cause of failure is that the artifact is published but not to any of the repositories where Ivy knows to look. To solve this, you need to tell Ivy where to look for the artifact. For example, if you were using the Play web framework, you'd need to add the repository where the releases are published, like so:

```
libraryDependencies += "com.typesafe.play" %% "play" % "2.2.0"

resolvers += "Typesafe releases" at "http://repo.typeasfe.com/typesafe/
      releases"
```

Not only do you declare a dependency on Play, but you also include the location where you can find the artifact. Now Ivy knows to look in the repo.typesafe.com server for artifacts when resolving for this project.

Sometimes you need to tell Ivy how to look for files. This is usually the case when dealing with pure Ivy repositories as opposed to Maven-style repositories (the default in sbt). This happens frequently when using sbt plugins.

sbt plugins are usually published using Ivy-style conventions (see appendix A for details). This means the directory structure where an sbt plugin is found is generally not in the Maven style. If you're resolving sbt plugins from your own repository, you need to specify the resolver so that it knows to look for the Ivy style conventions. For example, if you wanted your build to use the Play sbt plugin as a dependency, you'd need the following configuration:

```
addSbtPlugin("com.typesafe.play" % "sbt-plugin" % "2.2.0")

resolvers += Resolver.url("Typesafe ivy releases", new URL( "http://
    repo.typeasfe.com/typesafe/releases"))(Resolver.ivyStylePatterns)
```

Here you use the `Resolver.url` method to create a new resolver. This method takes three arguments: a repository name, a URL, and the pattern you use when looking up artifacts. sbt provides a default `ivyStylePatterns` you can use for standard Ivy repositories, as used in the sbt ecosystem. Although Ivy repositories are mostly used for sbt plugins, a lot of internal projects may also use the Ivy-style layout for the added power of Ivy configurations.

The last potential error occurs when Ivy is correctly configured for where and how to resolve artifacts but doesn't have the appropriate credentials to access artifacts from the server on which they reside. The only way to know this is happening is if Ivy is looking in the correct location for a file but is still unable to resolve it. To fix this, you need to add credentials for the appropriate repository.

9.4.2   *Fixing resolution conflicts*

The next issue that can happen in projects is resolution conflicts—that is, when you're trying to use two dependencies that are incompatible with each other. Let's take a look at one possible example failure.

For the preowned-kittens.com website, you decided to use the secure social library provided for the Play web framework. This provides integration so users can log into your website using their Twitter, GitHub, or Facebook account. Also, you're using the Akka actors library to handle communicating over WebSocket between clients. Your dependency declaration is as follows:

```
libraryDependencies ++=
  Seq(
    "securesocial" %% "securesocial" % "2.1.2",
    "com.typesafe.akka" %% "akka-actor" % "2.1.3"
  )
```

But at runtime you're seeing an `IncompatibleClassChangeFormatException`, or some other odd, hard-to-diagnose error. In these instances, you most likely have some kind of version conflict. Let's investigate what versions of libraries are getting used for your project. Conveniently, sbt dumps the resolution reports for every project under the target/resolution-cache/reports/ directory. Let's look at the contents in your example project:

```
$ ls target/resolution-cache/reports/
ivy-report.css                                           preowned-
    kittens-preowned-kittens_2.10-optional.xml          preowned-kittens-
    preowned-kittens_2.10-runtime.xml
ivy-report.xsl                                           preowned-
    kittens-preowned-kittens_2.10-plugin.xml            preowned-kittens-
    preowned-kittens_2.10-scala-tool.xml
preowned-kittens-preowned-kittens_2.10-compile-internal.xml  preowned-
    kittens-preowned-kittens_2.10-pom.xml               preowned-kittens-
    preowned-kittens_2.10-sources.xml
preowned-kittens-preowned-kittens_2.10-compile.xml      preowned-
    kittens-preowned-kittens_2.10-provided.xml          preowned-kittens-
    preowned-kittens_2.10-test-internal.xml
preowned-kittens-preowned-kittens_2.10-docs.xml         preowned-
    kittens-preowned-kittens_2.10-runtime-internal.xml  preowned-kittens-
    preowned-kittens_2.10-test.xml
```

There's one report for every Ivy configuration used. In this case, it's the runtime scope that's causing issues, so let's look at the report marked runtime. Each of these reports is XML but also includes some formatting so it can be loaded and viewed in a web browser. Figure 9.2 shows what the runtime scope looks like in Firefox (note: Chrome blocks using XSLT from a local path, so the page doesn't display correctly).

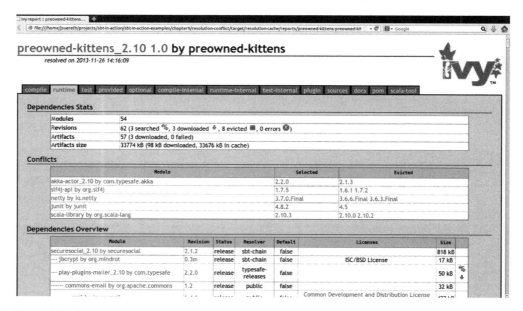

Figure 9.2 Runtime scope shown in Firefox

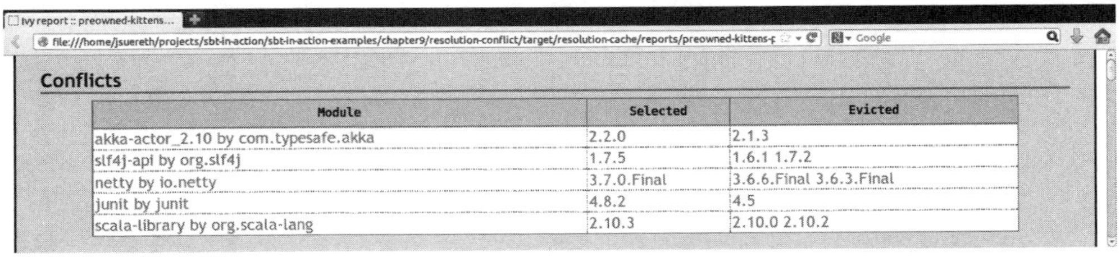

Figure 9.3 Five conflicts are shown.

This screen is split into several sections. First is a set of statistics informing you how long resolution took and how much the algorithm had to search to find your dependencies. The next section is the most important, because it shows conflict resolution. Let's look a bit closer, as shown in figure 9.3.

Here you can see that there were five total dependency conflicts in the application. This shows you which versions were requested and which versions are being used. In this case, it looks like the Akka version you want, 2.1.3, is being evicted in favor of version 2.2.0. To figure out who's requesting this version of Akka, you can click the module name and it'll take you to a deeper analysis, as shown in figure 9.4.

Here it shows that while your build is asking for Akka 2.1.3, a dependency on Play 2.2.1 and akka-slf4j 2.2.0 is bumping the Akka version request to 2.2.0. If you click these modules, you'll see that these requests are coming from secure social, as shown in figure 9.5.

Now that you know there's an issue, there are two possible fixes:

- Use libraries that are compatible.
- Attempt to force Ivy to use the older version you want.

For the first option, this is a matter of hunting down library versions and looking for ones that are compatible. Sometimes it's easier and sometimes it's not, but it's usually the best option. The second option is a bit riskier, because forcing your project to use

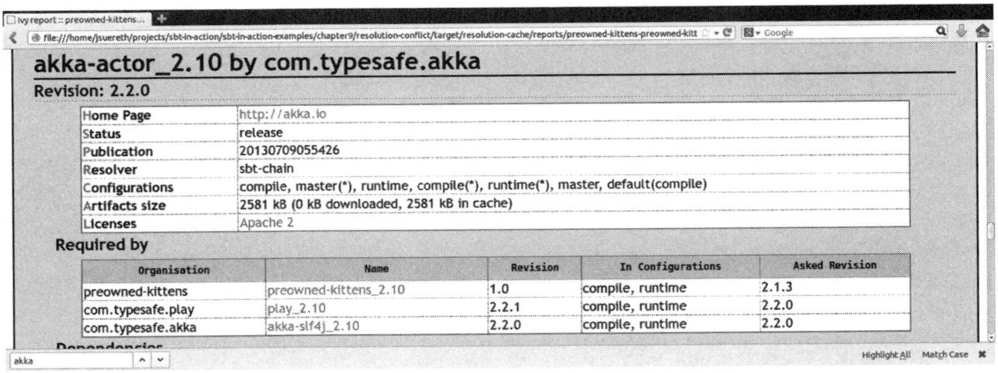

Figure 9.4 Deeper analysis shows a dependency.

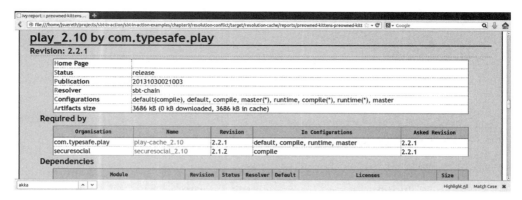

Figure 9.5   The requests are coming from secure social.

an older version of something may also mean binary incompatibilities, or worse, security vulnerabilities. But if you need to do that, you can use the `exclude` feature to ensure the libraries you want are resolved correctly. Fix your current resolution to use the version of Akka you desire:

```
libraryDependencies :=
  Seq(
    ("securesocial" %% "securesocial" % "2.1.2").exclude(
        "com.typesafe.akka", "akka_2.10").exclude(
            "com.typesafe.play", "play_2.10"),
    "com.typesafe.akka" %% "akka-actor" % "2.1.3"
  )
```

Here you modify the library dependencies so that you exclude both the Akka and Play dependencies declared by secure social. This prevents any transitive dependency in secure social from bumping the Akka version. If you reload the build and run `update` in the sbt console, the new dependency report shows no more conflict on Akka, as shown in figure 9.6.

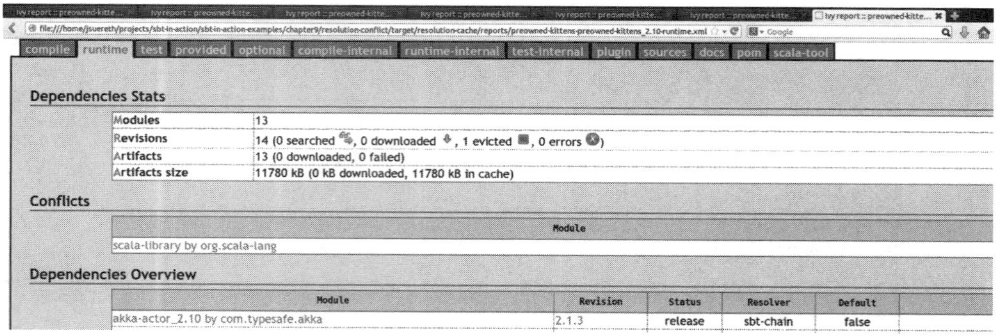

Figure 9.6   No conflict on Akka

Only the version of Scala is bumped, whereas the version of Akka used remains at 2.1.3. Although you've managed to get Ivy to resolve the versions you want, this actually won't work for your project. You'll still get runtime exceptions thrown, just in different places.

In practice, some dependency conflicts aren't resolvable. In these instances, it's best to look for an alternative library to use. Luckily for the preowned-kittens website, you can drop the requirement for Akka 2.1.3 and all dependencies you have on it, because all the libraries you've used have versions against Akka 2.2.0.

9.5 Summary

In this chapter we reviewed some of the most common sbt issues in the order in which they're encountered, along with how to start resolving them. The good news is that once you've gotten your projects resolved, compiled, and building, any failure you encounter after this point is usually introduced by your own development, and it's a sign that the build is working successfully. With sbt, the main way to begin debugging is to follow the flowchart shown in figure 9.7.

This should help diagnose most of the errors that occur in sbt and hone in on possible solutions. In the next chapter, we'll look in more depth at the underlying task API used by sbt, as well as some truly interesting things you can do with sbt's execution engine, including defining your own build scripts via commands.

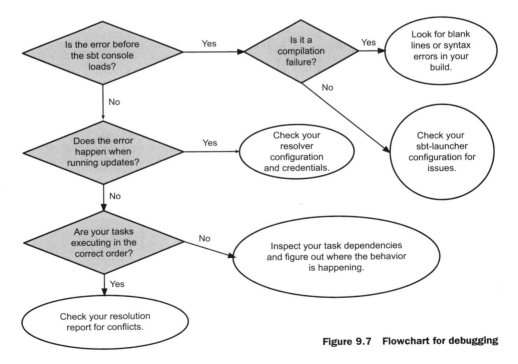

Figure 9.7 Flowchart for debugging

Part 4

Extending sbt

In Part 4, we'll build on the ground covered in Part 3. You'll define a workflow using commands and look at how to define a plugin so that you can share your tasks with others.

Automating workflows with commands **10**

This chapter covers

- A simple `release` command
- Improving discoverability of a command with help messages
- Chaining actions in a command
- Using custom tasks in the release script
- Custom parsing with commands

Sometimes executing one task isn't enough; there are several things that need to happen. Rather than creating an external script file that can run sbt more than once, sbt provides a commands API that can be used to create workflows that go beyond doing one thing. Let's start with an example.

Throughout the chapter, you'll work on the release script for the preowned-kittens website. This script involves a lot of different components, and you'd like it to be as simple as release 1.0 for your developers. To protect your company from issuing bad releases, the script should also have safety measures baked in, such as these:

- Ensuring all the tests run and pass
- Ensuring there are no uncommitted changes
- Creating and pushing a version control tag

10.1 *Creating a simple command*

Let's start with creating the simplest `release` command you can. This command should run all your unit tests before publishing the project. For the release script, you're going to keep the configuration separate from the main build of the project for two reasons:

- It keeps clutter out of the main build.sbt, which describes the structure of the project.
- The script of automated tasks is a separate concern from the main structure, generally adapted at separate times from the main build.

As discussed in chapter 2, sbt will load any .sbt file it finds in the root directory of your project. Create a release.sbt file with what you see in the following listing.

Listing 10.1 Creating a `release` command

```
val ReleaseCommand = Command.command("release") {          ◁──  Creates a basic command
  state =>                                                        called "release"
    "test" :: "publish" :: state                          ◁──
}
                                                                 Schedules actions to run
                                                                 after this command returns

commands += ReleaseCommand                                ◁───  Adds the new command to your build
```

In this listing, you first construct a `Command` object for your release script. This `Command` object will ensure that the string `"release"` is parsed on the sbt prompt to fire the command. When this string is parsed, the body of the command will run. This body is passed in the state of sbt (an `sbt.State` instance).

The `sbt.State` instance contains all the information about the current sbt build, as well as the next operation for the sbt engine to execute. The `::` method is used to prepend new operations onto the build state to execute after the `release` command finishes.

Scala's operator precedence and ::

`sbt.State`'s `::` method is designed to mimic the `List.::` method in Scala. When creating a list in Scala, you can write

```
1 :: 2 :: Nil
```

to get the list `List(1,2)`. Although the `::` method may appear to be defined on `Int` for the expression `1 :: Nil`, it's actually defined on `List`. Part of Scala's special operator syntax rules state that if a method ends with the `:` character, the target of invocation is inverted. This means that instead of `1 :: Nil` being `(1).::(Nil)`, it's compiled as `Nil.::(1)`. The idea is to make the runtime order of the list match the order you see in code.

In sbt, this prepend method (`::`) can be used to add commands into the `sbt.State`. These commands will be run immediately after the current command returns. sbt uses the same `::` method as `List`, where the order of the command runs matches the order you write it in code. For example, `state.prepend("second")` `.prepend("first")` is considered more confusing than (`"first"` `::` `"second"` `::` `state`).

You'll use this command in the sbt prompt after reloading the build:

```
> release
[info] Passed: Total 0, Failed 0, Errors 0, Passed 0
[info] No tests to run for test:test
[success] Total time: 0 s, completed Jan 20, 2014 2:37:44 PM
[info] Wrote /home/jsuereth/projects/sbt-in-action/chapter10/target/scala-
    2.10/preowned-kittens_2.10-0.1-
    bb5e1018270f46fa2eb2848cfd9f51d1b6de4b3f.pom
[info] :: delivering :: preowned-kittens#preowned-kittens_2.10;0.1-
    bb5e1018270f46fa2eb2848cfd9f51d1b6de4b3f :: 0.1-
    bb5e1018270f46fa2eb2848cfd9f51d1b6de4b3f :: release :: Mon Jan 20
    14:37:44 EST 2014
[info]     delivering ivy file to /home/jsuereth/projects/sbt-in-action/
    chapter10/target/scala-2.10/ivy-0.1-
    bb5e1018270f46fa2eb2848cfd9f51d1b6de4b3f.xml
[info]     published preowned-kittens_2.10 to /home/jsuereth/.ivy2/local/
    preowned-kittens/preowned-kittens_2.10/0.1-
    bb5e1018270f46fa2eb2848cfd9f51d1b6de4b3f/poms/preowned-kittens_2.10.pom
[info]     published preowned-kittens_2.10 to /home/jsuereth/.ivy2/local/
    preowned-kittens/preowned-kittens_2.10/0.1-
    bb5e1018270f46fa2eb2848cfd9f51d1b6de4b3f/jars/preowned-kittens_2.10.jar
[info]     published preowned-kittens_2.10 to /home/jsuereth/.ivy2/local/
    preowned-kittens/preowned-kittens_2.10/0.1-
    bb5e1018270f46fa2eb2848cfd9f51d1b6de4b3f/srcs/preowned-kittens_2.10-
    sources.jar
[info]     published preowned-kittens_2.10 to /home/jsuereth/.ivy2/local/
    preowned-kittens/preowned-kittens_2.10/0.1-
    bb5e1018270f46fa2eb2848cfd9f51d1b6de4b3f/docs/preowned-kittens_2.10-
    javadoc.jar
[info]     published ivy to /home/jsuereth/.ivy2/local/preowned-kittens/
    preowned-kittens_2.10/0.1-bb5e1018270f46fa2eb2848cfd9f51d1b6de4b3f/ivys/
    ivy.xml
[success] Total time: 0 s, completed Jan 20, 2014 2:37:44 PM
```

The terminal output shows sbt running the `test` command and then moving onto the `publish` command. Although this output doesn't display the specific task that's running, the debug output will show each command that's executed, prefixed with a `>`.

The core of the sbt engine is the command processor, which will take all commands scheduled on the `sbt.State` instance and execute them until none remain. The release script you've designed is creating a new set of commands to execute and then letting the command processor take control. What happens if one of these commands fails? Let's take a look:

```
> release v0.1.0
[success] Total time: 0 s, completed Feb 26, 2014 4:36:11 PM
[info] Integration tests successful
[trace] Stack trace suppressed: run last test:test for the full output.
[error] Error: Total 0, Failed 0, Errors 0, Passed 0
[error] Error during tests:
[error]     FailingTest
[error] (test:test) sbt.TestsFailedException: Tests unsuccessful
[error] Total time: 0 s, completed Feb 26, 2014 4:36:11 PM
```

A failure in any command leads to the remaining commands not executing. This is a feature of the error-handling command that's registered. On error, sbt executes a command that's meant to recover from that error. The default error handler clears the remaining command strings and schedules the shell command. The command engine process is outlined in figure 10.1.

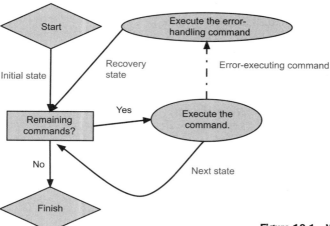

Figure 10.1   Workflow of sbt's command engine

sbt doesn't register individual commands for every possible task in a build. Instead, it registers a command called act that's able to take any input string and determine which task on the build to execute. But the act command isn't the only way to execute tasks. Let's look at another command called all.

10.2   Running tasks in parallel

Now you'll ensure that the integration tests for the preowned-kittens project are run. The simplest way is to add the it:test task to the list of commands you wish to run in the release script:

```
val ReleaseCommand = Command.command("release") {
  state =>
    "test" :: "it:test" :: "publish" :: state       Integration tests will
}                                                     run after unit tests.
```

Although this ensures that the integration tests are run, it would be much better if you could run integration tests in *parallel* with unit tests to ensure your build is as fast and efficient as possible. Although all commands have to be sequentially executed, there's one command that lets you break this restriction: all.

The all command lets you specify multiple tasks to execute on the sbt build. These tasks are executed in *parallel*. To ensure that test and integration tasks are run in parallel, you can modify the release.sbt file to look like the following:

```
val ReleaseCommand = Command.command("release") {
  state =>
    "all test it:test" :: "publish" :: state
}
```

Integration tests will run in parallel with unit tests if there are no dependencies between them.

Now, when running the release command, integration tests and unit tests can run in parallel before attempting to publish. The all command ensures that all specified tasks are successful before returning. The syntax of the all command is simple:

```
all (<space> <task string>)*
```

Each task to execute is separated by spaces. If the task takes arguments, like the run-Main input task, you can place those arguments in line and then add an additional task to run. For example,

```
all runMain com.jsuereth.MainApp test
```

will run the runMain com.jsuereth.MainApp task as well as the test task. This is because sbt uses a full parser library, and the task's parser is used against as much of the string as possible before looking for another task to run. Additionally, the all command allows only one task with arguments to be called in the list of tasks.

Although running tasks in a command is useful, you'll want to expand your release command so that it's more flexible than just running a set of tasks.

10.3 Parsing input with commands

So far, you've been using commands with simple names, but commands in sbt are actually more general. A command does two things:

- Parses a command string (parse)
- Takes the current state of the build and returns a new state (effect)

The way to think of commands is as things that can *parse* a string and then act on that (the effect). Let's look at the release command again:

```
val ReleaseCommand = Command.command("release") {        ⟵─── Parse
  state =>
    "all test it:test" :: "publish" :: state              ⟵─── Effect
}
```

Here you can see the two phases. For reading, the release command only reads the string "release". But commands can actually use any parser for the read phase.

You're going to use some of the tricks you learned in chapter 7 to define a parser that will also accept valid version strings before returning.

Although this code is using the simplest way to construct a command, you can use the more sophisticated constructor, which allows you to specify a custom parser for the command. Table 10.1 shows the ways of constructing a command.

Table 10.1   Ways to construct a command

Method	Argument List 1	Argument List 2	Argument List 3
command	name: String help: Help	effect: State => State	
apply[T]	name: String help: Help	parser: State => Parser[T]	effect: (State, T) => State
single	name: String help: Help	effect: (State, String) => State	

For those not familiar with Scala, the notion of multiple argument lists may be foreign, especially when combined with the special syntax used when defining functions and default arguments. Let's reexamine your initial command code and dig into the Scala tidbits required to see how this works:

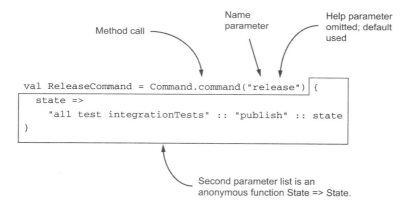

There are two things at work in this syntax. First, Scala has *default* parameters. For the command methods, this means that the Help parameter can be omitted and an empty help message is autogenerated for you. The second is a combination of Scala features that lets you treat an argument list that accepts one function as a code block. In this case, the second argument list expected a function State => State.

To provide a parser to the Command.apply method, you can use similar syntax as before, but this time there will be three argument lists with the last two as anonymous functions:

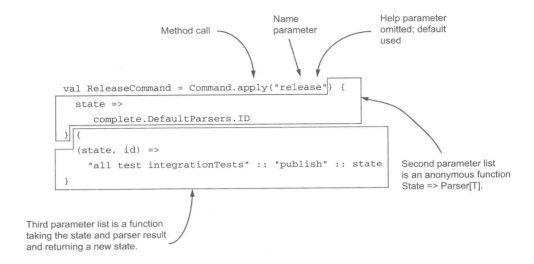

Although this is valid Scala syntax, and possibly convenient for some, the line that contains } { feels particularly grating. In addition, anonymous functions tend to be hard to debug. You'll modify the `release` command to explicitly define methods to handle the behavior of the command:

```
import complete._
import DefaultParsers._

def releaseParser(state: State): Parser[String] = ID

def releaseAction(state: State, version: String): State = {
    "all test integrationTests" :: "publish" :: state
}

val ReleaseCommand =
  Command.apply("release")(releaseParser)(releaseAction)
```

Here, rather than using anonymous function literals, you're directly passing methods. Not only is this code cleaner to read, but a named method is easier to debug when things go wrong.

Now that we have the Scala mechanics out of the way, let's begin focusing again on improving the release script. You'd like to have it require passing a version number that will be used to tag the Git repository as well as version the project itself. The sbt-git plugin has a feature that will modify a project's version number to match an underlying version tag. If the project has a Git tag called v<some version number>, then the sbt-git plugin will make the project's version be <some version number>. You're going to add this feature to your project.

First you need to add the sbt Git plugin to your project. Add this line to the project/plugins.sbt file:

```
addSbtPlugin("com.typesafe.sbt" % "sbt-git" % "0.6.2")
```

Modify the build.sbt file as follows:

```
// Must be at the top
import com.typesafe.sbt.SbtGit._

git.baseVersion := "0.1"

// Alter the default project setup for git versioning
def PreownedKittenProject(name: String): Project = (
  Project(name, file(name))
  .settings(versionWithGit:_*)
  ...
)
```

The `sbt-git` plugin is an old-style plugin. Previously in sbt, plugins would have users add the plugin settings explicitly to the project factory method. To use `sbt-git`, you've appended the `versionWithGit` settings into the common project factory method. Note that we've elided the other `.settings` definitions on the project for brevity, but be sure to check the example code for the full definition.

Now, when loading your build, the Git plugin will check for tags. If it doesn't detect a version tag, it will append the current Git commit SHA to the version. Let's take a look in the sbt console after reloading the build definition:

```
> version
[info] 0.1-bb5e1018270f46fa2eb2848cfd9f51d1b6de4b3f
```

git.baseVersion   Current Git commit

Now you'll create a fake tag and see the Git plugin pull in the new version number. Here's the sbt console session:

```
> git tag v0.2

> reload
[info] Loading global plugins from /home/jsuereth/.sbt/0.13/plugins
[info] Loading ...
> version
[info] 0.2
```

Note that the `git` command is added by the `sbt-git` plugin and allows you to run Git directly from within sbt. This allows you to directly tag the codebase and check the version number that's returned. Now that you have the Git plugin wired into the build, you can use it to create the tag as part of your release script. For now, you'll use the built-in NotSpace parser for the version number. Modify release.sbt:

```
def releaseParser(state: State): Parser[String] =
  complete.DefaultParsers.NotSpace

def releaseAction(state: State, version: String): State = {
```

```
    "all test integrationTests" ::
  s"git tag ${version}" ::
  "reload" ::
  "publish" ::
  state
}
val ReleaseCommand =
  Command.apply("release")(releaseParser)(releaseAction)
```

Now the `git` tag is created immediately after successful completion of both the tests and integration tests. Next, the build is reloaded, because the version key is a *setting*. Version is only evaluated on build load and requires the release script to reload the build to get the correct version.

Take a look at the new script in the sbt console:

```
> release 1.0
[info] Updating {file:/home/jsuereth/projects/sbt-in-action/chapter10/
      }chapter10...
[info] Resolving org.fusesource.jansi#jansi;1.4 ...
[info] Done updating.
[info] Passed: Total 0, Failed 0, Errors 0, Passed 0
[info] No tests to run for test:test
[success] Total time: 0 s, completed Feb 26, 2014 8:12:43 PM

[info] Loading global plugins from /home/jsuereth/.sbt/0.13/plugins
[info] Loading project definition from /home/jsuereth/projects/sbt-in-action/
      chapter10/project
[info] Set current project to preowned-kittens (in build file:/home/jsuereth/
      projects/sbt-in-action/chapter10/)
[info] Packaging /home/jsuereth/projects/sbt-in-action/chapter10/target/
      scala-2.10/preowned-kittens_2.10-0.2-sources.jar ...
[info] Updating {file:/home/jsuereth/projects/sbt-in-action/chapter10/
      }chapter10...
[info] Wrote /home/jsuereth/projects/sbt-in-action/chapter10/target/scala-
      2.10/preowned-kittens_2.10-0.2.pom
[info] Done packaging.
[info] Resolving org.fusesource.jansi#jansi;1.4 ...
[info] Done updating.
[info] Packaging /home/jsuereth/projects/sbt-in-action/chapter10/target/
      scala-2.10/preowned-kittens_2.10-0.2-javadoc.jar ...
[info] Done packaging.
[info] Packaging /home/jsuereth/projects/sbt-in-action/chapter10/target/
      scala-2.10/preowned-kittens_2.10-0.2.jar ...
[info] Done packaging.
[info]     published preowned-kittens_2.10 to /home/jsuereth/.m2/repository/
      preowned-kittens/preowned-kittens_2.10/0.2/preowned-kittens_2.10-0.2.pom
[info]     published preowned-kittens_2.10 to /home/jsuereth/.m2/repository/
      preowned-kittens/preowned-kittens_2.10/0.2/preowned-kittens_2.10-0.2.jar
[info]     published preowned-kittens_2.10 to /home/jsuereth/.m2/repository/
      preowned-kittens/preowned-kittens_2.10/0.2/preowned-kittens_2.10-0.2-
      sources.jar
[info]     published preowned-kittens_2.10 to /home/jsuereth/.m2/repository/
      preowned-kittens/preowned-kittens_2.10/0.2/preowned-kittens_2.10-0.2-
      javadoc.jar
```

```
[success] Total time: 0 s, completed Feb 26, 2014 8:12:44 PM
>
```

Here the tests are all run successfully before the `publish` task is called. The only downside to the `release` command is that it doesn't display when individual tasks are run, although these are available in the debugging output. You can see them if you turn on debug logging. In the sbt console, type `debug`, with the caveat that this will turn on many more messages, so the output isn't shown. It's useful when debugging the command but otherwise can remain off.

Although the new script is nice, you still need to fix the parser used for the version number. Luckily, you only need to refactor the `releaseParser` method defined in release.sbt, as shown in the next listing.

Listing 10.2 Parser for version numbers

```
def releaseParser(state: State): Parser[String] = {

  val version = (Digit ~ chars(".0123456789").*) map {        ◁────── Requires version
  case (first, rest) => (first +: rest).mkString              ◁──     strings to be a digit
  }                                                                   with any number of
                                                                      digits or . following

  val complete =                                                      Converts the parsed
    (chars("v") ~                                                     characters into a String
      token(version, "<version number>")) map {                      Requires version tags
        case (v, num) => v + num                          ◁──        to start with "v"
      }                                                   

  Space ~> complete              ◁──        Tab completion should
}                                           show this string instead
                                            of all possible numbers.
```

Requires version strings to be a digit with any number of digits or . following

Converts the parsed characters into a String

Requires version tags to start with "v"

Tab completion should show this string instead of all possible numbers.

Requires a space after the release command and before the version string; ignores the space in the returned String.

Now you can try out the new `release` command in the sbt terminal:

```
> release<tab>
> release v
> release v<tab>
<version number>
> release v0.2
[info] Updating {file:/home/jsuereth/projects/sbt-in-action/chapter10/
    }chapter10...
[info] Resolving org.fusesource.jansi#jansi;1.4 ...
[info] Done updating.
[info] Passed: Total 0, Failed 0, Errors 0, Passed 0
[info] No tests to run for test:test
[success] Total time: 0 s, completed Feb 26, 2014 8:12:43 PM

[info] Loading global plugins from /home/jsuereth/.sbt/0.13/plugins
[info] Loading project definition from /home/jsuereth/projects/sbt-in-action/
    chapter10/project
```

```
[info] Set current project to preowned-kittens (in build file:/home/jsuereth/
    projects/sbt-in-action/chapter10/)
[info] Packaging /home/jsuereth/projects/sbt-in-action/chapter10/target/
    scala-2.10/preowned-kittens_2.10-0.2-sources.jar ...
[info] Updating {file:/home/jsuereth/projects/sbt-in-action/chapter10/
    }chapter10...
[info] Wrote /home/jsuereth/projects/sbt-in-action/chapter10/target/scala-
    2.10/preowned-kittens_2.10-0.2.pom
[info] Done packaging.
[info] Resolving org.fusesource.jansi#jansi;1.4 ...
[info] Done updating.
[info] Packaging /home/jsuereth/projects/sbt-in-action/chapter10/target/
    scala-2.10/preowned-kittens_2.10-0.2-javadoc.jar ...
[info] Done packaging.
[info] Packaging /home/jsuereth/projects/sbt-in-action/chapter10/target/
    scala-2.10/preowned-kittens_2.10-0.2.jar ...
[info] Done packaging.
[info]     published preowned-kittens_2.10 to /home/jsuereth/.m2/repository/
    preowned-kittens/preowned-kittens_2.10/0.2/preowned-kittens_2.10-0.2.pom
[info]     published preowned-kittens_2.10 to /home/jsuereth/.m2/repository/
    preowned-kittens/preowned-kittens_2.10/0.2/preowned-kittens_2.10-0.2.jar
[info]     published preowned-kittens_2.10 to /home/jsuereth/.m2/repository/
    preowned-kittens/preowned-kittens_2.10/0.2/preowned-kittens_2.10-0.2-
    sources.jar
[info]     published preowned-kittens_2.10 to /home/jsuereth/.m2/repository/
    preowned-kittens/preowned-kittens_2.10/0.2/preowned-kittens_2.10-0.2-
    javadoc.jar
[success] Total time: 0 s, completed Feb 26, 2014 8:12:44 PM
>
```

As you press the Tab key, the space and the v character are automatically added. After this, pressing Tab instructs the user to enter a version number.

The last thing you'd like to do in your release script is to make sure that there are no local Git changes before releasing. You can do this by adding a new custom task that will perform the check and then adding it into the release script. First you'll create the custom task that will check for local index changes. Add the following to your release.sbt file:

```
val checkNoLocalChanges =
  taskKey[Unit]("checks to see if we have local git changes. Fails if we
    do.")

checkNoLocalChanges := {
  val dir = baseDirectory.value
  val changes =
    Process("git diff-index --name-only HEAD --", dir) !! streams.value.log
  if(!changes.isEmpty) {
    val changeMsg = changes.split("[\r\n]+").mkString(" - ","\n - ","\n")
    sys.error("Git changes were found: \n" + changeMsg)
  }
}
```

In the event that the Git process returns differences, the task will throw an exception. sbt's task system will catch this and mark the task as failed. For the release script, this means it will stop processing remaining commands and call the command error handler. By default, the sbt command error handler will drop all remaining tasks and ask for another task via the shell. You'll add the `checkNoLocalChanges` task to the release script; modify your release.sbt file as follows:

```
def releaseAction(state: State, version: String): State = {
    "checkNoLocalChanges" ::
    ("all test integrationTests" ::
    s"git tag ${version}" ::
    "reload" ::
    "publish" ::
    state)
}
```

You can immediately use it on the sbt command line without making a local Git commit:

```
$ sbt
> release v1.0
[trace] Stack trace suppressed: run last *:checkNoLocalChanges for the full
    output.
[error] (*:checkNoLocalChanges) Git changes were found:
[error]     - chapter10/release.sbt
[error] Total time: 0 s, completed Feb 26, 2014 3:05:11 PM
```

Now the release script is appropriately stopping after it detects local Git changes. You can no longer accidentally release code that hasn't been checked in or tagged. Although this is wonderful, it would also be nice to inform other developers on the team how to use your `release` task.

10.4 Creating useful help messages

One of the core goals of sbt is that, although it allows custom tasks, it tries to promote discoverability and convenient documentation for users of builds. This translates into several terminal commands, such as `inspect`, `help`, and `tasks`. In chapter 3, you used the `inspect` command exclusively to discover the structure of the default sbt build. The `help` command is the equivalent for learning about other commands available for a build. Take a look at what the `help` command displays for your build in the following listing.

Listing 10.3   sbt> help

```
help                                    Displays this help message or
    prints detailed help on requested commands (run 'help <command>').
about                                   Displays basic information about
    sbt and the build.
tasks                                   Lists the tasks defined for the
    current project.
settings                                Lists the settings defined for the
    current project.
reload                                  (Re)loads the project in the
    current directory
```

```
projects                                    Lists the names of available
    projects or temporarily adds/removes extra builds to the session.
project                                     Displays the current project or
    changes to the provided 'project'.
set [every] <setting>                       Evaluates a Setting and applies it
    to the current project.
session                                     Manipulates session settings. For
    details, run 'help session'.
inspect [uses|tree|definitions] <key>   Prints the value for 'key', the
    defining scope, delegates, related definitions, and dependencies.
<log-level>                                 Sets the logging level to 'log-
    level'. Valid levels: debug, info, warn, error
; <command> (; <command>)*                  Runs the provided semicolon-
    separated commands.
~ <command>                                 Executes the specified command
    whenever source files change.
last                                        Displays output from a previous
    command or the output from a specific task.
last-grep                                   Shows lines from the last output
    for 'key' that match 'pattern'.
export <tasks>+                             Executes tasks and displays the
    equivalent command lines.
exit                                        Terminates the build.
--<command>                                 Schedules a command to run before
    other commands on startup.
show <key>                                  Displays the result of evaluating
    the setting or task associated with 'key'.
```

Here you can see the information about common sbt commands. For example, here's the portion of output that describes the inspect command:

`inspect [uses|tree|definitions] <key>`	Prints the value for 'key', the defining scope, delegates, related definitions, and dependencies

You can get further help information on inspect by typing help inspect on the sbt console:

```
> help inspect
inspect <key>

    For a plain setting, the value bound to the key argument is displayed
    using
        its toString method.
        Otherwise, the type of task ("Task" or "Input task") is displayed.
        "Dependencies" shows the settings that this setting depends on.
        "Reverse dependencies" shows the settings that depend on this setting.
    When a key is resolved to a value, it may not actually be defined in the
        requested scope. In this case, there is a defined search sequence.
        "Delegates" shows the scopes that are searched for the key.
        "Provided by" shows the scope that contained the value returned for the
        key.

        "Related" shows all of the scopes in which the key is defined.
inspect tree <key>
```

```
        Displays 'key' and its dependencies in a tree structure.
        For settings, the value bound to the setting is displayed and for tasks,
            the type of the task is shown.
inspect uses <key>
        Displays the settings and tasks that directly depend on 'key'.
inspect definitions <key>
        Displays the scopes in which `key` is defined
```

You can see that the help information for the inspect command is quite rich. Again, because sbt allows custom tasks, commands, and settings, runtime-level help becomes more important. Users will quickly become comfortable with the default tasks and commands but may need guidance on project-specific tasks.

Warning: conventions enable collaboration

Although sbt allows custom tasks and workflows, this doesn't mean that a project should create custom workflows for everything. Consistency across an organization can help developers span their activities across teams. When adding custom workflows in sbt, the first question you should ask is "How is my project different so that it requires something custom?"

For commands, sbt provides a Help object, which contains the help documentation for users. Create one of these in release.sbt for your users:

```
val releaseHelp = Help(
  Seq(                                              ◁────── Shown when you type
    "release <version>" ->                                 "help" in the sbt console
➥ "Runs the release script for a given version number"   ◁────── Second column
  ),
  Map(                                              ◁────── Defines help for "help
    "release" ->                                           release" in the sbt console
        """|Runs our release script.  This will:
           |1. Run all the tests.
           |2. Tag the git repo with the version number.
           |3. Reload the build with the new version number from the git tag
           |4. publish all the artifacts""".stripMargin
  )
)
```

Next you need to wire the help documentation into the release command. Modify the command definition in release.sbt as follows:

```
val releaseCommand = Command("release",
    releaseHelp)(releaseParser)(releaseAction)
```

Now you can try out the new help documentation in the sbt console:

```
> help

  release                      Runs the release script for a given version
    number
  ...
```

```
> help release
Runs our release script. This will:
1. Run all the tests.
2. Tag the git repo with the version number.
3. Reload the build with the new version number from the git tag
4. publish all the artifacts
```

You now have a fully implemented, automated, and discoverable release mechanism for your build.

10.5 Summary

In this chapter we showed you how to create a simple command that scripts together a set of tasks, both custom and built-in, which fully automates the release process of the preowned-kittens project. This command uses the following:

- The built-in Help API to allow newcomers to learn about and know how to use the release command
- A parser for version numbers that helps guide a user in how to type the release command and prevent bad input
- A call to the all command, to run some tasks in parallel

Although this chapter only covered using the sbt.State object to schedule more commands to run, it's actually possible to implement/access the entirety of the sbt engine via the this interface. Commands are the meat and potatoes of sbt, and most of sbt's core is written using commands, including the not-yet-released sbt server.

In practice, commands are most useful for scripting tasks, like the release task. When debating whether to write a custom task or a command, here are the questions to ask yourself:

- Do I need to reload the build or alter settings in my script?
- If yes, write a command.
- Do I need to run tasks in a specific order?
- If yes, write a command.
- Do I need to alter the core sbt.State object?
- If yes, write a command.

For everything else, use tasks.

As a rule of thumb, commands are generally used much less than input tasks—say a ratio of 2:1. This means a majority of your build will be settings/tasks, with a fraction being input tasks and a small portion being commands. The release command is usually the only custom command.

In addition, there exists an sbt-release plugin that provides a configurable release command for usage. For most projects, this plugin should be sufficient for automating release scripts, but there are instances where it isn't enough and you'll need to create a custom command.

Now that you've scripted the release process, we'll look at how to create an sbt plugin.

Defining a plugin

This chapter covers

- Getting to know the `AutoPlugin` interface and using it to make life easier for the user
- Testing a plugin with sbt scripted
- Using configurations in your plugin
- Adding incremental tasks
- Reusing code using Scala files

In this chapter we'll go into the nuts and bolts of constructing a plugin. Plugins are the primary vehicle of reuse within sbt. As you saw previously, when you want your build to do something, the first thing to do is look for a plugin. If you don't find one, go ahead and add the custom functionality. Once you have the functionality working in your own build, sbt plugins provide a means for you to share it with the rest of the sbt ecosystem.

What is a plugin? A *plugin* is a set of reusable sbt settings that users can include in their build without having to copy/paste them in. Most of the time users should be able to reuse existing settings and tasks and likely tweak a few values here and there for their build. In this chapter we'll look at how to provide those tasks, along with some recommendations as to how to set up your plugin to make it easy for the end user. You'll write a simpler version of the Scalastyle plugin that you saw earlier.

When should you write a plugin? The simple answer is when the plugin would benefit others. Let's use the example of the uber jar tasks you constructed in chapter 6—the IO and Process libraries. This chapter involved quite a lot of tasks and code. Is there another project that would benefit from using this code? Well, given that there already exists more than one plugin in the sbt ecosystem to package uber jars, I think that answer is yes.

The second question to ask is how to distribute your code for others. Here are your options:

- Copy/paste the code.
- Publish the code as a library.
- Publish the code as a plugin.

Each of these approaches has its advantages and disadvantages. The copy/paste option is quick to get up and running—no worries when you change the code; it won't break the original build. The downside is that any bug fixes will have to be recopied/pasted to others. This is usually the first and best style of reuse, but after one or two users, you quickly find yourself wanting a better distribution mechanism.

If you publish the code as a library, it can be more flexible for the user. They can create or refine whatever sbt tasks they need and only call into your code for the heavy lifting. This is similar to what you did with Apache Velocity in chapter 8, where you called into the Apache Velocity library from an sbt task. Another benefit of this approach is that your code may be of use outside sbt as well.

The final option is to create a full sbt plugin, which is the option that makes things easiest for the user. The necessary tasks are added automatically, and usually they only need to configure these tasks. But the trade-off of making it easier for the user is making it harder for you. There's more work involved in writing a plugin; you have to think more carefully about your tasks and their interfaces. And you have to make them general enough to be useful.

In this chapter you'll create a couple of plugins from scratch. The first will be a Scalastyle plugin, called `scalastyle-plugin`. The second will be a plugin to show the notion of dependencies between plugins. This will be `depend-plugin`.

A note about the project setup: apart from the first section on code reuse using Scala files, the projects described in this chapter follow a slightly different pattern from what you've seen before. The code for the plugins exists outside of the `preowned-kittens` project; this is because they'll be distributed as their own projects, which you can then reuse in other projects. Distribution of projects is covered in depth in the next chapter, "Distributing your projects," but you'll use the `publish-Local` command to push your plugin onto the local computer so that it can be resolved in other sbt projects. In addition to the `scalastyle-plugin` project, there will be a `scalastyle-test` project, which is separate from both the `preowned-kittens` and the `scalastyle-plugin` projects. When reading examples, please pay attention to where files are located because they'll explicitly denote either a `scalastyle-plugin` or `scalastyle-test` directory. There's a similar setup for the `depend-plugin` project.

11.1 *Reusing code using Scala files*

As we said previously, there's one simple way to share code between builds: copy/paste. This isn't as bad as it sounds. When you publish code, it needs to be general enough that it can apply to multiple projects but specific enough to be useful. Build code (or build configuration) tends in the other direction; it's hard to be general and is usually very specific. But in a big build, you often want to do the same thing in multiple submodules. You can do this by using the project subdirectory.

sbt compiles the *.sbt files in the project-root directory and the .scala files in the project directory, and then these are available to the build. Specifically, the classes and objects defined in the .scala files are available to both the root build and the submodules. This code can be used anywhere within the build, shared between the modules. Let's look at a simple example. You want to ensure that a particular version of a library is used in all of the builds, so you'll provide a helper method that provides the correct version. You'll use the build created for chapter 10, and the dependency is scala-logging, which is a logging library. You create this method in project/Project.scala, as shown in the following listing.

Listing 11.1 project/Project.scala

```
import sbt._

object BuildUtils {
  def loggingDependencies(): Seq[sbt.ModuleID] = {
    Seq("com.typesafe.scala-logging" %% "scala-logging" % "3.0.0")
  }
}
```

As you can see, this isn't particularly complicated. You can use it as follows:

analytics/build.sbt

```
libraryDependencies ++= BuildUtils.libraryDependencies()
```

When you reload the build, you can see the results: the Scala logging library is added to the dependencies for the analytics project:

```
> show analytics/*:libraryDependencies
[info]  List(..., com.typesafe.scala-logging:scala-logging:3.0.0)
```

This is a simple example, and obviously you can do a lot more than this, but it gives you another option to reuse code when using sbt. Let's move on to plugins.

11.2 *Introducing the AutoPlugin interface*

Let's start super-simple with your first plugin. The goal here is to create a plugin with a single task that prints Hello world. You'll then publish and consume this plugin from the test project to ensure your environment is correct before actually implementing the meat of your new Scalastyle plugin.

First you'll need a new project called `scalastyle-plugin`. This is pretty similar to what you've done before: you need a build.properties and build.sbt. In your project/build.properties, make sure that you have the correct version of sbt:

scalastyle-plugin/project/build.properties

```
sbt.version=0.13.7
```

Next you create a build.sbt:

scalastyle-plugin/build.sbt

```
version := "1.0"

sbtPlugin := true // (a)

organization := "org.preownedkittens.sbt"

name := "scalastyle-plugin"
```

The only new thing in this build.sbt is the `sbtPlugin` setting at (a), which is set to true. This tells sbt that you're creating a plugin. sbt will then add the necessary dependencies and settings to your project so that the project will be packaged and distributed as a plugin. As far as the build file is concerned, this `sbtPlugin` setting is the only major difference between a normal build and an sbt plugin build.

Next you need some code. sbt plugins are written in Scala,[1] so you create a file named src/main/scala/HelloPlugin.scala, which contains the code. We'll run through the process of the first plugin quickly, but don't worry; we'll come back to the details.

First you add an object that extends `sbt.AutoPlugin`:

scalastyle-plugin/src/main/scala/helloplugin.scala

```
object HelloPlugin extends sbt.AutoPlugin {
}
```

You then declare a task (a `TaskKey`) inside the object:

scalastyle-plugin/src/main/scala/helloplugin.scala

```
object HelloPlugin extends sbt.AutoPlugin {
  lazy val helloTask = taskKey[Unit]("Prints Hello world.")
}
```

Then you define the task as part of a sequence of settings, called `projectSettings`.

scalastyle-plugin/src/main/scala/helloplugin.scala

```
object HelloPlugin extends sbt.AutoPlugin {
  lazy val helloTask = taskKey[Unit]("Prints Hello world.")

  override def projectSettings = Seq(
    helloTask := println("Hello world")
  )
```

---

[1] You can do this in other JVM languages as well, but the use of macros in sbt makes this difficult in languages other than Scala.

```
}
```

> **Why is the plugin interface called AutoPlugin and not Plugin?**
>
> Prior to sbt 0.13.5, there was an sbt.Plugin interface. This interface did not include the ability to depend on settings in other plugins, and when it was wired into users' projects, it could cause subtle issues. The mechanism was rewritten in sbt 0.13.5 to provide a few benefits:
>
> - AutoPlugins have their settings indexed, which can improve user messages; for instance, listing the plugins included in a project.
> - AutoPlugins know their dependencies on other plugins, so sbt can ensure those plugins have their settings included in a project first. This fixes the majority of multi-plugin issues that existed previously.
>
> AutoPlugins have simpler inclusion/exclusion semantics. Primarily, users can disable poorly behaved AutoPlugins, whereas before they were required to use advanced features to disable.

You can now publish the plugin. But you'll publish it only to your local cache for now; you don't want to really publish it to everyone yet. We haven't covered publishing so far; please check out chapter 12 for more details on publishing semantics. For now, run publishLocal. This pushes to your local Ivy cache on your local computer:

```
> publishLocal
[info] Packaging /home/mfarwell/code/sbt/sbt-in-action-examples/chapter11/
    target/scala-2.10/sbt-0.13/scalastyle-plugin-1.0-sources.jar ...
...
[info] Done packaging.
[info]  published scalastyle-plugin to /home/mfarwell/.ivy2/local/
    org.preownedkittens.sbt/scalastyle-plugin/scala_2.10/sbt_0.13/1.0/jars/
    scalastyle-plugin.jar
...
[info]  published ivy to /home/mfarwell/.ivy2/local/org.preownedkittens.sbt/
    scalastyle-plugin/scala_2.10/sbt_0.13/1.0/ivys/ivy.xml
[success] Total time: 1 s, completed 07-Jul-2014 10:58:16
```

You've now published your plugin locally, so you can use it from another project on the same machine. As mentioned earlier, you'll experiment with the plugin by creating a completely separate project, called scalastyle-test, from which you can import the plugin by specifying it in a plugins.sbt. Set up the following build files in a new directory:

scalastyle-test/build.sbt

```
version := "1.0"

organization := "org.preownedkittens"

name := "scalastyle-test"

enablePlugins(HelloPlugin)
```

scalastyle-test/project/build.properties

```
sbt.version=0.13.7
```

scalastyle-test/project/plugins.sbt

```
addSbtPlugin("org.preownedkittens.sbt" % "scalastyle-plugin" % "1.0")
```

Then you can run it (in scalastyle-test):

```
$ sbt hello
Hello world
[success] Total time: 0 s, completed 5 mai 2014 06:43:16
```

Yay, it works! We'll cover a better testing solution for this later on using the scripted plugin. You can also see the description that you set when you defined the task:

```
$ sbt "tasks -V"
...
fullResolvers              Combines the project resolver.
hello                      Prints Hello world.
incCompileSetup            Configures aspects of incremental compilation.
...
```

This is about as simple as it gets for publishing a plugin, but this covers the basic structure for your plugin. We went through this rather quickly, so let's now take some time and cover the same stuff but in more detail.

11.2.1 *Taking a closer look—the plugin definition*

Let's start with the build.sbt. You added the following line:

```
sbtPlugin := true
```

The effect of this flag is to tell sbt that you're building a plugin, and it has three major consequences:

- The libraryDependencies for the project are automatically updated to include all of the sbt libraries so you can use the same methods available in a build.sbt file.
- When sbt publishes the plugin, it will mark the plugin as being compatible with the binary version of sbt being used to compile the project. For example, if you're building a plugin on sbt 0.13.5, it will be marked as compatible with the sbt 0.13.x series, so any sbt 0.13.x version can use the plugin.
- It automatically generates a file called sbt/sbt.autoplugins that winds up in the packaged plugin jar. This contains a list of all plugin objects, that is, those objects that extend sbt.AutoPlugin. This file is used by sbt to automatically load settings when it loads a project.

Next let's look at HelloPlugin.scala, starting with the task declaration:

```
lazy val helloTask = taskKey[Unit]("Prints Hello world.")
```

Here, the first parameter to the taskKey method is the description of the task that will appear when you do tasks -V. Although help messages are always important, they're even more critical when defining reusable plugins. In the plugin object, you also override the projectSettings method:

```
override def projectSettings: Seq[Setting[_]] = Seq(
  ... settings go here ...
)
```

This method is called by sbt to find the list of settings and tasks that should be included on sbt projects. Note that you can have both settings and tasks in this list. In fact, the Seq[Setting[_]] can be viewed as a comma-separated list of build.sbt statements. Each element in the Seq is a setting or a task definition that sbt will append to the user's build.sbt. In the scalastyle-test build, you were manually enabling the plugin in build.sbt with the enablePlugins() method. You can prevent the user from having to do this by using the autoImport feature of AutoPlugins, which we'll cover later.

Finally, you need to define the behavior of helloTask in the settings:

```
helloTask := println("Hello World")
```

This line is exactly the same as it would be in a build.sbt file. As you may remember from chapter 3, each expression in a build.sbt file is either a Setting[_] or Seq[Setting[_]] instance. In fact, every key op initializer expression is an instance of Setting[_], which you can place inside the project sequences, meaning you can almost copy/paste directly from build.sbt files into the plugin's .scala definition of settings.

11.2.2 *Taking a closer look—task and setting dependencies*

Let's now take a deeper dive into task dependencies. When you run a task, it may have dependencies on other tasks or settings. Add to the helloTask task a dependency on, say, the location of the main Scala sources: scalaSource in Compile:

scalastyle-plugin/src/main/scala/helloplugin.scala

```
import sbt.Keys._

override def projectSettings = Seq(
  helloTask := println("Hello " + (scalaSource in
  Compile).value.getAbsolutePath)
)
```

You use the setting (scalaSource in Compile), which has a type SettingKey[File], and map to a simple File, which you can then use. When you run this, you'll get the following output:

```
$ sbt hello
Hello /home/mfarwell/code/sbt/scalastyle-test/src/main/scala
```

This is the way to introduce dependencies between settings and tasks in your plugins. Note that you're using scalaSource from the Compile configuration; this differs from the Test. configuration in that you're getting the directory used to compile production code, not unit-testing code or other configured code types. In sbt, configurations can be added by plugins, which we'll talk about in section 11.4.

There are other settings and tasks available to depend on. You can use any key; the default keys defined by sbt are available in the sbt.Keys object. For instance, if you'd like to stop using println and use the official streams for sbt, this is easy; this is called sbt.Keys.streams:

```
helloTask :=
    streams.value.log.info("Hello " +
(scalaSource in Compile).value.getAbsolutePath)
```

Here you use the log.info method. When run, it will look like this:

```
[info] Hello /home/mfarwell/code/sbt/scalastyle-test/src/main/scala
```

In your plugins, you should use the log methods provided by sbt rather than println; the user can filter the output to see only errors or warnings, and the output will be saved so that you can use the last command:

```
> set logLevel in Global := Level.Warn
[info] Defining */*:logLevel
[info] The new value will be used by no settings or tasks.
[info] Reapplying settings...
[info] Set current project to sbt-test (in build file:/C:/code/sbt/t/)
> hello
[success] Total time: 0 s, completed 11 mai 2014 11:54:39
> last hello
[info] Hello foobar
>
```

Finally, one more thing: you can depend on other settings defined in the same plugin. You'll define a key that contains a message that you print out, called helloMsg. First you define the setting:

```
lazy val helloMsg = settingKey[String]("message for hello task")
```

Then you put it into projectSettings:

```
override def projectSettings = Seq(
  hello := ...
  helloMsg := "default message"
)
```

Now you can use the setting as a dependency in your task:

```
hello := {
    val args: Seq[String] = spaceDelimited("<arg>").parsed
    val sourceDir = (scalaSource in Compile).value
    streams.value.log.info("Hello " +
helloMsg.value + " " + sourceDir.getAbsolutePath)
  }
```

The output is the following:

```
$ sbt hello
[info] Hello default message /home/mfarwell/code/sbt/scalastyle-test/src/
    main/scala
```

You can now change the default message in your build.sbt in the scalastyle-test project:

scalastyle-test/build.sbt

```
...

org.preownedkittens.sbt.HelloPlugin.helloKey := "new message"

$ sbt hello
[info] Hello new message /home/mfarwell/code/sbt/scalastyle-test/src/main/
    scala
```

We've now covered the basics of defining a plugin, along with dependencies on other settings. Next we'll look at how you can add automated tests for your plugins.

11.3   *Testing a plugin with the scripted plugin*

Now that the `HelloPlugin` works, you can start adapting this into something that's actually useful. In the rest of the chapter, you'll implement a Scalastyle plugin. Scalastyle is a style checker that will run over your code and enforce various team coding-style requirements during the build. These sorts of tools can dramatically help unify the look and feel of a codebase for a team across each developer.

To begin, you'll add a new plugin object to the same project. Yes, you can have more than one plugin in a plugin project. This may simplify your distribution. Create a new ScalastylePlugin.scala file with the contents shown in the following listing.

> **Listing 11.2   scalastyle-plugin/src/main/scala/ScalastylePlugin.scala**

```
object ScalastylePlugin extends sbt.AutoPlugin {
  override def projectSettings = Seq(
    scalastyleConfig := baseDirectory.value / "scalastyle-config.xml"
  )

  lazy val scalastyleConfig = SettingKey[File]("configuration file for
    scalastyle")
}
```

This is similar to the previous plugin, except this time the configurable setting is the `scalastyleConfig` key. The `scalastyleConfig` key will store the configuration for the style-checking rules for a project. The default will look for a scalastyle-config.xml file in the root directory of the project.

Next you need to add a task that will run Scalastyle using the config file specified. But to be able to run Scalastyle, you'll need it available to you. Scalastyle is both a command-line tool and a Scala library. For the sbt plugin, you can depend directly on the Scalastyle library and execute it within the sbt tasks directly, rather than using the command line. Go ahead and add a dependency in the plugin's own build.sbt, similar to how you added dependencies for other projects:

scalastyle-plugin/build.sbt

```
libraryDependencies ++= Seq("org.scalastyle" %% "scalastyle" % "0.5.0")
```

Now declare the `taskKey` that you'll use to run Scalastyle:

scalastyle-plugin/src/main/scala/scalastyleplugin.scala

```
lazy val scalastyleConfig = settingKey[File]("configuration file for
    scalastyle")
lazy val scalastyle = taskKey[Unit]("Runs scalastyle.")
```

Declare the definition:

scalastyle-plugin/src/main/scala/scalastyleplugin.scala

```
override def projectSettings = Seq(
  scalastyleConfig := baseDirectory.value / "scalastyle-config.xml",
  scalastyle := {
    val sourceDir = (scalaSource in Compile).value
    val configValue = (scalastyleConfig in Compile).value
    val s = streams.value
    doScalastyle(configValue, sourceDir, s.log)
  }
)
```

This is pretty much the same as what you used for the `HelloPlugin`, except that you're calling the method `doScalastyle`, which you haven't yet defined. This is common practice in sbt plugins:

- Define a method to do the work.
- Define settings/tasks that call that method.

Next you'll define the method that will do the work; you can ignore the internals of Scalastyle because you don't need the details for the purpose of this book. The implementation of `doScalastyle` in the following listing will run the style checker on all Scala code it finds, count the number of errors found, and display that number using the logger.

Listing 11.3   scalastyle-plugin/src/main/scala/ScalastylePlugin.scala

```
def doScalastyle(config: File, sourceDir: File, logger: Logger): Unit = {
  if (config.exists) {
    val messages = runScalastyle(config, sourceDir)
    val errors = messages.collect { case x: StyleError[_] => 1 }.size
    logger.info(errors + " errors found")
  } else {
    sys.error("%s does not exist".format(config))
  }
}
private def runScalastyle(config: File, sourceDir: File) = {
  val configuration =
      ScalastyleConfiguration.readFromXml(config.absolutePath)
  new ScalastyleChecker().checkFiles(configuration,
Directory.getFiles(None, List(sourceDir)))
}
```

Note that if you don't have a configuration file, sbt will return an error for the task. For testing purposes, you can copy the Scalastyle configuration from chapter 8 into the appropriate location, the top-level directory in the `scalastyle-test` project. Run the `scalastyle` task in the test project:

```
$ sbt scalastyle
[info] 5 errors found
[success] Total time: 0 s, completed 26 mai 2014 10:13:06
```

So far, so good. But there's a problem now: how can you more easily test your plugin? To test, you've been publishing, jumping between projects, reloading definitions, and crossing your fingers; this isn't easy to do and it's very manual. You need to add some automated tests to have the turnaround time between developing and verification be a lot quicker. As you saw in chapter 5, there are a lot of different testing frameworks. But the unit-testing frameworks that you used in chapter 5 are harder to apply when talking about testing a plugin.

If you follow the best practice of splitting the implementation and the setting configuration, you can use these unit-testing frameworks to test the bulk of your behavior. But there's a lot more involved with checking the wiring in sbt, and plugins tend to write to files, change state, and generally be hard to unit test. You require a better model to test the full plugin, and this is provided by the `scripted` plugin.

The basic idea of the sbt `scripted` plugin is this: you create a number of scenarios. A scenario consists of some sbt project files, a set of tasks to run, and a set of expectations: do you expect this file to exist, should this task succeed, is the content of this file as expected? The `scripted` plugin for sbt does this: it sets up the environment, runs sbt with your freshly compiled plugin, and tests the results of the commands that you execute.

As an example, you can test that if there's no valid configuration file, then the `scalastyle` task will fail. First add the `scripted` plugin to the `scalastyle-plugin` build:

scalastyle-plugin/projects/plugins.sbt
```
libraryDependencies <+= (sbtVersion) { sv =>
  "org.scala-sbt" % "scripted-plugin" % sv
}
```

Here you use a little trick that uses the current sbt version to add the correct version of the `scripted` plugin; the version corresponds to the sbt version.[2] Unlike most sbt plugins, `scripted` is tied to sbt itself. The `scripted` plugin is actually a core plugin, maintained as part of sbt itself.

Then, in the `scalastyle-plugin` build.sbt you add the settings for the `scripted` plugin:

---

[2] We're using the older (0.12) syntax here, `<+=`. This means "Using the value of this setting, construct a new value."

scalastyle-plugin/build.sbt

```
ScriptedPlugin.scriptedSettings

scriptedLaunchOpts <++= version apply { version =>
  Seq("-Xmx1024M", "-XX:MaxPermSize=256M", "-Dplugin.version=" + version)
}

scriptedBufferLog := false
```

> ### Why are you adding settings directly?
> At the time of writing, the `scripted` plugin is not an AutoPlugin and hasn't been converted to the new syntax. Before AutoPlugins, sbt plugins would require users to manually reference `Seq[Setting[_]]` from Scala objects.

Here you take the default settings for `scripted` and add a couple of JVM parameters and, importantly, you'll set the Java system property `plugin.version` to the version of the `scalastyle` plugin you're building. This is so `scripted` can pick it up when it runs. Note that the `scripted` plugin always runs a separate JVM. You tell `scripted` not to buffer output to ensure nothing important is missed when it runs; `scripted-BufferLog` is set to `false`.

You can then run the `scripted` task:

```
$ sbt scripted
[warn] Attempting to overwrite
    C:\Users\mfarwell\.ivy2\local\org.preownedkittens.sbt\scalastyle-
    plugin\scala_2.10\sbt_0.13\1.0\jars\scalastyle-plugin.jar
[warn]  This usage is deprecated and will be removed in sbt 1.0
... lots more output
```

There will probably be lots of warnings at this point from sbt advising that you shouldn't publish the same file more than once; you can safely ignore these for now, but it gives you a clue as to how the `scripted` plugin works. Because you defined the version to be a production version—that is, 1.0—sbt is warning you that you shouldn't publish production releases more than once. You can fix this by changing the version number to be a Snapshot or setting the `isSnapshot` setting for the plugin project to `true`.

But where do you put the `scripted` tests now? The directory src/sbt-test will contain the tests. You'll add a test. The scripted test directory has two levels: the first level is a group directory that contains a set of tests, each of which is in its own directory. This underlying test-instance directory contains all of the files that apply to a given test.

For this first test, you'll place it in the test group `config` and call the test instance `does-not-exist`. This means the directory containing the test files should be src/sbt-test/config/does-not-exist. In this directory, you'll create an sbt project and a test-script file. First define the build for the sbt project that you'll test:

scalastyle-plugin/src/sbt-test/config/does-not-exist/build.sbt

```
org.preownedkittens.sbt.ScalastylePlugin.projectSettings

org.preownedkittens.sbt.ScalastylePlugin.config := file("does-not-exist.xml")
```

Then define the plugins.sbt in the following listing.

Listing 11.4   scalastyle-plugin/src/sbt-test/config/does-not-exist/project/plugins.sbt

```
{
  val pluginVersion = System.getProperty("plugin.version")
  if (pluginVersion == null)
    throw new RuntimeException("""The system property 'plugin.version' is not
    defined. Specify this property using the scriptedLaunchOpts -
    D.""".stripMargin)
  else addSbtPlugin("org.preownedkittens.sbt" % "scalastyle-plugin" %
pluginVersion)
}
```

This file is where you pick up the plugin.version that you're testing. You don't want to hardcode a particular version in each test, so you'll use the Java property variables to add this dynamically, which you added to the launch options previously. Next you need to specify the test script for your test: this contains what to do and what to expect. You do this using a file called test in the test project directory. In your case, it will look like this:

scalastyle-plugin/src/sbt-test/config/does-not-exist/test

```
# test that a missing config file causes error
> clean
-> scalastyle
```

We won't describe the full syntax for scripted tests here, but the most important options are as follows:

```
#            starts a comment
> name       sends a command to sbt and tests if it is successful
$ name       executes a file command and tests if is successful
-> name      sends a command and tests if is successful, but expecting it to
       fail
-$ name      executes a file command and tests if is successful, but expecting
       it to fail
```

A file command is something like touch, delete, exists, copy—these are commands defined by the scripted plugin that manipulate files directly. Your test does a clean and then runs scalastyle. It expects the clean task to succeed and the scalastyle task to fail. This is what you want because the does-not-exist.xml file does not exist. Try this test out. You want to run all of your config tests, so use scripted config/*:

```
$ sbt "scripted config/*"
[info] Loading project definition from ...
[info] Set current project to scalastyle-plugin (...)
....
```

```
[info] Done packaging.
...
Running config / does-not-exist
...
[info] java.lang.RuntimeException: does-not-exist.xml does not exist
...
[info] [error] (*:scalastyle) does-not-exist.xml does not exist
[info] [error] Total time: 0 s, completed 26 mai 2014 11:14:47
[info] + config / does-not-exist
[success] Total time: 14 s, completed 26 mai 2014 11:14:47
```

This command produces a lot of output, which we've cut down here. The scripted plugin is performing three steps:

- It packages your plugin and publishes it locally (using publish-local).
- For each directory under src/sbt-test and that matches the input filter (for example, the config/* you passed in), it will run an update. This will be in a temporary build directory, not the local one.
- In the temporary build directory, it will run the tasks specified in your test script file. If everything goes according to plan, you'll get a success at the end; otherwise, you'll get an error and the whole task will fail.

You'll note that in the output shown here, there are errors; these are coming from the scalastyle plugin, but you're expecting these (indeed, you're testing for them), so at the end you're getting a success. With no parameters on the command line, the scripted plugin will run all tests that it finds under src/sbt-test, but you can specify a group (as shown previously) or a specific test instance to run on the command line (don't forget to put the quotes in the right place):

```
$ sbt "scripted config/does-not-exist"
```

You can put more than one test on the command line if you want. You can certainly use the scripted plugin to ease testing of your plugins. Indeed, sbt itself has over 200 scripted tests.

11.4 Using configurations in your plugin

In the scalastyle plugin, you made use of the scalaSource setting inside the Compile configuration:

scalastyle-plugin/src/main/scala/scalastyleplugin.scala
```
scalastyle := {
  val sourceDir = (scalaSource in Compile).value
  val configValue = scalastyleConfig.value
  val s = streams.value
  doScalastyle(configValue, sourceDir, s.log)
}
```

This is a good thing: you don't want the user to have to tell scalastyle where to find the sources, so you use the default sbt settings for production source files.

But it begs a question: what happens if you want to run a `scalastyle` task on your testing sources as well? The obvious (and wrong) solution is to create another task called `scalastyleTest`, which uses the test source location (`scalaSource in Test`) in the method as well. Here's an example:

scalastyle-plugin/src/main/scala/scalastyleplugin.scala

```
scalastyleTest := {
  val sourceDir = (scalaSource in Test).value
  val configValue = scalastyleConfig.value
  val s = streams.value
  doScalastyle(configValue, sourceDir, s.log)
}

lazy val scalastyleTest = taskKey[Unit]("Runs scalastyle.")
```

You add a `scalastyleTest` task that runs the same `doScalaStyle` method against the test sources. This will work, but there's still another problem: what happens if you need a different Scalastyle configuration file for the test sources? It often happens that you want different rules for main and test sources.

Rather than creating another two tasks for the different combinations, you can use sbt's configurations to help you here. First, we'll remind you how setting and task scoping works. Each setting or task can have a different value depending upon three axes: project scope (this project versus that project), configuration scope (`Test` versus `Compile`), and task (`compile` versus `test` versus `scalastyle`). Your `config` setting can therefore have different values for the `Compile` and `Test` configurations, so in your build.sbt you can say:

```
scalastyleConfig in Test := file("scalastyle-test.xml")

scalastyleConfig in Compile := file("scalastyle-compile.xml")
```

This, along with a default global value that you set in the plugin, means that this will work in all cases. You can also have different values for tasks, depending on the configuration:

scalastyle-plugin/src/main/scala/scalastyleplugin.scala

```
scalastyle := {
    val sourceDir = (scalaSource in Compile).value
    val configValue = (scalastyleConfig in Compile).value
    val s = streams.value
    doScalastyle(configValue, sourceDir, s.log)
  },
scalastyle in Test := {
  val sourceDir = (scalaSource in Test).value
  val configValue = (scalastyleConfig in Test).value
  val s = streams.value
  doScalastyle(configValue, sourceDir, s.log)
}
```

Now you're defining two values for one `taskKey`, `scalastyle`. If you run `test :scalastyle`, it will check the style of the test sources, whereas a vanilla `scalastyle` will check the style of your production sources. Additionally, because of configuration

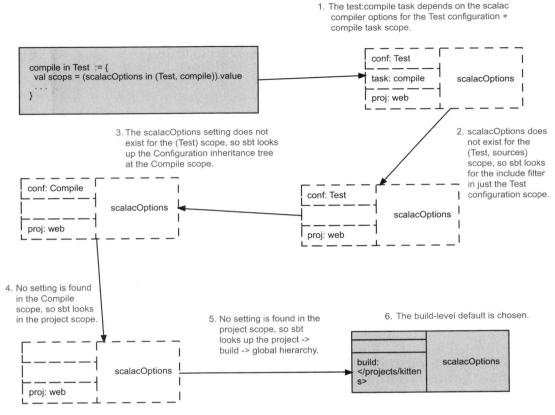

Figure 11.1 Example of scope delegation within sbt

inheritance, the `scalastyleConfig` values will both come from the `Compile` configuration unless the user has overridden it in the `Test` configuration. That's the beauty of sbt's config delegation. Figure 11.1 shows an example of scope delegation within sbt, and figure 11.2 shows resolution and inheritance diagrams for sbt scopes.

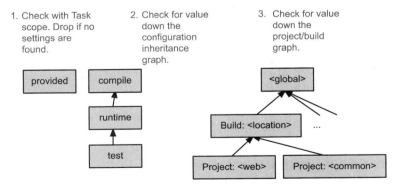

Figure 11.2 Resolution and inheritance diagrams for sbt scopes

Finally, there's still some code duplication. The `scalastyle` task is being defined twice in almost exactly duplicate fashion. You can remove this by using sbt's `inConfig` mechanisms.

First move the `scalastyle` task setting into its own sequence, where you don't use any configuration scoping:

```
def rawScalaStyleSettings: Seq[Setting[_]] =
  Seq(
    scalastyle :=  {
      val sourceDir = scalaSource.value
      val configValue = scalastyleConfig.value
      val s = streams.value
      doScalastyle(configValue, sourceDir, s.log)
    }
  )
```

This mirrors a `projectSettings` definition, except that it's standalone. Now you can take this definition of a setting and alter its dependencies. That is, for the entire sequence of settings, when a task or setting declares dependencies, you can shift these dependencies to be inside a different scope. sbt provides one method for each scope axis to do this: `inConfig`, `inProject`, `inTask`. For your purposes you'll use the `inConfig` method, as shown in figure 11.3.

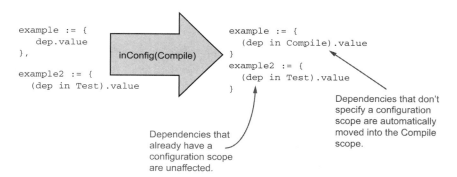

Figure 11.3 Configuration mapping using `inConfig`

Because the `scalastyle` task should be on both the `Test` and `Compile` configurations, use the `inConfig` method to alter the `projectDependencies` appropriately in the `scalastyle` plugin object to be the following:

```
def rawScalaStyleSettings: Seq[Setting[_]] =
  Seq(
    scalastyle :=  {
      val sourceDir = scalaSource.value
      val configValue = scalastyleConfig.value
      val s = streams.value
      doScalastyle(configValue, sourceDir, s.log)
    }
  )
```

```
override def projectSettings: Seq[Settting[_]] =
    inConfig(Compile)(rawScalaStyleSettings) ++
    inConfig(Test)(rawScalaStyleSettings) ++
    Seq(
      scalastyleConfig := file("scalastyle-config.xml")
    )
```

Here the `projectSettings` sequence is first given the `rawScalaStyleSettings` with its dependencies adapted into the `Compile` configuration. Then it's given the same settings with the dependencies adapted into the `Test` configuration. After this, you append the raw settings you had before. Viola! You've just reused the same task setting in multiple configurations. As you may recall from chapter 5, when you added the integration test settings, this used the same mechanism to take all the settings used for the `Test` tasks and migrate them into the `IntegrationTest` configuration.

11.5 Adding incremental tasks

One of the interesting things that the Scalastyle plugin does is that it always processes every file of the source code. This isn't necessarily a problem in the case of your project—your test project is quite small. But on a bigger, more realistic project, this may take too long to run every time. If you're using the ~ command to rerun tasks, this could result in large amounts of output each time you save a file in the project.

It would be nice to add an incremental option to your `scalastyle` task, to check only the files that have changed since the last time you ran `scalastyle`. How do you go about this? You need to limit the files processed to those that have a modified date later than the last call, so you'll need to store this somewhere. A file in the target directory is the obvious choice.

First add a setting to your existing tasks and call it `scalastyleIncremental`. If this value is `true`, you process only those files that have been saved since the last time `scalastyle` was run. This is simple and quick:

scalastyle-plugin/src/main/scala/scalastyleplugin.scala

```
override def projectSettings = Seq(
  scalastyleConfig := baseDirectory / "scalastyle-config.xml",
  scalastyleIncremental := false,
  ...

  lazy val scalastyleIncremental = settingKey[Boolean]("scalastyle does
    incremental checks")
```

To be able to tell which files have been updated, you'll need to save the last run date somewhere; convention dictates that it should be in the target directory, so that's where you'll put it. You'll need to pass this in as well:

scalastyle-plugin/src/main/scala/scalastyleplugin.scala

```
scalastyle := {
  val sourceDir = scalaSource.value
  val configValue = scalastyleConfig.value
  val inc = scalastyleIncremental.value
  val targetValue = target.value
```

```
  val s = streams.value
  doScalastyle(configValue, sourceDir, inc, targetValue, s.log)
}
```

And, of course, because of the inConfig usage, all of this configuration also shows up for scalastyle in Test.

You'll save the time of the last run into target/scalastyle.lastrun. Next you need a couple of methods to find the Scala files that have changed since your last run, if there were any. For this, you'll use the sbt.IO file, searching and filtering methods that you first looked at in chapter 8:

scalastyle-plugin/src/main/scala/scalastyleplugin.scala

```
private def lastModified(lastRun: Long)(file: File) = file.lastModified >
    lastRun
private def changedFiles(sourceDir: File, lastRunFile: File) = {
  val lastRunDate = try {
    read(lastRunFile).trim().toLong
  } catch {
    case _: Exception => 0L
  }
  (sourceDir ** "*.scala").get.filter(lastModified(lastRunDate))
}
```

Finally, you change doScalastyle (and runScalastyle) to use the incremental flag; if it's true, you use the files that are returned by the changedFiles function:

scalastyle-plugin/src/main/scala/scalastyleplugin.scala

```
def doScalastyle(config: File, sourceDir: File, incremental: Boolean,
    targetDir: File, logger: Logger): Unit = {
  val lastRunFile = targetDir / "scalastyle.lastrun"

  if (config.exists) {
    val sources =
      if (incremental) changedFiles(sourceDir, lastRunFile)
      else List(sourceDir)

    val messages = runScalastyle(config, Directory.getFiles(None, sources))
    val errors = messages.collect{ case x: StyleError[_] => 1}.size

    sbt.IO.write(lastRunFile, "" + new java.util.Date().getTime())
    logger.info(errors + " errors found")
  } else {
    sys.error("%s does not exist".format(config))
  }
}

private[this] def runScalastyle(config: File, sources:
    List[org.scalastyle.FileSpec]) = {
  val configuration =
    ScalastyleConfiguration.readFromXml(config.absolutePath)
  new ScalastyleChecker().checkFiles(configuration, sources)
}
```

Then you compile, deploy, and run—the first time you process all of the files. The second time, however, you get 0 files processed and 0 errors. The next time you edit a source file in your test project, it will be reanalyzed by Scalastyle.

11.5.1 Adding incremental tasks with .previous—a sneak preview of 1.0

sbt 1.0 is adding a number of different features, including `.previous`, which works much like the `.value` method on task keys that you've seen before, except that `previous` returns the value of the task from the previous time that it was run, not the current execution.

This can be used to implement what was implemented in section 11.5 but using sbt built-in functionality. As of the time of writing (version 0.13.6), the feature is still being implemented, but let's see what you can do with what's already out there. First, add another task and call it `scalastylePrevious`. This task will behave in the same way as the `scalastyle` task. Note that this is a task, not an `inputTask`:

scalastyle-plugin/src/main/scala/scalastyleplugin.scala

```
lazy val scalastylePrevious = taskKey[Long]("Runs scalastyle.")
```

Note also that the task must return a value, so you're declaring this task to return a `Long` value. You need to return a value; otherwise, sbt can't give you the value of the previous run. The value of this task will be the time the task was run, stored as the number of milliseconds since 01/01/1970. As you saw in section 11.4, this is easy to obtain. Next you add the task with the dependent tasks:

scalastyle-plugin/src/main/scala/scalastyleplugin.scala

```
import sbt.Cache._

override def projectSettings = Seq(
  ...
  scalastylePrevious := {
    val sourceDir = (scalaSource in Compile).value
    val configValue = (scalastyleConfig in Compile).value
    val inc = incremental.value
    val streamsValue = streams.value

    doScalastylePrevious(configValue, sourceDir, inc, scalastyle2.previous,
      streamsValue.log)
  }
```

Note that you're passing the value of `scalastyle.previous` into the `doScalastylePrevious` method. This is similar to the `doScalastyle` method created before.

scalastyle-plugin/src/main/scala/scalastyleplugin.scala

```
def doScalastylePrevious(config: File, sourceDir: File, incremental: Boolean,
    lastRun: Option[Long], logger: Logger): Long = {
  if (config.exists) {
    val sources = if (incremental) changedFilesPrevious(sourceDir, lastRun)
    else List(sourceDir)

    val messages = runScalastyle(config, Directory.getFiles(None, sources))
    val errors = messages.collect{ case x: StyleError[_] => 1}.size
```

```
    logger.info(errors + " errors found")
    new java.util.Date().getTime()
  } else {
    sys.error("%s does not exist".format(config))
  }
}
```

You return the current date and time in the last line. `scalastylePrevious.previous` is an `Option[Long]`, so in `changedFilesPrevious` you check to see whether it has a value, and if it does, you use that. Otherwise, you use 0 (the beginning of time; well ... the beginning of time for computers):

scalastyle-plugin/src/main/scala/scalastyleplugin.scala

```
private def changedFilesPrevious(sourceDir: File, lastRun: Option[Long]) = {
  val lastRunDate = lastRun.getOrElse(0L);
  (sourceDir ** "*.scala").get.filter(lastModified(lastRunDate))
}
```

Now you no longer have to manage the `lastRunFile` or take care where it gets created. There's no need to pass around `targetValue` either, because sbt will do all of this for you.

11.6 *Making things easy for the user—more about the AutoPlugin interface*

The `AutoPlugin` interface fixes a number of plugin problems that existed before sbt 0.13.5, the major ones being difficulties with plugin dependencies and ease of use for the user. Let's look at how the new interface solves these issues.

Imagine you have a plugin (let's call it `DependPlugin`, because we're creative) that depends on the `ScalastylePlugin` discussed earlier. The `DependPlugin` is designed to declare common settings you want to reuse across the entire company. You can declare in `DependPlugin` that you depend on `ScalastylePlugin`, and sbt will make sure the `scalastyle` plugin settings are also included on projects that depend on `DependPlugin`. In addition, you can then further configure the `scalastyle` settings with customizations for your company.

Let's again start with creating a basic plugin, which prints `Hello`:

depend-plugin/build.sbt

```
version := "1.0"

sbtPlugin := true

organization := "org.preownedkittens.sbt"

name := "depend-plugin"
```

src/main/scala/dependplugin.scala

```
package org.preownedkittens.sbt

import sbt._
```

```
import sbt.Keys._
object DependPlugin extends sbt.AutoPlugin {
  lazy val depend = taskKey[Unit]("Prints Hello depend.")

  override def projectSettings = Seq(
    dependTask := streams.log.info("Hello depend")
  )

  override def requires = Seq(ScalastylePlugin)
}
```

This is similar to the HelloPlugin that you saw before. The major difference is the requires method. This method declares the plugins that this plugin depends on. This method serves two purposes:

- It means that whenever the user enables your plugin, they also get the ScalastylePlugin.
- It means that the scalastyle plugin settings are always added to the build before any settings you define; that is, your plugin can adapt the default settings of the scalastyle plugin however it wants.

You can build the plugin and publish locally as you did before. Now, to use this plugin, you must enable it on the build.sbt as you did before:

depend-test/build.sbt
```
version := "1.0"

organization := "org.preownedkittens"

name := "depend-test"

enablePlugins(DependPlugin)
```

depend-test/project/plugins.sbt
```
addSbtPlugin("org.preownedkittens.sbt" % "depend-plugin" % "1.0")
```

Again, you use the enablePlugins method in build.sbt to turn the plugin on for the build. Because depend has a dependency on scalastyle, this will, additionally, enable the scalastyle plugin on the project. If the user explicitly disables the scalastyle plugin, the depend plugin won't be added to the build. You can do this via a list of enabled plugins for projects via the plugins command in the sbt prompt.

In addition to automatically adding dependent settings, AutoPlugins can also define methods, values, or keys that will be available in .sbt files via the autoImport feature of AutoPlugin. If, as a plugin writer, you declare autoImport to be a stable identifier (either an object or a val), the plugin user no longer needs to run the projectSettings to get access to the tasks or settings that you create (within the autoImport). You can require that the plugin be enabled for your project. In your DependPlugin definition, you define autoImport and define your input task inside it:

depend-plugin/src/main/scala/dependplugin.scala

```
object DependPlugin extends sbt.AutoPlugin {
  import autoImport._

  override def projectSettings = …
  override def requires = ...

  object autoImport {
    lazy val depend = taskKey[Unit]("Prints Hello depend.")
  }
}
```

When you publish it, you can create a new task that depends on the `test` task:

depend-test/build.sbt

```
version := "1.0"

organization := "org.preownedkittens"

enablePlugins(DependPlugin)

lazy val dependtest = taskKey[Unit]("depends on a key from autoImport")

dependtest := depend.value
```

Now you can run the `dependtest` task:

```
depend-test$ sbt dependtest
[info] Hello depend
```

`AutoPlugin` has another method that you can override, `trigger`, which defines under what circumstances your plugin will be activated. By default it's `noTrigger`; this is the behavior you saw previously. In `noTrigger` mode, you force the user to explicitly enable your plugin. If you change the trigger to `allRequirements`, then the plugin gets automatically enabled when all of its required plugins are also enabled on the project. If you define a plugin with no requirements, but a trigger of `allRequirements`, it's enabled on all projects automatically.

Use the autoenabling feature with care; it may be a bad idea to force a user to import all of your settings. But if you do use it, the user will always have the option of using `disablePlugin` to prevent your plugin from getting included. Generally, a trigger of `allRequirements` should be used for plugins that depend on and adapt other plugins. For example, the `sbt-pgp` plugin takes the settings defined in the `IvyPlugin` and adds PGP signatures to artifacts generated. Having the `sbt-pgp` plugin automatically included on any project using Ivy would be okay, but adding PGP settings to every project, regardless of whether or not the user wants it, may not be useful.

Let's look a bit more at the requirements feature of `AutoPlugin`s. What's a requirement? It's a set of other plugins that a plugin requires to function. Additionally, a plugin can designate plugins it won't work with, as exclusions in the requirements. For example, if there are two competing uber jar packaging plugins, they can declare that they conflict with each other so users are unable to specify both in the same project.

Although the DependPlugin is meant to be a companywide plugin that's explicitly enabled, let's pretend that it's actually an extension to Scalastyle that adds default style rules and is instead meant to be used wherever Scalastyle is used. You'll modify the trigger for the DependPlugin to be allRequirements:

depend-plugin/src/main/scala/dependplugin.scala
```
object DependPlugin extends sbt.AutoPlugin {
  override def projectSettings = ...

  override def trigger = Plugins.allRequirements

  override def requires = Seq(ScalastylePlugin)

  object autoImport = ...
}
```

You also need to remove the DependPlugin from being enabled in build.sbt, but instead enable ScalastylePlugin:

depend-plugin/build.sbt
```
version := "1.0"

organization := "org.preownedkittens"

name := "depend-test"

enablePlugins(ScalastylePlugin)
```

Note that you're enabling the ScalastylePlugin here, but that the DependPlugin is automatically enabled when you enable the ScalastylePlugin. You can view this by running a task defined only on the DependPlugin:

```
depend-test$ sbt depend
[info] Hello depend
depend-test$
```

In addition to the features shown, AutoPlugin has a few more methods, as shown in table 11.1.

Table 11.1 AutoPlugin methods

Method	Semantic
def projectConfigurations: Seq[Configuration]	Adds new Configuration objects to the project. These will participate in Ivy resolution and scope lookup. When adding custom configurations, always register them here.
def buildSettings: Seq[Setting[_]]	Settings that will be injected into the "build global" level. These will all have a scope of "in ThisBuild" and are shared among all projects within the build.
def globalSettings: Seq[Setting[_]]	Similar to buildSettings but are global across builds and shared between all builds and projects loaded in an sbt instance. Note: we haven't talked about multibuild sbt instances, which are an evolving feature of sbt.

11.7 Summary

In this chapter you learned how to reuse code within sbt. In practice, build setting reuse should take the following flow:

- Oh, I need this setting in this other build. Copy-paste.
- I really need this function available in all my builds. Release a library.
- I'd like to reuse settings/tasks I've defined in many other builds. Release a new plugin.
- I'd like to create a plugin that captures the standard settings for my company. An AutoPlugin that depends on all the standard plugins for your company and tweaks their settings.
- I'd like to extend an existing plugin with new features. An AutoPlugin with an allRequirements trigger and appropriate depends method.

Plugins represent a great way to join the sbt community, both through improving existing plugins and submitting your own. It's through the community that sbt is able to expand its reach to many varieties of build tasks. Now go and discover how to publish your projects and plugins so that the world can use them.

Part 5

Deploying your projects

In the final section, you'll learn how to distribute your project. We'll examine different deployment options, and how you can determine which one is right for you.

Distributing your projects

This chapter covers

- Common methods of deploying JVM applications
- Publishing common libraries/artifacts into a company repository
- Generating a zip-based distribution
- Creating a Linux distribution

One of the most important and often overlooked aspects of software development is deployment. No project is useful in pure code form: it must be given to others. The best way to distribute your code generally depends on several factors, including what the code is intended to do. Is the code a library? Does it define a service? Is it meant to be run in a cluster? In addition, the tools available for running programs can alter whether a given deployment option is a good idea.

The key rule of any build administrator is to ensure the requirements of all the stakeholders of a build are met. Builds are generally a key bridge between three things: the developer, the machine, and the system administrator. This chapter focuses on the handoff between the developers and the system administrators.

In this chapter we'll cover two types of projects and a few deployment options for libraries and services. Figure 12.1 shows a simple decision tree for determining how to deploy libraries and services. sbt's default build is optimized for the right

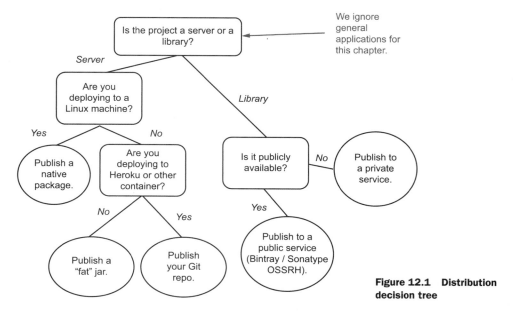

Figure 12.1   Distribution decision tree

side of the decision tree: publishing private and public libraries. First we'll look at the hooks to do this for library code you'd like to share between projects.

12.1   *Publishing a library*

One of the most touted benefits of using software libraries, languages, and frameworks is that of code reuse. But code reuse usually means distributing libraries in a way that others can consume. For JVM projects (Java, Scala, Groovy, and Clojure), this means publishing Maven artifacts to a Maven repository, either an internal company repository or the open source Maven Central repository of libraries.

The default build in sbt is optimized for publishing open source libraries to Maven repositories. The built-in `package` task automatically takes your code and creates a jar file containing the .class files for the project and any resources defined for the build. This means that with almost zero configuration, sbt is able to build publishable artifacts for library authors. There are three mechanisms to publish within sbt, as shown in table 12.1.

Table 12.1   Mechanisms for publishing within sbt

`publish`	Publishes the project's artifacts to a remote repository (Maven or Ivy)
`publishLocal`	Publishes the project's artifacts to the local machine's shared Ivy repository for use with other local projects
`publishM2`	Publishes the project's artifacts to the local machine's Maven cache for use with other local Maven projects

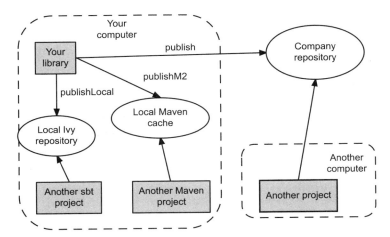

Figure 12.2 Library distribution and consumption

Each of these tasks represents a different mechanism for integrating your library with other projects. Figure 12.2 offers another way to view these publish tasks.

As figure 12.2 shows, the different publish tasks go to different locations. Although the local Ivy repository and the local Maven cache are well-defined locations, the publish task is flexible in where it can publish, and it's also the most important of the three. The publish task is how you ensure artifacts from one developer are usable by other developers.

Let's go back to the preowned-kittens project, where the team has grown large. You'd like to have one developer working on the core library while the other developers work on either the analytics or the website. The first thing to do is pull the core libraries into their own Git repository and give them their own build:

```
name := "core-library"

organization := "com.preowned-kittens"

version := "1.0.1"

libraryDependencies += "junit" % "junit" % "4.10" % "test"
```

The build currently only defines information about the library. It's using sbt's default configuration for building, and it depends on JUnit for testing. Now you'd like to publish the new core library you've created so that you can try to use it in your other builds. The first decision to make is whether to publish to Maven or Ivy. Generally, publishing to Maven is the best (and default) option because more tools are compatible with Maven repositories. But the publish style can be customized with the publish-MavenStyle setting.

Next you need a location to publish the library so that everyone knows where and how to find it. Generally, Ivy and Maven repositories are HTTP services where files can be downloaded or POST/PUT-ed. These serve as central locations where all shared binary artifacts are distributed/used among team members.

Because this is your first time sharing binary artifacts for the preowned-kittens team, you'll purchase a new Artifactory Online account and run a remote artifactory. By default, this comes with some repositories you can publish to. For our purposes, the URL of the repository is http://preowned-kittens.artifactoryonline.com/preowned-kittens/mvn-releases. When publishing, the documentation for your repository manager or company should give you the URL of where you publish. To configure the publish location in the preowned-kittens project, add the following to the build.sbt file:

```
publishTo := Some("preowned-kittens-release" at "http://prowned-
    kittens.artifactoryonline.com/preowned-kittens/mvn-releases")
```

Because you're publishing to a Maven repository, the only other configuration you need is the credentials (username/password) for your account. These credentials are needed to publish the artifacts, but they don't belong in the project itself. sbt provides a means to configure these credentials for your build without having to check them into source control to run: place the configuration inside the global directory.

sbt, by default, will load build settings from .sbt files in the ~/.sbt/0.13/ directory. This means that for all your sbt projects, you can create a set of settings that will be applied to all of them. For publishing, create a ~/.sbt/0.13/users.sbt file with the following:

```
credentials += Credentials("Artifactory Realm", "preowned-
    kittens.artifactoryonline.com", "joe.developer", "my-encrypted-
    passphrase")
```

This will add the artifactory credentials to every project you load with sbt, allowing you to publish as needed. The credentials are composed of four parts:

- *The realm*—The challenge string issued by the HTTP server when it asks for a password
- *The host*—The hostname of the server the credentials are for
- *The username*—Your Artifactory Online username
- *The passphrase*—Your Artifactory Online passphrase

Most remote repositories require credentials, but those that don't should be considered suspect. As of sbt 0.13.5, if a repository requires credentials that aren't configured properly, you'll see an error message like this:

```
> publish
…
[error] Unable to find credentials for [ArtifactoryRealm @ preowned-
    kittens.artifactoryonline.com]
[error]   Is one of these realms mispelled for host preowned-
    kittens.artifactoryonline.com]:
[error]   * ArtifactoryRelam
```

In this error message, you can see the HTTP authentication realm requested and all the configured credentials within sbt. This should help identify whether or not credentials are configured and what authentication realm the server is requesting.

12.2 *Publishing locally*

Now that you have the account, you can push your library to all other developers within the company. But sometimes you want to test the library changes locally against dependent projects before pushing to other developers. For example, when adding a new validation method to the analytics library, you'd like to run the analytics test suite to ensure this new API doesn't break the downstream projects. sbt has the notion of a local repository to solve this problem.

The local repository is a directory on your computer (<HOME>/.ivy2/local) where artifacts from all local builds can be pushed and seen by other sbt projects. This means you can pretend to publish a library on your machine and have other builds see it.

Take a look at the publishLocal task on the preowned-kittens build:

```
$ sbt
> publishLocal
...
[info] Done packaging.
[info] Packaging /home/jsuereth/projects/sbt-in-action/chapter11/analytics/
       target/scala-2.10/analytics_2.10-1.0.jar ...
[info] Done packaging.
[info]     published website_2.10 to /home/jsuereth/.ivy2/local/
    com.preownedkittens/website_2.10/1.0/poms/website_2.10.pom
[info]     published website_2.10 to /home/jsuereth/.ivy2/local/
    com.preownedkittens/website_2.10/1.0/jars/website_2.10.jar
[info]     published website_2.10 to /home/jsuereth/.ivy2/local/
    com.preownedkittens/website_2.10/1.0/srcs/website_2.10-sources.jar
[info]     published website_2.10 to /home/jsuereth/.ivy2/local/
    com.preownedkittens/website_2.10/1.0/docs/website_2.10-javadoc.jar
[info]     published ivy to /home/jsuereth/.ivy2/local/com.preownedkittens/
    website_2.10/1.0/ivys/ivy.xml
[info]     published analytics_2.10 to /home/jsuereth/.ivy2/local/
    com.preownedkittens/analytics_2.10/1.0/poms/analytics_2.10.pom
[info]     published analytics_2.10 to /home/jsuereth/.ivy2/local/
    com.preownedkittens/analytics_2.10/1.0/jars/analytics_2.10.jar
[info]     published analytics_2.10 to /home/jsuereth/.ivy2/local/
    com.preownedkittens/analytics_2.10/1.0/srcs/analytics_2.10-sources.jar
[info]     published analytics_2.10 to /home/jsuereth/.ivy2/local/
    com.preownedkittens/analytics_2.10/1.0/docs/analytics_2.10-javadoc.jar
[info]     published ivy to /home/jsuereth/.ivy2/local/com.preownedkittens/
    analytics_2.10/1.0/ivys/ivy.xml
```

Here you can see that the artifacts are pushed into the /home/jsuereth/.ivy2/local directory with a similar layout to what you'd see on the remote Artifactory server. From this point, any resolution on local projects will pick up the releases in the local directory.

Clean-slate development

To minimize cache issues, sometimes it's helpful to clear your ~/.ivy2/local directory to see what other remote developers do. It's generally safe to remove without corrupting your Ivy cache, and doing so ensures that all dependencies you use in your builds come from a remote public/private resource.

12.3   *Publishing a simple server*

You can now distribute libraries both locally and remotely, but we haven't really gotten into the interesting aspect of software: creating an application that can actually run somewhere. Using the Java platform, you have myriad solutions for running software, but we'll focus on two types of deployable applications: those used by a majority of existing sbt builds, as shown in table 12.2.

Table 12.2   Deployable applications

Fat jar	You squish all your binaries and resources into the same jar file that gets pushed out to servers.
Bundle	You grab all binaries and resources and add/combine them with metadata to create an installable bundle. Examples: deb files, rpm files, war files, and msi files.

We already talked about creating fat jars for the website project in chapter 6, and we showed the `sbt-assembly` plugin in section 8.2. Let's look again at how to define a fat jar using the assembly plugin.

To include the assembly plugin, add the following line to plugins.sbt:

```
addSbtPlugin("com.eed3si9n" % "sbt-assembly" % "0.11.2")
```

And add the following configuration to website/build.sbt:

```
import AssemblyKeys._

assemblySettings
```

Now you can call the `assembly` task on the website project and generate a fat jar that can be passed directly to the `java` executable to run your application. This is a super-convenient distribution mechanism, because this one file contains all the necessary dependencies for your application and it's simple to start it up.

A rich ecosystem of plugins

In addition to the assembly plugin, there's also the `one-jar` plugin and the `proguard` plugin that can create fat jars. All of these plugins perform the same work but with different philosophies. `sbt-assembly` has support for merging typesafe-config, which tends to be better for creating play/akka bundles.

Now that the build can bundle your core project as a single jar, you can publish this jar using Ivy in addition to the raw jar. To do this, you'll add the one jar to the set of artifacts that Ivy will publish.

Add the following to the website/build.sbt file:

```
lazy val assemblyArtifact = Def.setting {
  artifact.value.copy(classifier = Some("assembly"))
}

artifacts += assemblyArtifact.value

packagedArtifacts +=
  Assembly -> assemblyArtifact.value
```

> ### Temporary settings
> The first part of this code creates a temporary setting using the `Def.setting` method. A temporary setting is a value that can be used like a setting but that can't be discovered by the user (it never lives inside a key). Temporary settings may depend on other settings and may also be assigned into a setting key later but are otherwise invisible within the setting system.

To publish the assembly jar as an artifact, the first thing to do is create a temporary setting that stores the `sbt.Artifact` instance describing the file you want to publish. This artifact instance is the same as the one used for your normal jar, except you add the classifier `assembly`. For more information on artifacts and classifiers, please check out appendix A, "Ivy."

Once the artifact temporary setting is created, append the value to the list of artifacts published by the analytics project and build a new `sbt.Artifact -> File` mapping for the `packagedArtifacts` task. Now when calling `publish` or any other publish task, Ivy will publish the assembly jar in addition to the regular artifacts.

Next, publish the website jar into the local repository to make sure the configuration is correct. First make sure to reload the sbt build to pull in the new settings; then run `website/publish`:

```
> reload
...
> website/publish
...
[info]      published website_2.10 to http://prewoned-
     kittens.artifactoryonline.com/preowned-kittens/mvn-releases/com/
     preownedkittens/website_2.10/1.0-20140706T223209/website_2.10-
     assembly.jar
...
[success] Total time: 9 s, completed Jul 6, 2014 6:34:17 PM
```

Here you see that the assembly artifact (`website_2.10-assembly.jar`) is pushed into the repository correctly. Now you can use the regular Ivy publish mechanism to release the website.

12.4 *Generating a distribution*

Every project eventually gets deployed somewhere, be it on a user's machine or to some server or cloud. Although there are numerous platforms that can host applications, the sbt community has slowly been standardizing on one mechanism of generating distributions: the `sbt-native-packager` plugin.

The `sbt-native-packager` plugin provides a means to describe your application and hooks to bundle it for various runtimes, including these:

- RedHat/CentOS RPMs
- Debian/Ubuntu DEB packages
- Windows MSIs (w/ Windows Service Support)
- Docker packages
- Raw zip/tgz bundles

You'd like to get the `preowned-kittens analytics` project distributed and running in production. This project is a server that will every so often update your owner-to-kitten match index for the website to use.

You'll set up the `sbt-native-packager` to deploy the `preowned-kittens analytics` server project, first as a raw zip that can be handed off to the devops team at preowned-kittens.com. To start, you need to add the `sbt-native-packager` plugin to the project.

First create the project/packager.sbt file with the following contents:

```
addSbtPlugin("com.typesafe.sbt" % "sbt-native-packager" % "0.7.1")
```

Next you need to enable the native packager for the `analytics` project so that its tasks and settings to generate a zip are available.

> **Transitionary plugins**
>
> As of the writing of this book, the native packager has not been converted from the old-style plugins to the new `AutoPlugin` interface. Thus, details of this plugin may deviate from how upgraded plugins are used within sbt.

First open the analytics/build.sbt file and add the following to the top of the file:

```
import com.typesafe.sbt.SbtNativePackager._
import NativePackagerKeys._
```

These are the imports of utility keys used by the native packager. This ensures that the helper methods from the native packager are callable without the long package prefix. Next add the following to the bottom of the analytics/build.sbt file :

```
//-----------
// Packaging
//-----------

mainClass := Some("org.preownedkittens.Analytics")

packageArchetype.java_server
```

The comment denotes to future readers that the next section of build configuration is about packaging. The first setting declares the `main` class for the project explicitly. Although sbt will automatically detect a `main` class if it exists, it's a good idea to pick one. Later you'll write this `main` class to start up the analytics server.

The next line is `packageArchetype.java_server`. This provides all the settings required by the `sbt-native-packager` to package the analytics project as a server. This means the native packager will automatically construct startup/shutdown hooks for platforms it understands, as well as generate a start script for the project.

You can immediately try out the native packager by running the `stage` task in the sbt console. Here's the output from the sbt terminal :

```
> stage
[info] Wrote /home/jsuereth/projects/sbt-in-action/chapter12/analytics/
    target/scala-2.10/analytics_2.10-1.0-20140706T191954.pom
[info] Packaging /home/jsuereth/projects/sbt-in-action/chapter12/common/
    target/scala-2.10/common_2.10-1.0-20140706T191954.jar ...
[info] Done packaging.
[info] Main Scala API documentation to /home/jsuereth/projects/sbt-in-action/
    chapter12/analytics/target/scala-2.10/api...
model contains 5 documentable templates
[info] Main Scala API documentation successful.
[info] Packaging /home/jsuereth/projects/sbt-in-action/chapter12/analytics/
    target/scala-2.10/analytics_2.10-1.0-20140706T191954-javadoc.jar ...
[info] Done packaging.
[info] Wrote /home/jsuereth/projects/sbt-in-action/chapter12/common/target/
    scala-2.10/common_2.10-1.0-20140706T191954.pom
```

The `stage` task creates the same directory layout as the final distribution but in the local target directory. For the `analytics` project, the staged release is located in analytics/target/universal/stage/ with the following contents :

```
$ tree analytics/target/universal/stage/
analytics/target/universal/stage/
??? bin
?   ??? analytics
?   ??? analytics.bat
??? lib
    ??? com.preownedkittens.analytics-1.0-20140706T195759.jar
    ??? com.preownedkittens.common-1.0-20140706T195759.jar
    ??? org.scala-lang.scala-library-2.10.4.jar
```

This is known as the universal distribution from the native packager. It includes all the underlying jar files used by the project, as well as start scripts for all known platforms, as shown in table 12.3.

Script	Format	Platform Supported
analytics	Bash	Linux (all) Mac OS X Windows (cygwin)
analytics.bat	CMD.exe	Windows (all)

Table 12.3 Supported platforms by script

Now that the script has been created, you can try it out in the Linux terminal (exit out of sbt if needed):

$ ./analytics/target/universal/stage/bin/analytics

```
Running analytics....
```

Currently, the project prints that it's running and quits. That's because the current implementation, which we didn't show before, prints out that it's running and quits. Here's the current server main method:

analytics/src/main/scala/main.scala

```
package org.preownedkittens

object Analytics {
  def main(args: Array[String]): Unit = {
    println("Running analytics....")
  }
}
```

Now that you have the basic packaging working, the devops team at preowned-kittens has asked to be able to alter the configuration for the application. But you haven't actually exposed any configuration!

You'll start getting the configuration files in place for the project. To add files to the package, you can place them in the src/universal directory. Any directories found underneath src/universal are preserved. In addition, creating a conf directory has special meaning to the sbt-native-packager plugin. Any directory called conf is automatically treated specifically as configuration when generating native packages for various platforms, which you'll see in section 12.5.

First you need to create a configuration.properties file:

analytics/src/universal/conf/analytics.properties

```
database.url=jdbc:derby:/tmp/dummy.db;create=true
```

Now, from the Linux command line, run sbt stage and see where this file winds up in the package:

```
$ sbt stage
$ tree analytics/target/universal/stage/
analytics/target/universal/stage/
??? bin
?   ??? analytics
?   ??? analytics.bat
??? conf
?   ??? analytics.properties
??? lib
    ??? com.preownedkittens.analytics-1.0-20140706T195759.jar
    ??? com.preownedkittens.common-1.0-20140706T195759.jar
    ??? org.scala-lang.scala-library-2.10.4.jar
```

Both the conf directory and the analytics.properties file show up in the distribution. The next step is to figure out how to get the server to find and read this file.

The sbt native packager is autogenerating the shell script, which starts the project. The `sbt-native-packager` documentation (http://www.scala-sbt.org/sbt-native-packager/archetypes/java_app/customize.html) outlines a few hooks to the scripts, primarily via Java properties. Let's use these hooks to pass the installed location of configuration to the running application. Add the following lines to the analytics/build.sbt file:

```
bashScriptExtraDefines += """addJava "-Danalytics.properties=${app_home}/../
    conf/analytics.properties""""

batScriptExtraDefines += """set _JAVA_OPTS=%_JAVA_OPTS% -
    Danalytics.properties=%ANALYTICS_HOME%\\conf\\analytics.properties"""
```

These two definitions add code into the generated .bat or bash file. The new code interacts with the autogenerated script to ensure the following option is passed when your application is started:

```
-Danalytics.properties=/path/to/distribution/conf/analytics.properties.
```

Inside the `analytics` project, this setting can be used to find the correct properties file.

Now you need to read in the new properties configuration file. Modify analytics/src/main/scala/main.scala to the following:

```
package org.preownedkittens

import java.io._
import java.util.Properties

object Analytics {
  def main(args: Array[String]): Unit = {
    val propsFile = new File(sys.props("analytics.properties"))
    val props = new Properties
    val in = new FileInputStream(propsFile)
    try props.load(in)
    finally in.close()
      println("Running analytics....")
      println(s"* database: ${props.get("database.url")}")
  }
}
```

This changes the simple server main script to load the properties file using the configured system property, and then it prints the result of reading the database file value after loading.

To test whether the configuration is making it to runtime, you first need to restart/reload the sbt terminal and then run `stage` again:

```
    $ sbt
    > stage
    > exit
    $ ./analytics/target/universal/stage/bin/analytics
Running analytics....
* database: jdbc:derby:/tmp/dummy.db;create=true
```

Now you can see that the analytics server is able to find and load the properties file. You can add all the configuration hooks that the system administrators for preowned-kittens.com have been asking for.

Packaging for Heroku

For those who use Heroku to deploy servers, the `sbt-native-packager stage` task is used by the Heroku build pack. Heroku and the `sbt-native-packager` make a great way to prototype and deploy services you'd like to test.

Once you're comfortable with the look of the analytics/target/universal/stage directory, you can generate a zip file for the system admins to use. To do so, run the `universal:packageBin` task:

```
> analytics/universal:packageBin
...
[info] /home/jsuereth/projects/sbt-in-action/sbt-in-action-examples/
     chapter12/analytics/target/universal/analytics-1.0-20140709T133026.zip
[success] Total time: 8 s, completed Jul 9, 2014 9:30:39 AM
```

Here you can see that an analytics/target/universal/analytics-1.0-20140709T133026 .zip file was created. This zip has the same contents as the staging directory and can be directly passed off to the DevOps or system administrators.

12.5   *Creating a Linux distribution*

Those pesky system admins have been complaining that the zip file you've been sending them is hard to automate and install. They'd prefer a Debian package file, because the preowned-kittens.com site is run on Debian servers.

The `sbt-native-packager` comes with baked-in support for Debian. First you should ensure you have the `dpkg` command-line tool available on your system. For Ubuntu, it's as simple as running `apt-get install dpkg`. Try it out by running the `debian:packageBin` task in the sbt console:

```
> debian:packageBin
[trace] Stack trace suppressed: run last analytics/debian:debianControlFile
     for the full output.
[error] (analytics/debian:debianControlFile) packageDescription in Debian
     cannot be empty. Use
[error]   packageDescription in Debian := "My package Description"
[error] Total time: 1 s, completed Jul 6, 2014 4:52:49 PM
>
```

This error is telling you that you haven't fully configured all the information required to generate a proper Debian file. After reading the `sbt-native-packager` docs for what Debian requires (http://www.scala-sbt.org/sbt-native-packager/DetailedTopics/ debian.html#plain-debian-packaging), you'll see that you need to add the following to the end of analytics/build.sbt:

```
maintainer := "Josh Suereth <pet-them-all@preowned-kittens.com>"

packageSummary := "Analytics server for prewoned-kittens.com"

packageDescription := """Contains the analytics of kitten-owner
    compatibilities."""
```

Now reload sbt and rerun the `debian:packageBin` task:

```
> reload
...
> debian:packageBin
...
[info] Altering postrm/postinst files to add user analytics and group
    analytics
[info] dpkg-deb: building package 'analytics' in '/home/jsuereth/projects/
    sbt-in-action/chapter12/analytics/target/analytics-1.0-
    20140706T211050.deb'.
[success] Total time: 4 s, completed Jul 6, 2014 5:10:57 PM
```

Hooray, you have an installable Debian file! If you look at the context, you can see it includes a lot of Debian-specific additions. Here's the list of files that are used to generate the package:

```
$ tree analytics/target/analytics-1.0-20140706T210759/
analytics/target/analytics-1.0-20140706T210759/
??? DEBIAN
?   ??? conffiles
?   ??? control
?   ??? md5sums
?   ??? postinst
?   ??? postrm
?   ??? prerm
??? etc
?   ??? analytics -> /usr/share/analytics/conf
?   ??? default
?   ?   ??? analytics
?   ??? init
?       ??? analytics.conf
??? usr
?   ??? bin
?   ?   ??? analytics -> /usr/share/analytics/bin/analytics
?   ??? share
?       ??? analytics
?           ??? bin
?           ?   ??? analytics
?           ??? conf
?           ?   ??? analytics.properties
?           ??? lib
?           ?   ??? <analytics jar>
?           ?   ??? <commons jar>
?           ?   ??? <scala jar>
?           ??? logs -> /var/log/analytics
??? var
    ??? log
```

```
?   ??? analytics
??? run
    ??? analytics
```

In addition to placing the universal package, `wholesale`, in the /usr/bin/analytics location, the native packager adds the files listed in table 12.4.

Table 12.4   **Additional files generated**

File/Directory	Purpose
/usr/bin/analytics	Symlink to the Bash script in /usr/share/analytics/bin/analytics. Ensures the analytics server shows up in the path of Debian.
/var/log/analytics	Location to dump log files.
/var/log/run/analytics	Location used to store active process ID in Debian server start scripts.
/etc/analytics	Symlink to the configuration directory /usr/share/analytics/conf/. Ensures system admins find configuration files in expected location.
/etc/default/analytics	Server start configuration file. This file is an upstart convention.
/etc/init/analytics.conf	Upstart configuration. Ensures your server is started at startup with this Linux system.
DEBIAN/*all files*	Raw configuration files used by the `dpkg` tool to generate the Debian package.

That's a lot of generated files! The benefit is that most of the fine-tuned controls that system administrators need are included in these files, including mechanisms to tune memory and properties.

But the system administrators have a new complaint: your Debian file doesn't declare any dependencies, so they don't know which version of Java to install! You'll add a dependency to the package so that you require a compatible JRE to be installed that your package can use to run the server.

Add the following to analytics/build.sbt :

```
debianPackageDependencies in Debian ++=
  Seq("java7-runtime-headless", "bash")
```

This line configures dependencies on other Debian packages. A survey of the Debian ecosystem shows that all JRE packages are required to provide a virtual package called `javaX-runtime-headless`, where `X` denotes the major version of Java. `java7-runtime-headless` denotes that your server relies on the existence of a Java7 JRE but doesn't require any of the Swing UI hooks. The second dependency requires the Bash program to run the startup script.

Now the `analytics` project is fully configured to be deployed on a Debian server.

> **What Debian packages can you use?**
>
> If you're running a Debian system, you can use the `dpkg-query -1` command to display installed packages, including descriptions. Additionally, you can go to the https://www.debian.org/distrib/packages website to find available packages per Debian distribution.

12.6 Summary

In this chapter, you learned how to

- Publish common libraries into a shared repository
- Create fat jar distributions that can be published to a shared repository
- Generate a native Debian package, complete with dependency specifications

These techniques are super-valuable to ensure a successful project launch and continued health. As stated previously, builds are a key bridge between three entities: the developer, the machine, and the system administrator. This chapter focused on the handoff between the developers and the system administrators.

When designing packaging, remember the following:

- Does this software get used by other developers?
- Deploy a shared library.
- Does this software get deployed in production?
- Negotiate with the system administrator on what they need.

While this chapter only covered creating fat jars and deploying Debian packages, there are many other mechanisms of building and deploying your software. We recommend checking out the plugins shown in table 12.5, depending on need.

Table 12.5 Plugins for building and deploying software

Plugin	Description
`sbt-native-packager`	Windows MSIs, Linux RPMs or DEBs and Docker images
`sbt-assembly`	Fat jars
`sbt-app-bundle`	OS X bundles
`xsbt-web-plugin`	WAR files
`xsbt-proguard-plugin`	Obfuscated/minified fat jars (Android)

appendix A:
What you need
to know about Ivy

Modern software development on the JVM makes heavy use of automated dependency resolution and management. This is where instead of downloading jar files and dumping them into your project, a tool is responsible for determining which jar files are needed by your dependencies and automatically resolves these jars for use in your build.

There are two alternative dependency resolution libraries for Java: Aether and Ivy. Aether is extracted from the build tool known as Maven, whereas Ivy was built from scratch. Both tools are able to interoperate with each other to some extent; albeit, there are some fundamentally different concepts to each. sbt makes use of Ivy for some of its advanced features.

Let's take a quick look at the core concepts in Ivy and how they show up inside sbt.

A.1   Modules

The module is the fundamental unit of released project in Ivy. A module is made up of three things: identification information, a set of artifacts, and a set of configurations. The identification information is used to find modules within repositories. The artifacts are the actual files (for example, jars) that were associated with the project. The set of configurations defines the grouping of artifacts. For example, the configuration `test` would contain all artifacts used for testing.

Let's start digging into module identification.

A.2   Module identification

The identification information consists of three core attributes:

- *Organization*—An identification for the company, team, or individual responsible for a project. Usually it's a reverse domain name, like com.typesafe or org.apache.
- *Name*—Identifies the name of a project within an organization. Examples are junit and akka-actors.
- *Version*—A version number for the project.

240

In sbt, you specify this information via the three-form % syntax you've seen before; for example:

```
libraryDependencies += "com.typesafe" % "config" % "1.0.2"
```

In this sbt setting, the configuration module is represented with organization of `com.typesafe`, a name of `config`, and a version of `1.0.2`.

Although this represents the core information about modules, modules may also have additional attributes used to uniquely identify themselves. For example, sbt adds these additional attributes when publishing/resolving sbt plugins:

- `sbtVersion`—The version of sbt used to compile the plugin
- `scalaVersion`—The version of Scala used to compile the plugin

These additional attributes help distinguish between, for example, the sbt-pgp-plugin version 0.9 for sbt 0.12 and the sbt-pgp-plugin version 0.9 for sbt 0.13. Although these two modules share the same organization/name/value, the contents of the jar file artifacts are different and must be resolved differently.

These extra attributes are added via the convenience method `addSbtPlugin`:

```
addSbtPlugin("com.jsuereth" % "sbt-pgp" % "0.6")
```

This method automatically appends the extra configuration for the current sbt and Scala versions. But you can specify these directly using the following method:

```
"com.jsuereth" % "sbt-pgp" % "0.6" extra ("scalaVersion" -> "2.10",
    "sbtVersion" -> "0.13")
```

This syntax comes in handy if you're using a sbt plugin as a library because you'll need these extra attributes for Ivy to properly resolve the external plugin.

A.3 Artifacts

Artifacts in Ivy are the single files associated with the module. Examples of artifacts include the jar library for a project, documentation bundles, or testing code.

Artifacts carry their own identification, consisting of the following:

- *Name*—The name of this file within the module distribution.
- *Type*—The type identifies the purpose of the artifact within the module. Examples of type identifiers include conf, jar, docs, srcs, dll, and sql. sbt directly uses this value to determine which artifacts should be included on the classpath. See the `classpathTypes` setting for more information.
- *Extension*—This identifies a specific filename extension if the type of the artifact doesn't make this clear. Examples include html, tar.gz, and zip.

A.4 Differences in Ivy and Maven

Although sbt uses Ivy, Maven remains a popular build tool with its own abstraction around modules and artifacts. Whereas Ivy requires all artifacts to be specified in the metadata for projects, Maven leaves additional artifacts unspecified. This leads to extra download requests when trying to resolve what artifacts exist. In Maven, this resolution is on demand, but for Ivy to generate the full module config it must do it up front. sbt has custom hooks into Ivy that disable the automatic lookup for sources/javadocs. If you wish to reconstruct the full artifact information, you need to run the updateClassifiers command.

Although the artifact name and type can to some extent specify the intended use of an artifact, this doesn't qualify the *aggregate* intent of the artifacts. Aggregate intent means that several artifacts should be used together or included together for some purpose. For example, I may include native libraries (DLLs, SOs, or jnilibs) separately from my jar as artifacts, but they're both part of the library. To associate these artifacts together, use configurations.

A.5   *Configuration*

Configurations represent groupings of artifacts and dependencies. For example, if I'm deploying software that may be used within a servlet container or standalone, I can provide the dependencies and artifacts differently for these two scenarios, using different configurations.

More importantly, I can deploy all my associated files together. For example, by default sbt will deploy all API documentation and source bundles inside a module via configurations. In Maven or Ant, this behavior must be configured separately.

sbt embraces these configurations in its setup. The configurations used in sbt to delineate tasks also generally align with Ivy configurations. For example, the test configuration in sbt makes use of artifacts resolved into the test configuration of Ivy, by convention.

When specifying library dependencies in sbt, there's an optional configuration setting you can include. You've seen this when specifying test dependencies like the following:

```
libraryDependencies += "org.specs2" % "specs2_2.10" % "1.14" % "test"
```

The last string in the % sequence denotes how artifacts in the remote module should be mapped into the local configuration. So far, you've used sbt's shorthand for Ivy configuration mappings on dependencies. Table A.1 lists example sbt configuration settings, how these map to Ivy configuration mappings, and what these mean. A good way to read the mapping string "A->B" is "my A uses their B."

Table A.1   Ivy configurations and classpaths

sbt configuration	Ivy mapping	Meaning
N/A	compile->compile	The remote's compile artifacts in your local project's compile configuration.
runtime	runtime->compile	The remote's compile artifacts are used when running the local project, but not for compilation.

Table A.1 Ivy configurations and classpaths (*continued*)

sbt configuration	Ivy mapping	Meaning
`test`	`test->compile`	The remote's compile artifacts are used when compiling/running the local tests.
`test->test`	`test->test`	The remote's testing artifacts are used when building/running your tests.

For all practical purposes, sbt and Ivy perform a mapping of artifacts into various groupings, which sbt will use when compiling/running/testing your project. Figure A.1 offers another look at what's happening.

In this example, we show how remote dependencies are mapped to the local configuration buckets. specs2 is being added to the compile bucket, while Junit is being added to the `test` bucket. When sbt goes to compile, it grabs, among other buckets, the default bucket and uses the jars it finds. In this case, specs2 will be included as a dependency of your main project and used for your main project, whereas JUnit is used only when compiling/running tests. In both examples, you're taking the default artifacts from each module and using them.

But if you wanted to pull the testing classes from another project, as long as that project publishes its tests, you can do so using the `test->test` syntax. This solves one of the greatest annoyances of trying to share code in unit tests between two projects. Now that you understand how to specify artifacts and dependencies and map these files to the appropriate buckets within sbt, let's talk about the most important piece: how you obtain remote dependencies.

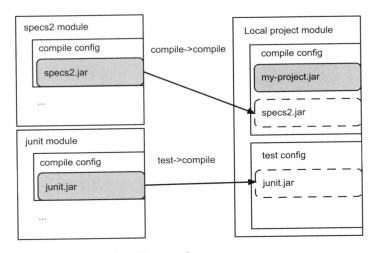

Figure A.1 Ivy configuration mappings

Lost in translation

When attempting to publish to Maven repositories, some of Ivy's features simply don't exist in Maven. Advanced configuration mapping is one such item. Most configuration mappings will be lost when publishing your project to a Maven repository.

A.6   *Resolvers*

Resolvers are the means of finding and (optionally) downloading module dependencies for a project. In sbt, resolvers are usually defined using two components:

- *The protocol*—How you download/find artifacts. Are they on the local disk? Do you use HTTP? SSH?
- *The layout*—Where artifacts are stored on the medium. In sbt this is usually done through the use of patterns.

sbt provides a set of built-in support for defining Ivy resolvers using patterns and protocols. This is done through the `sbt.Resolver` object, which has the helpers listed in table A.2.

Table A.2   sbt resolver types

Resolver	Protocol	Example Setting

file	Read from local files	`resolvers += Resolver.file(`
		`            name= "name",`
		`            baseDirector=file("/share/repo")`
		`) (Resolver.defaultIvypatterns)`

url	Read from HTTP server	`resolvers += Resolver.url(`
		`            name = "name",`
		`            url = "http://ivyserver.mycompany.com"`
		`) (Resolver.defaultIvyPatterns)`

ssh	Connect to remote file-system over SSH	`resolvers += Resolver.ssh(`
		`            name = "name",`
		`            hostname = "ivyserver.mycompany.com",`
		`            port = 22,`
		`            basepath = "/share/ivyrepo"`
		`) (Resolver.defaultIvyPatterns)`

sftp	Connect to remote FTP server	`resolvers += Resolver.sftp(`
		`            name = "name",`
		`            hostname = "ivyftp.mycompany.com"`
		`) (Resolver.defaultIvyPatterns)`

All of these examples use the resolver's `defaultIvyPatterns` setting to define where Ivy looks for files. Take a look at this in figure A.2.

Here the path of a repository is configured using [] blocks defining where each data item exists on the repository. Given this default path, let's see what a file-based

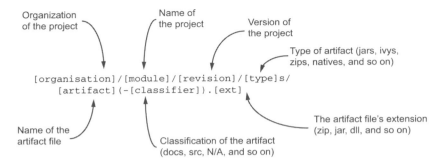

Figure A.2 Default resolver pattern

repository will look like for the `preowned-kittens` analytics project. Assuming you're looking into a directory, figure A.3 shows the path and files that would exist after publishing the `analytics` project.

As shown in figure A.3, the patterns defined previously are used to define the location of files in the file-based repository. Given the set of remote protocols and a pattern-based approach, sbt remains pretty flexible in how it can resolve or publish files.

Although this is the main way to configure sbt out of the box, it's still possible to dive into Ivy itself and create a custom resolver that can pull artifacts from anything, as long as the interface is extended properly.

sbt also includes special support for resolving from Maven repositories. This can be done using the `at` method added to strings; for example:

```
resolvers += "My Company Repository" at "http://repo.mycompany.com/repo"
```

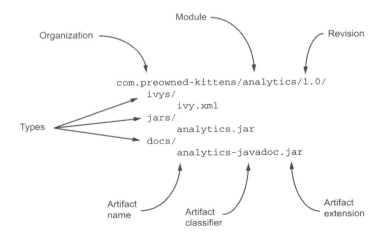

Figure A.3 Example file repository for default resolver

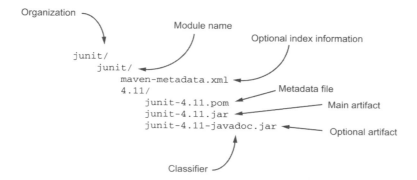

Figure A.4   Example Maven repository layout

Here you give the resolver a name and then specify the URI (which could be a local file) that indicates where to find artifacts using the Maven method. Maven repositories all have a similar format, which for the Junit artifact looks like figure A.4.

The major difference between Ivy and Maven here is that with Maven, the artifacts included with a module aren't explicitly specified and are unable to use different names than the Maven module itself. Although Ivy allows this option, it's not a frequently used feature. Let's look at an example.

Some projects—for example, the Java-COM bridge project, which enables Java-based applications to talk natively to applications written with Microsoft's COM networking—release not just a jar file but also some DLL files that are to be included. In the case of Jacob (the Java-COM bridge library), there are two files in addition to the pom and the jar:

- *x86.dll*—A dll compiled for 32-bit Windows
- *x64.dll*—A dll compiled for 64-bit Windows

This leads to a repository layout of

```
net/sf/jacob-project/
    jacob/
        1.14.3/
            jacob-1.14.3.pom
            jacob-1.14.3.jar
            jacob-1.14.3-x86.dll
            jacob-1.14.3-x64.dll
```

Within Maven, the pom defines the dependencies required for the jar itself, but it leaves no description of dependencies or behavior needed for the DLLs. In Maven, you can depend on the x86 DLLS via the following dependency declaration:

```
<dependency>
<groupId>net.sf.jacob-project</groupId>
<artifactId>jacob</artifactId>
<version>1.14.3</version>
<classifier>x86</classifier>
```

```
<type>dll</type>
    </dependency>
```

The issue here is that the dependencies for this classified/typed artifact are the same as for the jar itself. There's no way to express dependencies from this native DLL to any other. In Ivy, you can resolve this by attaching all x86 DLLs into a configuration and declaring dependencies on modules in other configurations.

For the Jacob project, the ivy.xml would declare three configurations:

- *default*—The configuration from which to find the Java artifacts
- *win-x86*—The configuration from which to find the x86-friendly DLLs
- *win-x64*—The configuration from which to find the x64-friendly DLLs

These configurations can depend on other configurations using the A->B syntax of Ivy. To include the x64 DLLs in the compile configuration of your project (similar to the previous Maven definition) you'd use the following line:

```
libraryDependencies += "org.specs2" % "specs2_2.10" % "1.14" % "compile->win-
    x64"
```

> **NOTE** This would work only if Jacob were deployed using Ivy's configuration feature. Although sbt attempts to adapt most Maven conventions into Ivy configurations (like source/javadoc jars), there's little consistency in how native DLLs, SOs, and JNILIBs are deployed, so this line won't function without first republishing Jacob.

In practice you can usually publish to either an Ivy or a Maven repository with no impact to your project. Using configurations and having the full description of all included files in the ivy.xml is an advanced feature that few projects use.

The second difference between Ivy and Maven is the use of optional index metadata files. In the previous example, there's a maven-metadata.xml file that's used to record the following:

- The various version numbers stored in the repository for this module
- The time the file was generated

This information is used to help speed up version searches when using a version range to specify a dependency. A version range in Maven is a way of saying, "I'd like any version between the 3.2 release and the 4.0 release but not 4.0 itself." Version ranges are generally accepted as being dangerous for these reasons:

- *They lead to unrepeatable builds.* If a project releases a new version, your published module and its dependencies will suddenly start using it. This can cause a once successfully building project to start breaking and is hard to track down.
- *They can (sometimes dramatically) slow down resolution.* Maven or Ivy will have to constantly check to see if new versions have been released, leading to increased HTTP calls.

Now that you know the core concepts of Ivy, let's look at the most important thing to know: how to resolve dependency conflicts.

A.7   *Resolving dependency conflicts*

It's an inevitable reality of depending on external projects that eventually there will be a scenario where two dependencies conflict over a third version of a dependency they require. For example, the `preowned-kittens analytics` project uses the Scala logging for Project and, perhaps, Hibernate. Both of these projects rely on SLF4J. Now you have to figure out the following:

- Is there a compatible version of the protocol buffers library that both Akka and Hadoop can use?
- What incantations do you need to put into sbt so that these versions are used instead of the automatically resolved dependencies?

In most conflicting dependency scenarios, Ivy is smart enough to handle the resolution for you. Let's take a look. First you'll make a simple analytics build file to demonstrate the issue, as in the following listing.

Listing A.1   build.sbt with dependency conflicts

```
name := "preowned-kittens"

version := "1.0"

resolvers += "maven-restlet" at "http://maven.restlet.org"

libraryDependencies += "org.specs2" % "specs2_2.10" % "1.14" % "test"

libraryDependencies += "org.hibernate" % "hibernate-core" % "3.6.7.Final"

libraryDependencies += "com.typesafe" %% "scalalogging-slf4j" % "1.0.1"
```

In this build, you rely on three libraries: specs2 for testing, Hibernate Core for persistence, and Scala-logging for logging. Hibernate and Scala-logging both rely on different versions of SLF4J. You can run the `update` command in sbt to see if Ivy is able to resolve the conflict, as shown in the next listing.

Listing A.2   Resolving Ivy dependencies in the sbt console

```
> update
[info] Updating {file:/home/jsuereth/projects/sbt-in-action/sbt-in-action-
    examples/appendix-c/}appendix-c...
[info] Resolving org.fusesource.jansi#jansi;1.4 ...
[info] downloading http://repo1.maven.org/maven2/org/hibernate/hibernate-
    core/3.6.7.Final/hibernate-core-3.6.7.Final.jar ...
[info]     [SUCCESSFUL ] org.hibernate#hibernate-core;3.6.7.Final!hibernate-
    core.jar (3391ms)
[info] downloading http://repo1.maven.org/maven2/antlr/antlr/2.7.6/antlr-
    2.7.6.jar ...
[info]     [SUCCESSFUL ] antlr#antlr;2.7.6!antlr.jar (471ms)
[info] downloading http://repo1.maven.org/maven2/commons-collections/commons-
    collections/3.1/commons-collections-3.1.jar ...
[info]     [SUCCESSFUL ] commons-collections#commons-collections;3.1!commons-
    collections.jar (586ms)
```

```
[info] downloading http://repo1.maven.org/maven2/org/hibernate/hibernate-
    commons-annotations/3.2.0.Final/hibernate-commons-annotations-
    3.2.0.Final.jar ...
[info]      [SUCCESSFUL ] org.hibernate#hibernate-commons-
    annotations;3.2.0.Final!hibernate-commons-annotations.jar (189ms)
[info] downloading http://repo1.maven.org/maven2/org/hibernate/javax/
    persistence/hibernate-jpa-2.0-api/1.0.1.Final/hibernate-jpa-2.0-api-
    1.0.1.Final.jar ...
[info]      [SUCCESSFUL ]
```

Ivy appears to have successfully resolved the conflict. But it's still a bit unclear, not knowing enough about Ivy, what it actually did. Take a look at the resolution report logs, which sbt dumps into the target/resolution-cache/reports/ directory:

```
$ ls target/resolution-cache/reports/
ivy-report.css
ivy-report.xsl
preowned-kittens-preowned-kittens_2.10-provided.xml
preowned-kittens-preowned-kittens_2.10-runtime-internal.xml
preowned-kittens-preowned-kittens_2.10-compile-internal.xml   preowned-
    kittens-preowned-kittens_2.10-runtime.xml
preowned-kittens-preowned-kittens_2.10-compile.xml            preowned-
    kittens-preowned-kittens_2.10-scala-tool.xml
preowned-kittens-preowned-kittens_2.10-docs.xml              preowned-
    kittens-preowned-kittens_2.10-sources.xml
preowned-kittens-preowned-kittens_2.10-optional.xml          preowned-
    kittens-preowned-kittens_2.10-test-internal.xml
preowned-kittens-preowned-kittens_2.10-plugin.xml            preowned-
    kittens-preowned-kittens_2.10-test.xml
preowned-kittens-preowned-kittens_2.10-pom.xml
```

There's one xml file that describes the Ivy resolution for each Ivy configuration. You can view these reports by opening any of the xml files in a web browser. If you open the compile configuration report, you'll see a table at the top that looks like table A.2 and lists the conflict resolution on dependencies.

Table A.3 Ivy resolution output

Module	Selected	Evicted
slf4j-api by org.slf4j	1.7.2	1.6.1
scala-library by org.scala-lang	2.10.1	2.10.0

Here you can see that Ivy detected two dependencies conflicts. The first was the SLF4J logging conflict between Hibernate and Scala-logging. The second, and one you weren't expecting, was a conflict between the Scala version your project desired and the Scala version depended on by Scala-logging.

As you can see, Ivy is able to evict the old dependency version and correctly choose the most recent dependency for the project. In almost every conflict scenario, Ivy is able to successfully choose the latest revision and get the project working correctly.

When the latest version isn't safe

Although it's usually okay to upgrade a library to the latest version, sometimes binary incompatibilities between versions can cause runtime failures using this approach. Automated dependency management can drastically reduce the amount of time you spend hunting down dependencies and ensuring they work together, but you're not completely out of the woods. When adding new dependencies or upgrading dependencies, we recommend checking the Ivy conflict-resolution reports so you can verify that the chosen version is safe and desired.

appendix B
Migrating to autoplugins

So you want to use autoplugins. This quick guide explains how to take an existing (< sbt 0.13.0) plugin and upgrade it to the new `AutoPlugin` interface.

The sbt 0.13.5 release brought the developer preview of the new interface for plugins in sbt, called `sbt.AutoPlugin`. The new interface aims to fix two primary issues with sbt plugins:

- The ability for plugins to *automatically* and *safely* register themselves into a user's build
- The ability for plugins to *depend on other plugins*

Before we discuss migrating, let's look at how most plugins looked prior to sbt 0.13.5.

B.1 *Older sbt plugins*

Most plugins in the ecosystem are nothing more than jar files that contain a set of utility methods for the sbt DSL, one or more of which will be references to `Seq[Setting[_]]` that users can inject into their build.sbt files. For example, the `sbt-assembly` plugin you used in chapter 12 looks similar to the following:

```
object SbtAssembly extends sbt.Plugin {
    def assemblySettings: Seq[Setting[_]] = …
    lazy val mergeStrategy = taskKey ...
}
```

This object extends the `sbt.Plugin` interface. By default, sbt makes all members of such objects available inside build.sbt files. Although the older plugin API did include features to automatically add settings to sbt projects, these features led to innumerable problems in user builds, and the sbt community abandoned the features.

From a user's perspective, all plugins required some addition to build.sbt. For example,

```
name := "my-project"
```

```
assemblySettings
```

would add the `sbt-assembly` plugin settings to the build. But there was no inspection as to what plugins were added, and worse, if plugins depended on each other, it was up to the user to know in which order plugin settings needed to be added to avoid explosions.

B.2   *Migrating to autoplugins*

Migrating to autoplugins in the new version of sbt is a two-part process:

1 Move the sequence of settings you want to add to a project into the `project-Settings` method of `AutoPlugin`.
2 Move all the build.sbt DSL methods you wish for users to have into an `auto-Import` object.

For the `sbt-assembly` plugin, the new layout would look like the following:

```
object SbtAssembly extends sbt.AutoPlugin {
  def projectSettings: Seq[Setting[_]] = …
  object autoImport {
    lazy val mergeStrategy = taskKey …
  }
}
```

As you can see, it's not a major change, but there are two benefits:

- You can define settings that should be automatically added to builds.
- The build.sbt API you expose is limited to just the `autoImport` object, letting you have full control over what's exposed. (In the past, even methods like `projectSettings` would be exposed in build.sbt.)

Now the user will need to modify their build to make use of the autoplugins. The previous build.sbt would be changed to the following:

```
name := "my-project"

enablePlugins(SbtAssembly)
```

But autoplugins are actually a lot safer to include by default if they depend on other plugins. For example, if the `SbtAssembly` plugin is designed to work with any Ivy-based project, you can automatically enable it when the `IvyPlugin` is enabled for a project:

```
object SbtAssembly extends sbt.AutoPlugin {
  def requires = IvyPlugin
  def trigger = allRequirements
  def projectSettings: Seq[Setting[_]] = …
  object autoImport {
    lazy val mergeStrategy = taskKey …
  }
}
```

There are two important additions here:

- Overriding the `requires` method to define a plugin dependency
- Overriding the `trigger` method so the plugin is automatically added to projects

By declaring that the `SbtAssembly` plugin depends on the `IvyPlugin` (included in sbt by default), the assembly plugin will be added to *all* projects that are also Ivy projects. But it can be explicitly disabled by the user using the `disablePlugins` method:

```
name := "my-project"

disablePlugins(SbtAssembly)
```

This flexibility makes the out-of-the-box experience of using sbt plugins much better and allows plugin authors to control their dependencies and know that settings they wish to add to builds will be contributed in the right order.

We hope to see the sbt community embrace the new Plugin API and a richer, more diverse ecosystem take over.

appendix C
Advanced setting/task API

Although this book covers the core of sbt, one thing we didn't get to touch on as much as we desired was the advanced features of the task/setting system. These features aren't widely used, but they still come in handy when needed. Here we'll lay out a few use cases and how to achieve them in sbt.

C.1 Optional settings

It's possible to define a `SettingKey[Option[String]]` to represent a setting that may not be set, but sometimes the user may experience having to write this:

```
optionalSetting := Some("value")
```

Instead, sbt provides a mechanism to find out if a particular key has a value. If you want to allow the `optionalSetting` key to not exist in your build, you can use the `?` method to assess its value:

```
myTask := {
   val theValue = optionalSetting.?.value.getOrElse("default")
   println(theValue)
 }
```

Here the `?` on a given key creates a new `Intialize[Option[String]]`, which you can call the `.value` on to grab the optional `String` value. The big benefit here is that if a user never sets the `optionalSetting` key with a value, it won't break the build.

C.2 Failing tasks

Sometimes it's desirable to allow tasks to fail. You'd like to catch whether or not a task you depend on fails and to then perform different actions. You can achieve this by converting a `TaskKey` into its `TaskResult`, like this:

```
myTask := {
   otherTask.result.value match {
       case Inc(failure) =>  handleFailure(failure)
       case Value(result) => result
   }
 }
```

Here you use the `result` method to turn the `TaskKey[T]` into an `Initialize [TaskResult[T]]`. You then grab the value and pattern match to capture either the failure (Inc) case or the success result (Value). The benefit here is that trying to run myTask won't fail even if otherTask does fail.

C.3 *Dynamic tasks*

There are times when you may want to choose between running two tasks dynamically. Normally in sbt all tasks have to be tied into a key to be executed. But sbt does provide the ability to create a *dynamic task*—that is, a task that generates and executes other tasks.

A dynamic task looks like the following:

```
someTaskKey := Def.taskDyn {
    Def.task {  doStuff(); }
}
```

The Def.taskDyn method defines an Initialize[Task[_]], which is allowed to dynamically generate tasks. The example is trivial, where you generate a task that calls the doStuff method. Although this example doesn't need to be dynamic, let's look at an example that does.

Imagine you have an sbt task that can read a configuration file and generate data. But what you'd like to do is have the user configure one or more configuration files and then read the configured files and run a different task for each of them. This would look as follows:

```
def generateData(configFile: File): Initializer[Task[Unit]] = Def.task {
    // We can use .value here for any other key,
    // and the passed in config file.
}

lazy val dataGenConfigFiles = settingKey[Seq[File]]("Config files for
    generating data")

dataGenConfigFiles := Seq(...)

lazy val dataGenAll = taskKey[Unit]("Generate all the data for all config
    files")

dataGenAll := Def.taskDyn {
    val tasks =
        for {
            file <- dataGenConfigFiles.value
        } yield generateData(configFile)
    tasks.joinWith(_.join)
}
```

This code has the following shape:

- A method that takes the dynamic input and returns a task (generateData)
- A setting that is super-configurable and will lead to additional tasks
- An exposed key that will run all of the dynamic tasks, joined together

The funniest looking piece is the `joinWith(_.join)` call. This call is digging into the `Initialize[Task[_]]` types. `joinWith` allows you to join two `Initialize` objects. The `join` method is used to aggregate two tasks so that they run together.

C.4   *Composing InputTasks*

InputTasks, in general, can't compose with regular tasks because they require some kind of input string to run. But you can directly pass this input string into an Input-Task to turn it into a regular task using the `toTask` method. Here's an example where you'll create a new task that uses the `run` task with preconfigured input:

```
lazy val runGenerator = taskKey[Unit]("Runs the generator")

runGenerator := {
   val input = s"com.jsuereth.GeneratorMain ${sourceDirectory.value}
      ${target.value}"
   (run in Compile).toTask(input).value
}
```

Here the `runGenerator` task is defined by constructing a string, which is then passed to the parser for the `run` InputTask, creating a new `Task[Unit]`, which you then execute.

index

MORE TITLES FROM MANNING

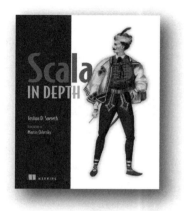

Scala in Depth

by Joshua D. Suereth

ISBN: 9781935182702
304 pages
$49.99
May 2012

Scala in Action

by Nilanjan Raychaudhuri

ISBN: 9781935182757
416 pages
$44.99
April 2013

Scalatra in Action

by Dave Hrycyszyn, Stefan Ollinger,
and Ross A. Baker

ISBN: 9781617291296
325 pages
$44.99
December 2015

For ordering information go to www.manning.com